SOCIAL CONSTRUCTION OF GENDER INEQUALITY IN THE HOUSING SYSTEM

To Ray
affectionately

Kan Wah Chan
5 Jan. 98

To Ching

Social Construction of Gender Inequality in the Housing System

Housing Experience of Women in Hong Kong

KAM WAH CHAN

Ashgate

Aldershot • Brookfield USA • Singapore • Sydney

Published by
Ashgate Publishing Ltd
Gower House
Croft Road
Aldershot
Hants GU11 3HR
England

Ashgate Publishing Company
Old Post Road
Brookfield
Vermont 05036
USA

British Library Cataloguing in Publication Data

Chan, Kam Wah
 Social construction of gender inequality in the housing
 system : housing experience of women in Hong Kong
 1. Women - Housing - Hong Kong 2. Women - Hong Kong - Social
 conditions
 I. Title
 363.5'92'095125

Library of Congress Catalog Card Number: 97-74511

ISBN 1 84014 163 8

Printed and bound by Athenaeum Press, Ltd.,
Gateshead, Tyne & Wear.

Contents

Figures and tables

Acknowledgements

Many people have offered generous help in the process of writing my PhD thesis in the University of Bristol, on which this book is based. Particularly, I am indebted to my supervisor Professor Peter Townsend whose suggestions and advice have been extremely stimulating and enlightening. Professor Townsend's sharing of his rich experiences in conducting academic research and his immense knowledge of social policy analysis have guided me to overcome numerous difficulties and obstacles in my project. I am grateful to Professor Michael Harloe, the external examiner of my PhD thesis, who has given valuable comments and encouraged me to publish my thesis.

I am also indebted to Professor Sophie Watson, who was the supervisor of my thesis at the early stage. Professor Watson's inspiring and insightful suggestions have helped to lay a solid foundation for my study. My research has also been improved through informal discussions with Professor Ray Forrest, whose extensive knowledge in urban and housing studies was a constant source of inspiration for my study.

Special thanks are due to Mr Robin Snell who offered generous help in proof reading and English editing. This invaluable assistance has made this book much more readable. Thanks are also due to the women interviewed. Without their generosity in sharing their precious experience, this study would not have been possible. Similarly, the cooperation and patience of the social workers and housing officers whom I interviewed are also very much appreciated. At the same time, I would also like to record my thanks to all my friends who helped in arranging the interviews. Support from the Hong Kong Polytechnic University is also important, without the Staff Development Programme the completion of my PhD study would be much more difficult.

Finally, I am extremely grateful to my dearest companion Lai Ching Leung, who shared my ambitions, aspirations and anxieties throughout my work. Without her support and encouragement this book would have remained an impossible dream.

Exchange rate

All currency are in Hong Kong Dollars (HK$)
1 British Pound = 12 HK$ roughly, in 1992/93
1 US dollar = 7.8 HK$ roughly, in 1992/93

Part One

THEORY AND METHODOLOGY

1 Introduction

Gender inequality in housing is seldom an issue of concern in Hong Kong, which is also true in most countries in the world. At the early stage of my study, when I raised the concern for this issue most of my colleague thought that it was not a relevant issue in Hong Kong. They asserted that unlike people in Western countries who place more emphasis on individual rights and competition, Chinese people cherish harmony and cooperation. Therefore, they argued that gender inequality in general and conflicts between the two sexes is not as serious as that in Western countries, not to mention gender inequality in the housing system. Of course, this is only a myth rather than the reality.

The invisibility of the problem does not mean that there is no significant gender inequality in the housing system, despite the beliefs of most policy planners, politicians, academics, and even some social activists in Hong Kong. On the contrary, there is every reason to believe that the situation in Hong Kong is even worse than in Western countries, given the dominant patriarchal Chinese culture and the minimal government intervention in social services in this colonial capitalist state.

In Western countries, although there is increasing concern about women's situation in the housing system (Watson, 1988; Weisman, 1992; Gilroy and Woods, 1994; Morris and Winn, 1990, chapter 4; Birch, 1985; Matrix, 1984; Little et al., 1988; Moser and Peake, 1987; Brion and Tinker, 1980; *International Journal of Urban and Regional Research*, 1978; *Antipode*, 1984; *Built Environment*, 1984; *Signs*, 1980), this issue is still marginal in policy analysis and housing studies. That is why there has been increasing concern to reinstate the gender dimension in housing studies (Pugh, 1990; Munro and Smith, 1989; Madigan et al., 1990; Watson, 1986b).

This problem is unlike those in the education and employment systems which are more explicitly linked to gender inequality. It is more subtle and is easily obscured. Housing problems are usually perceived as problems of physical spatial planning, or technological problems of design and management, which are more related to 'value free' scientific knowledge rather than to ideological practice and gender discrimination. In fact, sometimes ideological domination is so thorough that even women themselves feel that they are happy with the existing housing system and home life. However, it would be extremely erroneous to conclude that housing and home life is not oppressive for women.

In this study the term 'housing' is not only limited to the physical meaning of brick and mortar, it also includes the design of the environment, the provision of community facilities, allocation of housing resources and more importantly the nature of home life and the social relations embedded in housing. Of course, it is academically interesting to explore further the meaning of home, housing, household, or residence (Kemeny, 1992, chapter 1; Saunders and Williams, 1988; Saunders, 1989; Dickens, 1989), but that is not the main concern of this study. For this book, it suffices to say that the term housing is used to encompass all the spatial and social aspects relating to the home and the living environment.

One of the aims of this study is to reveal that gender inequality is prevalent in the housing system in Hong Kong. My stance is that the housing system does not only reflect existing inequality in gender relations, but it also helps to reinforce these social relations.

It is commonly believed that even though some women such as lone mothers and battered women may face serious housing problems, these are individual cases of mishap rather than consequence of gender inequality in the housing system. Even worse, some may argue that the misfortunes of these women have resulted from their own failure to maintain a happy family and their inability to solve their own problems, and that therefore it has nothing to do with the structure of gender inequality. These arguments are extremely popular in a laissez-faire capitalist system such as Hong Kong, where economic concerns dominate social policy planning (Walker, 1988).

Therefore, a more important aim of this book is to challenge the traditional conceptualization of women's housing problems as rooted in individual incompetence or in the breaking up of particular families. Traditional explanations of social problems tend to put the blame on the individual, assuming the problem is the result of individual inadequacy or misfortune. This book argues that women's housing problems are socially constructed by our patriarchal social system coupled with our laissez-faire capitalist system in Hong Kong. These two systems mutually reinforce each other to form a rigid web of gender discrimination which permeates all social systems, our family, our employment, our education, as well as the housing system. This influence is so far reaching that it predominates at the ideological level, the structural level, and in everyday social interactions. Women's housing problems are socially constructed and women's subordinate position in society is reinforced by a gender biased housing system.

To refute the common sense belief that there is no specific housing problem for women, here are some examples to highlight the extent of the problem. There are numerous problems facing women in our housing system. Women with different family backgrounds, ages, class, ethnicity, or education may experience housing inequality differently. Roughly, we can divide these problems into two major

4

categories: 1) access to housing resources; and 2) discrimination in housing design and planning.

First, let us briefly look at women's access to housing resources. Many studies in Western countries have pointed out that women have less access to housing resources as compared to men (e.g. see Brion and Tinker, 1980; Watson and Austerberry, 1986; Austerberry and Watson, 1983; Coleman and Watson, 1987; Hardey, 1989). There are also numerous examples in Hong Kong. For example, lone mothers are not regarded as a priority group in applying for public housing. Sheltered housing services for battered women are extremely underdeveloped. Single women have extreme difficulties in finding appropriate accommodation both in the public and private housing market. Provision of housing for elderly people, mostly affecting women, is far behind social demand. In private housing this inequality in resource distribution is even more obvious. Male home owners far out-numbered that of female. Even in the case of joint ownership between husband and wife or between brothers and sisters, it is obvious that men always have greater control over housing property. It is even worse in traditional villages in rural areas in Hong Kong, where women are still not allowed to inherit land and housing property from their families.

Second, there is obvious discrimination against women in the design of housing and urban planning (Weisman, 1992; Little et al., 1988; Matrix, 1984; Women and Geography Study Group of Institute of British Geographers, 1984). For example, the design of housing and the community is based on the assumption that women are the carers for the family. Consequently, child care and homemaking services are not taken seriously in the development of community services. The underdevelopment of these services increases the burden on women (Bowlby, 1988; Roberts, 1984). The problem is further exacerbated in new towns where women are more isolated from their established social support network in the urban centre. The transportation system also neglects women's needs for getting around and constrains women's mobility (Pickup, 1988). This is true both for travel outside the community and inside it. Housing design encourages privatism in family life, thus hindering the development of neighbourhood support which is essential to reduce women's burdens of homemaking.

In short, the limited access to housing resources and the discrimination against women in housing design contribute to increase their burdens of homemaking, confine women to their homes, reinforce their subordination within the family and their dependency upon men.

Given the diverse nature of the problems facing women in the housing system, it is impossible and too confusing to deal with all the problems in a single study. This book picks up two of the most critical issues to illustrate how gender inequality is being constructed in the housing system. The first issue is lone mother's housing problem. I choose this issue because it is very evident that lone mothers, especially in the low income working class, are facing great difficulties in solving their housing problems. However, it is contentious to explain the causes of lone mothers' housing problems. Generally, lone mothers' problems are not understood in the context of gender inequality. The causes of their problems have been reduced to individual inadequacy and inability to solve their own problems. Even worse, some people would blame lone mothers for divorcing their husbands or breaking up the family. This study tries to demonstrate that housing and other related problems for lone mothers have not arisen from their own inadequacy. On the contrary, it is because of their commitment to take care of the children coupled with discrimination against lone mothers in our patriarchal and capitalist society that they have been trapped in such a disadvantaged position.

The second problem I am going to deal with is women's experience in new towns. This problem is chosen to illustrate the fact that experience of gender inequality is not only confined to certain groups of 'vulnerable' women in very exceptional situation such as the lone mothers. On the contrary, gender inequality exists widely in the housing system. At present, more than 40 per cent of the population in Hong Kong is living in new towns, and this is still increasing rapidly. We cannot say that women in new towns are a minority or a 'vulnerable' group. Yet, housing conditions in new towns could affect women's life chances adversely, albeit more subtly.

By focusing on housing problems of lone mothers and women in new towns we can see that gender inequality in the housing system exists extensively. The manifestation of this inequality may vary for women of different backgrounds. Sometimes the problem is more acute, such as the situation of lone mothers; sometimes it is more subtle and inconspicuous, such as the case of women in new towns. By looking at these two critical examples, we can better understand how gender inequality is constructed in the housing system.

This book starts by pointing out that housing studies has largely neglected the gender dimension (chapter 2). I am going to scrutinize critically the ideology underpinning the housing system and to examine the social basis of women's subordination in the housing system, so as to argue that the cause of women's housing problems lies in the gender biased housing system, not individual deficiency. In chapter 3, I try to ground these arguments in the Hong Kong context by examining policies and services in various social systems such as housing, employment and social welfare which have significant roles to play in constructing women's housing problems. Then, we discuss briefly the methodology adopted in this research in chapter 4, paying special attention to issues in conducting feminist research. In the data analysis of lone mothers' housing experience, we look at how lone mothers' problem solving ability is being restrained (chapter 5) on the one hand, and on the other hand how they are being discriminated and marginalized in the various type of housing (chapter 6). For the data analysis on women's experience in new towns, in chapter 7 we look at how women are being confined to their homes and subordinated within the family because of housing conditions in the new towns. In chapter 8, we turn to look at how women in new towns are being marginalized from, subordinated in or even excluded from the employment system. This book ends with a brief discussion of the theoretical and policy implications arising from this research (chapter 9).

2   Gendering the housing question

Why is that women's housing problem is so invisible, or even if visible, attributed to individual mishap? It is largely because traditional housing analysis is gender blind. Therefore, the first task of this book is to demystify common sense belief and to develop a theoretical explanation of the causes of women's disadvantaged position in the housing system. This study firmly rejects individualistic explanations. Instead, I insist that women's housing problems must be understood in the context of patriarchal domination in a capitalist society. In other words, women's housing problems are constructed in the society at the ideological level, the structural level, and the level of everyday social interaction. Of course, such a statement requires careful documentation and substantiation, which I shall seek to provide in the ensuing pages.

This chapter starts with scrutinizing and unveiling the ideological foundation of the housing system. It is only after taking off this pair of gender biased spectacles that we can see the reality more clearly. This paves the way for developing an appropriate approach to study the housing problems, which is the second task of this chapter. Various approaches including environmental determinism, the 'add on' approach, and the deconstruction approach will be scrutinized in order to develop an appropriate orientation.

Women's disadvantaged position in housing does not exist independently of other forms of women's subordination in society. That is, gender inequality in the housing system must be understood in the context of women's subordination at home and at work. In fact, male domination is so extensive because various social systems and state policies mutually reinforce each other to form a rigid structure of inequality. Therefore, the third part of this chapter turns to look at how different social systems and state policies are working together to construct women's disadvantaged position in the housing system.

In discussing the structuring of women's disadvantaged position, it is important to note the active role played by the system of patriarchy and the capitalist state. In doing so, we have to face questions such as: what is patriarchy? What is the role of the state? What is the relation between patriarchy and the capitalist state? I am going to deal with these questions in the fourth part of this chapter.

Finally, we end up with integrating the arguments put forward in this chapter to develop a preliminary framework of analysis, which provides guidelines for analyzing data in this research.

Ideology of housing

Before we can fully understand the dimension of gender inequality in the housing system, first of all we must unveil the ideology underpinning the housing system which obscures the reality. Obviously the planning of housing policy and delivery of housing services are based on a set of ideological assumptions of how our society works. Therefore, it is important to have an in-depth review of the ideology underlying the housing system. There are two major ideologies: 1) the domestic ideal; and 2) familial ideology.

Before we go into detail discussion of the domestic ideal and familial ideology it must be clarified that housing and urban development is not purely ideological driven, there are other political and economic reasons. However, what concerns us here is how housing development in industrial capitalist societies echoes the dominating patriarchal values, which contributes to perpetuate women's subordination and gender division in society.

Domestic ideal

Modern housing design is greatly influenced by an idealized conception of the traditional style of living which Davidoff et al. termed the 'domestic ideal' (Davidoff et al., 1976). Under this ideology, the most ideal home is portrayed as one that is located in the country side or suburban area, isolated from the hectic life in the city centre. It should be quiet, clean and warm and should be separated from the work place, so that the breadwinner can enjoy and relax in this haven after the exhausting work in the day. Furthermore, the house should be self-contained and detached from the neighbour so as to preserve a high level of privacy (Saegert, 1980; McDowell, 1983a, 1983b; Crow, 1989). Of course, I am not arguing that this ideology is the cause of suburbanization,[1] instead we can say that suburbanization inevitably reflects the dominant ideology of our society at large.

Anyway, it is very doubtful whether this idealized home life and community ever existed widely in the past, even in the rural areas. Or, this idealized imagery mainly reflects the middle class, Western, white and masculine culture and life style. For the low income families, the ethnic minorities and the working class, a lot of them are living in slum or congested environment, instead of the ideal home in a suburban area.

8

The portrait of home as haven for men contributes to obscure the subordination of women in the family. For women, the home is the work place, it often means long hours of dreary work without pay. Moreover, this idealized self-sufficient suburban housing serves to further isolate women in their home. It reinforces the development of privatism in family life in industrial capitalist societies. Consequently, women are trapped at home, performing increasingly demanding duties of child care and household chores. Furthermore, their needs to participate in the labour market and other social activities are neglected. It should be noted that some writers, like Saunders (1989; 1990, chapter 5), are critical of this argument. This is a matter of how we approach the women's housing question, which I am going to discuss in the following section.

As a British colony for more than one hundred years, inevitably urban planning and policy making in Hong Kong has been dominated by this Western, white and middle class ideology of housing. Lee (1985) has pointed out that this Westernized housing policy and urban development has had a significant impact on traditional family patterns and relationships in Hong Kong. However, in Hong Kong the suburbanization process does not only limit to the middle class as in some Western countries. Because of the scarcity of residential land in this small city, especially in the city centre, a large proportion of the working class has been decentralized to remote new towns. This massive relocation of the population to new towns and the rapid development of new Western style of dwellings has contributed to speed up the implantation of the domestic ideal in Hong Kong.

The dichotomization of home and work within this ideology has also been echoed in many mainstream urban and housing studies. Many of these studies tend to conceive of housing as merely a consumption good. That is housing is an arena for consumption activities, which is separated from the workplace where production activities are performed. For example, for Castells housing is conceived of as a major form of 'collective consumption' (Castells, 1977). Another example is Saunders's devotion to develop the 'sociology of consumption' (Saunders, 1986, chapter 8; Saunders and Williams, 1988), in which the consumption of housing is the major arena of study.

The major limitation of this conceptualization which concerns us here (see Warde, 1990 for more detailed critique) is that by emphasizing housing as consumption the productive nature of housing is being over-looked. As a consequence, the importance of women's productive role in housing and the maintenance of home is very much neglected. That is why Pugh (1990) calls for a new approach to housing theory, in which gender issues are more visible.

Familial ideology

The division of consumption/production, private/public or home/work is also closely related to the familial ideology underpinning the housing system in a patriarchal society. Similar to earlier qualification, it should be noted that housing is not purely designed or allocated with the notion of maintaining traditional forms of and relations in a family. But the consequence is that traditional familial ideology is perpetuated or reinforced.

Under this ideology, the family is regarded as a basic unit of society. It is portrayed as a harmonious social unit fuelled with love, care, warmth, and mutual concern. It is assumed that everyone in the family plays a specific role which contributes to the normal functioning of the family. It is assumed that the mother stays at home to take care of the children and the family, while the father is the breadwinner financing the family. The gender division of labour in the family is assumed to be 'natural', and every member of the family is assumed to be satisfied with their role and is assumed to benefit most by playing these roles. It is implied that conflicts, power and inequality seldom exist. Or, even if they exist, that these can be solved easily if everyone assumes their 'proper' role.

This traditional conception of family relations is very questionable (Gittin, 1985; Segal, 1983; Barrett and Mcintosh, 1982; Leonard and Hood-Williams, 1988). It is doubtful whether this set of harmonious family relationships really existed. It may only be an ideologically driven image of the family which helps to cover up the inequality and power conflicts within the family. In practice, it is always the women who have had to sacrifice their interests to maintain the harmony and stability of the family.

Besides these idealized relations within the family, there is also an idealized family form. This 'conventional' form of family is portrayed as one with a formally married couple living with their dependent children, and in Hong Kong it frequently includes families living with the elderly grandparents. In certain aspects Hong Kong is still very much affected by the traditional Chinese concept of the family. For example, cohabitation, single parent families, and couples without children are regarded as 'abnormal' to a certain extent, while these are generally acceptable in Western countries.

With the various social changes in modern society such as rapid industrialization, increasing employment opportunities for women and the raising of education standards in general, it would be problematic to assume that the 'conventional' family persists without change. On the contrary, new forms of family are becoming more common, not to mention the ever changing family relationships. There are more single parent families, married couples without children, singletons (because of death of spouse, divorce or never married), families of co-habitation (instead of in formal marriage), not to mention some less common family forms such as gay and lesbian couples, and some forms of communal and open marriage.

However, most housing policy planners, housing managers, social workers and other related professionals still firmly believe that the maintenance of the 'conventional' family is the basis of social stability. The result is that other 'unconventional' families are neglected and marginalized in the housing system (Watson, 1986a). Women suffer most from this discrimination against 'unconventional' families, because usually they have less access to financial resources than men for solving their housing problems, not to mention their heavier burden in homemaking and child caring. In order to solve their problems, many women are compelled to depend on men and the 'conventional' family in order to survive in the system, even though they are unhappy about their subordinate position at home.

Approaching women's housing questions

In emphasizing the oppressive nature of home life, care must be taken to avoid the pitfall of environmental determinism, which portrays the housing system as simply a tool employed by men to oppress women. At this stage, it is necessary to clarify this point by referring to discussion of various feminist approaches to the housing studies, and developing the appropriate approach for this study. Roughly, we can classify feminist approaches to housing studies into three major categories (see Watson, 1988, chapter 8 for similar categorizations): 1) environmental determinism; 2) the 'add on' approach; and 3) deconstruction approach.

Environmental determinism

Environmental determinism has a longer history of development as compare to the other two. It is especially conspicuous in some feminist studies in geography and urban planning (e.g. Matrix, 1984; Hayden, 1980; Coleman, 1990; see comment from Hillier, 1986 and Spicker, 1987). In this approach, housing and the living environment is postulated as an independent factor structuring women's experience. To a certain extent, housing and urban design seems to be a tool used by men to oppress women at home. Environmental determinists believe that by modifying housing design and urban structure, we can develop a more gender neutral living environment.

Although I very much agree that housing design and urban planning have a significant impact on gender inequality, I do not think that changing housing design and urban planning alone can achieve a 'non-sexist' city (Hayden, 1980 and 1981). It is because the most important issue is the social relations embedded in the housing system, not the housing and urban structure as such. That is why in this book I am not going to elaborate too much on the physical housing design as such, but will focus more on analyzing the gender relations embedded in the housing system.

The 'add on' approach

The main concern of the 'add on' approach is to reveal the disadvantaged position of women or the lack of resources allocated to women in the housing system (e.g. Brion and Tinker, 1980). This approach tends to postulate women as a disadvantaged group or set of groups with special housing needs, so as to argue that more housing resources should be allocated to them.

11

This approach is significant in fighting for more housing resources for women. By exposing the disadvantaged position of certain vulnerable groups of women in the housing system, it helps to build up social pressure to improve the distribution of housing resources, albeit to a very limited extent and usually confined to a very limited policy area.

The major limitation with this approach is that it does not challenge the gender blind assumptions in developing housing and related social services. It simply tries to add women on the list for special consideration. It seems to imply that women are being overlooked in the housing system because of mere negligence, instead of the structural inequality in the housing system. However, in most situations it is the housing system itself that creates the problems. As Clapham and Smith (1990) have pointed out, by emphasizing the 'special housing needs' of certain 'vulnerable' groups we are also reinforcing the misconception that they are relatively inferior or less capable of solving their own problems (see also Marcuse, 1989a). This may help to obscure the fact that most of their housing problems are being constructed by our social structure and everyday social interactions. Therefore, some feminists start to call for a more fundamental challenge to the ideology of housing policy planning and to the construction of women's dependency.

The deconstruction approach

The deconstruction approach advocates a more fundamental challenge to the ideology behind housing policy planning (see Watson, 1988, chapter 8). It points out that the disadvantaged position of women is constructed in the housing system itself, and is reinforced by other gender blind social systems. Therefore, the strategy of this approach is to reveal the process of how gender inequality is constructed in the housing system. For example, in their study on homeless women, Watson and Austerberry (1986) tried to demystify misconceptions about women and homelessness. By doing so, they revealed how women's homeless problems are being pushed aside through the gender blind definition of the problem.

The significance of this approach is that it reminds us that power inequality between the two sexes is subtle. It permeates completely into everyday social interactions. By critically scrutinizing taken for granted beliefs and social practices, the unfair distribution of power and housing opportunities between the two sexes can be revealed. It is only after exposing this absurdity and unfairness that there is any chance of developing a non-sexist housing policy and eliminating the inequality of gender relations.

Here, it is instructive to refer to a debate in recent years on the 'meaning of home' to women. In his study on people's perception of the meaning of home, Saunders (1989; 1990, chapter 5; see critique by Somerville, 1989) challenged feminist assertions that home is oppressive to women. He pointed out that in his research when people were asked about what the home means to them, there was no significant difference in response between men and women. Women did not perceive home negatively. Similarly to men, most women associated home with love, care, comfort, relaxation, family and kids, instead of with being oppressed, being tied down, or having long hours of dreary work. Saunders argued that most women are satisfied with their home life, and concluded that the home is not confining women and oppressing women as feminists asserted.

Saunders' argument is superficial. He neglected the fact that women are influenced by the dominant ideology in society. Although he did briefly refer to feminists argument of the structural and ideological domination of the patriarchal system, he rejected the argument simply by accusing this as '...denying the validity of what people tell us whenever we do not like what we hear' (Saunders, 1989:181). Of course, most feminists are not denying what people tell us, the problem is that Saunders did not listen carefully enough to what people tell him. If he had taken more patience to probe into women's experience in home life, he would have developed more insight in the manifestation of power in everyday social interaction.

Ideological domination is so effective that frequently even the oppressed feel that they are benefiting from existing practices. Most women think that their home is the best place that existing social system can provide. Of course it is problematic to conceive of the housing system as a simple tool for men to oppress women. However, we cannot conclude that gender inequality in housing does not exist simply because women love their home as much as men do.

In this respect, Foucault's study on power (Dreyfus and Rabinow, 1982; Smart 1985: 76-80; McNay 1992: 38-40) may shed some light on this issue. Power is not simply a repressive tool. Instead, power exists, constructs and reproduces itself throughout social interactions. In other words, power is not something imposed from the top down. It is like capillary action, which builds up from below and permeates throughout all social relations. Applying this conception of domination and power to Saunders's question, it is not surprising to learn that most women said that they are satisfied with their home life in a survey like this. The more important point, which Saunders has missed completely, is to study the mechanisms enhancing the functioning of this power relation combined with its ideological denial.

This has important implications for the study of gender inequality in the housing system. That is, besides paying attention to the structure of inequality, at the same time we have to understand how the individual interprets this situation. In other words, we have to study how women construct their concept of home life and how this conceptualization contributes to the maintenance of women's subordination in the society.

However, with its emphasis on analysis of social relations and social interactions, the deconstruction approach also runs the risk of neglecting structural dimensions such as social classes and the state (see discussion in Smart, 1985, pp.122-7), which are also important in understanding social inequality. In the worse instance, this may degenerate into explaining gender inequality purely in terms of cultural practice, or in terms of individual psychological reactions.

Therefore, the implications of this discussion for this research are that both the structural level and social interaction level are important to the analysis of gender inequality in the housing system. On the one hand, I aim to show the structural constraints on women which constructs their housing problems or limits their ability to solving the problems when they arise. On the other hand, I am aware that the manifestation of power is complex and subtle, and can only be fully understood in the context of everyday social interactions. Therefore, I also aim to deconstruct the dominant gender bias ideology and practice through revealing how existing gender inequality in housing is constructed and reinforced in everyday life experience.

Home versus work

Oppression and discrimination in the housing system do not operate in a vacuum. Women's disadvantaged position in the housing system is closely related to their subordinate position in society in general. The housing system and other social systems such as the family, employment and social welfare mutually reinforce each other to construct women's subordinate position and dependency in the family.

In order to fully understand the mechanisms constructing women's disadvantaged position in housing, we have to look at women's subordination at home and at work. By delineating the two axes in analyzing women's experience - home and work - it does not imply that they are independent of each other. In fact, women's experience at home and at work mutually reinforce each other to construct women's subordination in society at large.

This section starts with a general scrutiny of the social division of gender roles, that is the division between private and public, between home and work, between consumption and production. This helps to demystify the ideology rationalizing the gender division of labour in society at large. Then, we evaluate critically the taken for granted assumptions sustaining women's confinement at home and the subordination in the family system. Finally, the rationalization of women's marginal and subordinate position in waged work will be challenged.

The private-public division

One of the basic patriarchal assumptions in rationalizing women's subordination is that the gender division between male and female is a 'natural' social division of labour. 'Natural' in the sense that women's physiological and psychological traits are best for the private sphere and domestic affairs, while those of men are best for public life. Obviously, this reduction to biological determinism is completely useless for explaining the gender roles which are developed through social interactions (Oakley, 1972). As the refutation of biological determinism is well established in gender studies, I am not going to reiterate the arguments.

Here, it is more important to point out that this conceptualization of public-private division does not even reflect the social reality in modern societies. With closer scrutiny, it is not difficult to see that the demarcation of public and private is very arbitrary. Many women are involved in many 'public' activities both directly or indirectly. For example, many women participate in the labour market directly from time to time or even constantly; or, indirectly, many women are assisting their husbands in developing their career and business (Finch, 1983). Moreover, it is very doubtful why men's activities in earning money for the family is considered 'public'; while women's work in getting school places or medical services for the children is regarded as 'private'.

It is obvious that the private-public division is only an ideological demarcation that defines women's work as 'private' and confines women in the domestic sphere. In other words, by socially defining a 'public' sphere for men, women are being excluded or marginalized from this arena (Pateman, 1987; Elshtain, 1981; Imaray and Middletone, 1983). In fact, there is not much sense in distinguishing between public and private spheres when we realize that 'the personal is political'. Similarly, it is meaningless to separate production from consumption when we realize that housework is as productive as the work in the factories. Therefore some feminists are very critical of this dichotomy as a frame of analysis, while others have raised the concern for impacts of restructuring of the production and reproduction relations (Nicholson, 1992; Harman, 1983; Watson, 1991; McDowell, 1991).

Pointing out the vagueness of the private-public boundary does not imply that men and women share equal opportunities in work and home life. On the contrary, the patriarchal ideology continues to affect women's life chances in the work place and at home. Many women are still largely confined to so called 'domestic affairs', at the same time, they are discriminated, marginalized, subordinated, or even excluded from waged work.

Confining women at home

One of the consequences of the ideology of private-public demarcation is that women are under pressure to assume responsibility for homemaking and child care. That is one of the major reasons why women, as compared to their male counterparts, face more housing problems and are less equipped to solve their housing problems when they arise. Women are socialized, trained, and constructed to be carers throughout their life (Oakley, 1972). This socialization is so thorough that there are strong social sanctions on women who are not living up to social expectations. For example, in Chinese culture, women from broken families are always blamed for failing in their duty to take care of the family.

Many women even define their identity through the satisfaction of providing services to their husband and children. In her important discussion on labour of caring, Graham has pointed out that 'care defines both the identity and the activity of women in western society' (Graham, 1983, p.30). This is even more obvious in oriental society such as Hong Kong, where patriarchal culture is more predominant.

The ideology of caring is so dominant that it is commonly believed that the individualized care provided by women to their family members is the best form of caring (Dalley, 1988). Sometimes other forms of caring, such as collective care in child care centres or the sharing of caring duties between husband and wife, are completely ruled out.

Even worse, women's labour in caring is frequently debased because caring is not regarded as heavy work. Sometimes the duty of caring is even postulated as only a sentiment, not a form of labour. Many feminist studies have pointed out that caring is a form of work, in fact very demanding and burdensome work (Finch and Grove, 1983).

At the same time, it is believed that with the development of technology homemaking is becoming an effortless duty. Contrary to common sense beliefs, many feminist studies have shown that the modernization of housework benefits the capitalists more than women. Most women are not released from dreary household duties. On the other hand, because of the rising standard of hygiene and more complicated procedures of operating these household appliances, women may end up with more housework (Cowan, 1989; Roberts, 1991, pp.90-3).

The capitalist state also plays an active role in reinforcing this patriarchal ideology, and at the same time making use of this ideology to shed its responsibility for providing social services for the public. For example, backed up by the ideology that women are the best carers of their own children, provision of child care services in Hong Kong is minimal. Even if some child care services are available, the low quality of service and the inadequate provision reinforces common sense beliefs that individual care is always better than collective care. Another typical example is the promotion of community care policies in Hong Kong in recent years, which as many feminist studies have pointed out, shifts the burden of caring for the dependants from the state to women in the family (Land, 1991; Walker, 1982). The policy planners do not seem to care about the carers - the women taking care of the dependants in the family - because this is assumed to be the 'natural' duty of women.

With this burden of homemaking and child care, women are more likely to face housing problems especially when there is any change in housing conditions such as moving to a new town or moving home after divorce.

Marginalizing women at work

Women's domestic duties are not the only factor contributing to the construction of women's housing problems, the lack of employment opportunities has a significant part to play. Women have less financial resources to solve housing problems because of their disadvantaged position in the labour market. In Britain, it is well documented that one's occupational position and income have great influence on the level of housing deprivation (e.g. Townsend, 1979, chapter 13; Allen and Hamnett, 1991).

In Western countries, many feminist studies of work have already pointed out that women have less employment opportunities because of the serious occupational segregation between male and female (Murgatroyd, 1982; Dex, 1985; Hartmann, 1979; Thompson, 1989, chapter 7; Lonsdale, 1992). There is not much difference in the Hong Kong situation, if not worse (Chan and Ng, 1994, and chapter 3 of this book). Usually, men occupy higher paid or prestige jobs such as engineers, doctors, lawyers, managers, and lecturers. Women are expected to do less important jobs or caring jobs such as factory workers, secretaries, child care workers, and nurses.

Patriarchal ideology tries to rationalize women's subordinate position in the labour market by arguing that women are less skilful and less productive in work. So, it is insisted that women's subordination in the labour market is the result of free competition rather than gender discrimination.

This argument neglects the structural constraints on women that hinder their participation in the labour market, such as burden of homemaking and child care, less opportunities in education and occupational training, and the discrimination against women in the labour market.

At the same time, it also neglects the fact that the definitions of terms such as 'skill' and 'work' are largely sexually biased. As Phillips and Taylor have pointed out, frequently women's work is defined as unskilful while that of men is regarded as technical.

> Skill definitions are saturated with sexual bias. The work of women is often deemed inferior simply because it is women who do it. Women workers carry into the workplace their status as subordinate individuals, and this status comes to define the value of the work they do. Far from being objectives economic fact, skill is often an ideological category imposed on certain types of work by virtue of the sex and power of the workers who perform it (Phillips and Taylor, 1986, p.55).

That is, it is not the amount of work or the nature of the work that matter. It is a matter of how we define work. Even if both women and men are doing more or less the same job, women could be considered less skilful and therefore get less pay. For example, in Hong Kong, male bus drivers get higher pay than their female counterparts. The rationale given by the bus company is that male drivers are more skilful so that they can be assigned to drive various types of buses if required. But the fact is that female bus drivers are also qualified to drive all types of bus, which is in fact a basic requirement to get a bus driving licence. However, female drivers are only assigned to drive small size buses because they are assumed to be less skilful. Hence, male bus drivers get higher pay than female drivers. There are endless examples of this kind of inequality in the labour market.

In an extreme form of gender bias in definition of work, women's domestic labour is defined as not 'work', or at best 'unproductive' work. Of course, this is fallacious. I have already pointed out that domestic labour and caring for the dependants in the family is extremely tedious and laborious work. It is very common to see that women work very long hours in household chores, and yet, they are not considered as 'working' and their domestic labour is unpaid.

Some patriarchal enthusiasts would hastily defend the argument that domestic labour is not as 'productive' as paid employment, so it is not paid or not considered as 'productive work'. However, it is obviously problematic to define domestic labour as 'unproductive' or merely consumption activities (Dex, 1985, pp.104-10; Oakley, 1974). The process of taking a meal, or taking a rest in a quiet, clean and warm home may be considered as consumption (or reproduction of labour power). Nevertheless, the process of producing these services, such as cooking meals and cleaning the house, is obviously a 'production' process. It is quite illogical that a chef (most probably a man) in a restaurant producing a meal is well paid for his work, while a housewife doing the same cooking at home is unpaid. In reality, it is very questionable whether production and consumption activities are so distinctly separated. Even the 'consumption' activities at home can be regarded as the reproduction of labour power, which is an essential part of the process in production. The separation of production and consumption activities becomes an ideological rationalization to degrade women's work, and to sustain women's dependency and subordination.

It is important to note that the state and the capitalists are more than happy to sustain this patriarchal system. In fact, they play active roles and are part of the social structure which constructs women's subordination in society. For the capitalists, degrading women's work, marginalizing and subordinating women in the labour market, and keeping domestic labour unpaid helps to minimize the cost of labour. At the same time, by emphasizing women's duty in taking care of the family the state also shed some of its responsibility for solving social problems, such as providing minimal child care services and Public Assistance for lone parent families.

Of course, the above statement is an over simplification of the relation between the system of patriarchy and the capitalist state. It needs further clarification. Is the state a 'patriarchal state'? What is the role of the state in perpetuating patriarchy?

Patriarchal versus capitalist state

In modern society, the state intervenes in civil society so extensively that it is impossible to understand women's disadvantaged housing position without looking at the role of the state. Feminists in Western societies have long been arguing that the welfare state contributes in reinforcing women's subordination in the family (e.g. Wilson, 1977). In recent years, this interest has been expanded to the concern of how the modern state contributes to reinforce the patriarchy system in general (Sassoon, 1992; Dahlerup, 1992; Watson, 1990; Brown, 1992).

Before going into detail of the relation between patriarchy and the state, I have to clarify the term 'patriarchy'. It is difficult to develop a definition of patriarchy accepted by all theorists. The traditional meaning of patriarchy is 'rule by father'. However, this narrow, static and a-historical interpretation is not helpful in understanding the domination of man over women in the modern world. That is why some feminists argue that we should abolish the term patriarchy because it fails to convey the dynamic social process in which men dominate women (Rowbatham, 1979), while others argue that it is more appropriate to use the term 'gender division of labour' instead (Young, 1981).

However, I do not agree with abolishing the term patriarchy altogether, because a suitable development of the concept can serve as a social construct describing male domination in modern society. Broadly speaking, the concept of patriarchy can be expanded to include 'men rules' in general rather than limiting it to 'father rules'. Patriarchy can be interpreted as a system of ideology and practice that maintain men's domination over women. Of course, the exact form of patriarchy is not static or a-historical. Instead, it is changing over time and varies between different social contexts (Walby, 1990). Since my main concern in this book is not to define patriarchy or explore the social basis of patriarchy, we have to leave the question here.

Now, let us turn to the questions of the relation between patriarchy and the capitalist state.[2] In the feminist literature, there is a long debate on whether we should maintain the theoretical construct of patriarchy as a distinct system separate from capitalism (see Hartmann, 1979, 1981; comment from Walby, 1989, and the collection of papers in Sargent, 1981). There are two basic stances in this 'dual system thesis' debate. Those who object to the dual system stance argue that separating the two systems tends to conceive of patriarchy as a static system, which is independent of capitalist system. But, in fact, these two systems are well integrated to develop the particular form of gender inequality in modern capitalist societies. Patriarchy and capitalism cannot exist without each other. Therefore, it is better to conceptualize 'capitalist-patriarchy' as a unitary system that constructs class and gender inequality simultaneously.

On the other hand, those who support the dual system thesis argue that it will be analytically clearer to maintain the two theoretical constructs. For example, we know that the capitalist system has to maintain a pool of cheap labour in order to enhance profitability. However, it is with the superimposition of patriarchy that we can better explain why women, not men, frequently occupy these lower positions in the labour market.

Although it is conspicuous that the capitalist state contributes significantly to oppress women and reinforces the system of patriarchy, I still prefer to adopt a dual system approach to emphasize that influences from the two systems are relatively independent and yet integrated. It should be apparent that although patriarchy and capitalist systems mutually reinforce each other, they also have different origins and paths of development. Therefore, it is not surprising to see that sometimes these two systems are relatively autonomous (Dahlerup, 1992, pp.114-5), or even in conflict with each other. This qualification is especially important in the context of Hong Kong, where an extreme form of laissez-faire capitalism from the West is mingled with a patriarchal system under traditional oriental culture. A typical example of this conflict is that more and more women are drawn into the labour market in Hong Kong because of the capitalists' need for women's cheap labour. This is especially true under global economic restructuring which has boosted women's participation in the labour market in newly industrialized countries (Salaff, 1990). These increasing opportunities for women (at least for some women) could help them to attain a higher degree of independence financially or even socially.

However, I must immediately qualify that the conflicts between patriarchy and the capitalist system do not necessarily imply that capitalism helps to minimize gender inequality. Even if women have got their own employment and their own wage, it does not mean that it is equal. They still carry the double burden of work and home; and they are still occupying marginal and subordinate positions in the labour market. It is more exact to say that capitalism has helped to transform the manifestation of gender inequality, rather than to reduce it.

Although indisputably gender inequality is maintained and reinforced in this complex interaction between the two systems, it is never a simple and straightforward process. Gender inequality in the modern capitalist state is frequently obscured, hidden and subtle. In fact, the main theme of this book - gender inequality in the housing system - is a typical example in which inequality is not apparent before it is unveiled systematically. An important implication is that the exact pattern of interaction between the system of patriarchy and the capitalist state, and the manifestation of gender inequality has to be studied in a particular social and cultural context.

Implication for this research

Based on the above discussion, I have developed a highly simplified framework to explain the development and perpetuation of gender inequality in the housing system. Gender inequality in a capitalist society, such as Hong Kong, is constructed through the complex interactions between the patriarchy system and the capitalist system. These complex interactions result in a close and tough web of gender inequality permeating throughout the social structure and social practices, which is reflected in and backed up by state policies. The housing system developed under such a gender bias system reflects gender inequality on the one hand and reinforces this inequality on the other hand. Moreover, we should note that the housing system and other social systems such as the family, employment, social welfare and education mutually reinforce each other to form part of this web of gender oppression (see figure 2.1).

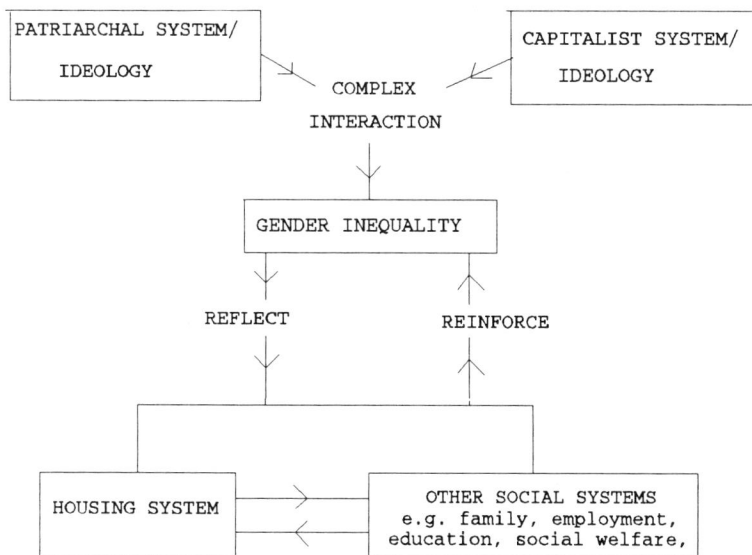

```
┌─────────────────────┐              ┌─────────────────────┐
│ PATRIARCHAL SYSTEM/ │              │ CAPITALIST SYSTEM/  │
│     IDEOLOGY        │  ↘  COMPLEX  ↙     IDEOLOGY        │
└─────────────────────┘   INTERACTION └─────────────────────┘
                              │
                              ↓
                   ┌──────────────────────┐
                   │  GENDER INEQUALITY   │
                   └──────────────────────┘
                     ↓                ↑
                  REFLECT          REINFORCE
                     ↓                ↑
        ┌────────────────────────────────────────┐
        │                                         │
┌─────────────────┐          ┌──────────────────────────────┐
│                 │    →     │  OTHER SOCIAL SYSTEMS        │
│ HOUSING SYSTEM  │          │  e.g. family, employment,    │
│                 │    ←     │  education, social welfare,  │
└─────────────────┘          └──────────────────────────────┘
```

Figure 2.1   Framework of analysis

Here, 'patriarchal system' refers to the ideology, social structure and social practices sustaining male domination and female's subordination in the society at large. This includes all the ideologies such as the domestic ideal and familial ideology underpinning the housing system; as well as other patriarchal ideology, such as private-public division of gender roles, which reinforces women's subordination in general.

'Capitalist system' refers to the ideology, social structure and social practices embedded in the laissez-faire capitalist system in Hong Kong, together with the state policies and actions reinforcing this system. This includes ideologies and practices such as minimal state intervention in social welfare, forcing the family (more exactly women in the family) to take up the burden of solving social problems, economic considerations dominating social policy making, capitalists and landlords exploiting the working class (especially women in the working class) without too many restrictions.

The system of gender inequality resulting from the complex interaction between the patriarchal system and the capitalist system permeates throughout all the social systems. For example, in the housing system women have less access to housing resources and urban planning does not take into consideration women's needs. In the family system, women are charged with the duty of homemakers and carers, thus confining their activities to the home, depriving their chances of other forms of social participation, and compelling them to depend on the family. In the employment system, women enjoy much less opportunity than men. Usually, women occupy less important jobs, or more women are of lower rank than men even though they are in the same occupation. Frequently, women are expected to quit their jobs under various circumstances such as the need to care for children or for dependent members of the family.

I need to emphasize that the process of social construction of gender inequality in the housing system operates on different levels, the ideological level, the structural level and the social interaction level. On the ideological level, most men and women are affected consciously or unconsciously by patriarchal logic such as the domestic ideal, familial ideology and gender division of social roles. This also further reinforces some of the capitalist logic which dominates the Hong Kong society. On the structural level, most of the social systems such as housing, family, employment, social welfare, and most state policies serve to reinforce women's disadvantaged housing position. However, the social structure is not a 'tool' used by men or by the state to oppress women. Gender inequality is developed and perpetuated in the complex daily social interactions, of which women are a part. That is, women are also an active agent reinforcing or undermining these social inequalities. In general, these social interaction processes are largely unconscious and are taken for granted, for both men and women. That is why male domination in our society is so extensive and deep rooted. Hence, it is important to reveal women's everyday life experiences of housing inequality so that we are more conscious of how women are being discriminated against, marginalized or subordinated in the housing system.

Conclusion

Concluding from the discussion in this chapter, it is obvious that the housing system is not a gender neutral entity, instead it is underpinned by gender biased ideologies and practices. The domestic ideal and familial ideology are two major ideologies dominating the housing system. Housing services developed in this system reinforce men's domination and women's subordination in society at large. However, the oppressive nature of housing policy is frequently neglected or underplayed.

Having said that, I have to clarify that housing is not a simple tool 'captured' by men to oppress women. For example, we cannot say that new towns are designed by men to trap women in their homes. Gender inequality in housing is not created directly from the design of the physical environment, as postulated by some environmental determinists.

Gender inequality in housing should be understood in the context of the complex interplay between the capitalist state and the patriarchal system, as well as the manifestation of power inequality between the two sexes in everyday life social interaction. An important implication is that besides paying attention to the structural constraints that limit women's housing opportunities, we also need to explore how gender inequality manifests in everyday housing experiences of women.

Frequently, manifestation of power inequality is so subtle that it is difficult to read off directly from the social structure. Foucault's analogy of power as capillary action, that building up from below instead of imposing from top down, has shed some light on discussion. For example, there is no legal limitations on lone mothers' access to private housing, however, discrimination from landlords/landladies has greatly reduced their housing choices. Another example is that new town development does not discriminate against women explicitly, it is in the context of the traditional gender division of labour that women are being confined at home in new towns. It is only through exposing the unreasonable power relations between the two sexes that more sensible housing policy can be developed.

This subtle power relationship is manifested both in the public and private sphere, both at home and at work. That is why we have to focus our attention on women's experience in work and at home to understand how gender inequality is being constructed in the housing system.

Although eventually the subordination of women is maintained by the complex social structure and social interactions, it may be modified in form at different historical time, space and social conjunctures. Therefore, the manifestation of gender inequality in the housing system should be understood within a specific social and historical context. For example, in the case of Hong Kong there are numerous factors influencing gender inequality in the housing system: the family forms and relations arising from traditional Chinese culture in a modern westernized city, the minimal interventionist attitude of the laissez-faire capitalist state, changing employment opportunities under the global economic restructuring (especially the development in Asian-Pacific rim), the scarcity of land in this small metropolitan city, the undemocratic colonial government, etc. So, this leads us to look in more detail the Hong Kong context in the next chapter, especially with respect to the situation of women and the development of housing policy.

Notes

1. Those who are interested please refer to various theoretical explanations of urban and suburban development, such as the classical ecology approach (Saunders, 1986, chapter 2; Bardo and Hartman, 1982, chapter 2), Harvey's (1978) emphasis on 'circulation of capital' and capital accumulation in the development of built environment, Logan and Molotch's (1987) emphasis on the role of activists in creating capitalist space; or refer to the theoretical debate on urban development and economic restructuring and flexible

accumulation (Henderson and Castells, 1987; Kephart, 1991; Gottdiener, 1985; Scott and Storper, 1986; Harvey, 1987; Sayer, 1989).

2. Here, I used the term capitalist state to represent the system of political domination of the state and the capitalist. It is not our major concern here to enter into the classical debate about the relations between capitalist and the state - e.g. Miliband vs.Poulantzas (see Poulantzas, 1973; Miliband, 1969). For simplicity, I use the term 'capitalist state' to refer to the integrated system of the state and capitalism, however, this does not imply that the state is a simple tool of the capitalists.

3 Women and housing in Hong Kong: the structural context

How does gender inequality arise in a population like Hong Kong, and with what effect? How do social policies and the social structure of Hong Kong contribute to reinforce gender inequality in the housing system? This chapter documents some important changes in the political economic system and state policies, and changes in social services such as housing, employment and social welfare. Such an account is important in understanding the situation of women in new towns and lone mothers in Hong Kong, which is the central concern of this book. I am therefore aiming to show how the structural context of women's life is essential to the explanation of their problems.

The first section of this paper focuses on the political and economic context of Hong Kong. The second section turns to the development of housing policy in Hong Kong and the housing problems arising in such a system. The third and fourth sections are on the employment system and the social welfare system respectively, which are two of the most important systems constructing women's disadvantageous position.

The political economic context

The rapid growth of Hong Kong from a small fishery village before the 1950s to a metropolitan city and an important financial centre in Southeast Asia in the 1990s seems like a fairy tale. Have women benefitted from this economic growth and the corresponding changes in the political system? In this section, a brief profile is provided so as to set the scene for our study of gender inequality in Hong Kong. It is not my main concern here to provide a detailed and comprehensive description of the social, political and economic context of Hong Kong (please refer to Miners, 1989; Schiffer, 1991; McLaughlin, 1993 for more detail).

In the last century, Hong Kong was only a small fishery port on the south coast of China. Hong Kong became a British colony in 1843 when it was ceded after the Opium War. Subsequently, the colony was extended to Kowloon and New Territories (see Appendix D and figure 7.1 for maps of Hong Kong) with a lease up to 1997.

Before the 1980s, like most of the traditional British colonies, the political system in Hong Kong was impervious and undemocratic. The formal political structure was completely controlled by the British together with a few Chinese elites. It was until early 1980s that direct elections were introduced in District Boards, which are consultative councils in local district affairs. For the central government level, it was not until 1991 that there was any direct election for the Legislative Council, which is a consultative council to the governor rather than a sovereign decision making body. However, the central decision making body of the government, the Executive Council, has never been open to election; and the governor of Hong Kong is still appointed by Britain. Under this circumstances, it is not surprising to see that most of the state policies favour the rich, the capitalists and the large corporations, especially the British. On the other hand, working class and the public is extremely under represented in the formal political structure.

As expected, women are almost completely neglected in the political structure. Up to the early 1980s before any direct election was instigated in Hong Kong, only 11 women (including local and British) had been appointed to the Legislative or Executive Council over 150 years of the colony's history (Wan, 1985, pp.75 & 77). Although the situation has improved a little bit in the 1980s and the 1990s, women are still extremely under represented. In early 1994, there were only 4 women amongst the 14 Executive Council members, and only 8 women amongst the 60 Legislative Council members (Hong Kong Government, 1994, pp.433-6). Not to mention the fact that most of the women appointed or elected are from middle and upper class elites rather than representatives of the female population as a whole.

The political structure of Hong Kong is changing rapidly due to the imminent transfer of sovereignty back to China in 1997. As a consequence of the restructuring of political power and economic interest in the last episode of the colonial history, the political structure has opened up a bit in relative terms. Although a few grassroots representatives have been able to squeeze into the otherwise impermeable political structure, the future is not too optimistic. The Chinese government has made clear that there is no way for Hong Kong to develop a democratic and self administrated polity.

With reference to gender issues, the Chinese government is equally conservative. For example, in early 1994 a social issue erupted on women's right to inherit land and housing properties in rural villages. The Chinese government officials openly declared that the patriarchal practice of inheriting properties by males should be maintained without change in rural villages.

At the same time, it is politically naive to believe that the British appointed colonial governor Chris Patten, who is talking about democracy everyday, is going to be able to improve the political and economic system significantly. Ironically, most of the conservative elites that the government relied on before the 1980s have turned their back on the British government and support the Chinese government because of economic interest. That is part of the reason why the governor is so eager to instal 'democracy' to wash out the betrayers appointed in the past. After all, democracy is only possible and sustainable if initiated from the public, not bestowed by a colonial government from top down.

Because the primary concern of the governor is not to build up a democratic system as such and to improving the social welfare of Hong Kong, social services are still far from adequate in meeting social needs or ineffective in solving social problems. Policies still mainly reflect the interests of the rich and the capitalists, albeit there is obvious shift of power from the pro-British to the pro-Chinese capitalists. Here, I have two important qualifications. First, by saying that state policies mainly reflect capitalist interests does not imply that the state is a simple functional tool serving the interest of the capitalists. State policies are the results of complex social processes. Second, state policies, especially housing and social welfare policies, are not static and remain unchanged over the years. Sometimes, they may even appear to be improving gradually. However, this limited improvement does not match the rapid economic growth, which we are going to look at in the following paragraphs. Furthermore, if we look into more details of the housing, employment and welfare system (later sections of this chapter), it is apparent that social polarization along class and gender dimensions, and relative poverty and deprivation still remain, and may have worsen (for further discussion see Skocpol, 1985; Skocpol and Amenta, 1986; Esping-Andersen, 1990; Poulantzas, 1973; Miliband, 1969). We are going to show that working class women in new towns and low income lone mothers are amongst those hardest hit.

For the economy of Hong Kong, the rapid economic boom seems like a miracle. The Gross Domestic Product per capita at current price rises from HK$4,000 in 1967 to HK$127,700 in 1992. Even calculated at constant prices, it has risen more than 4 times over the past 25 years (figure 3.1).

Before the 1950s, the economy of Hong Kong was relatively underdeveloped. It was only a small colony which had no significant economic value to the British government. The real significant change was in the early 1950s in which the Communist Party took over the regime of China. Hong Kong became a haven for the capitalists and the citizens escaping the sovereignty of the Communists. With this abundant supply of capital and labour, Hong Kong gradually built up its own economic foundation. In the 1960s and the 1970s the economy boomed rapidly with its labour intensive industry. Since the 1980s, the economy has been growing more rapidly (see figure 3.1) because of China's economic reform. Due to its geographical location and its special relation with Western countries, Hong Kong has become an important entrepot for China trade. With this rapid economic restructuring, the role of Hong Kong in providing financial and commercial services for trading in China and Southeast Asia has become more and more important, while its labour intensive industry is declining rapidly.

27

$ Thousand

140 -

120 -

100 -

80 -

60 -

40 -

20 -

0 -

```
68  70  72  74  76  78  80  82  84  86  88  90  92
```

Legend

— AT CURRENT PRICES

---- AT CONSTANT PRICES

127.7

49.4

12.0

4.0

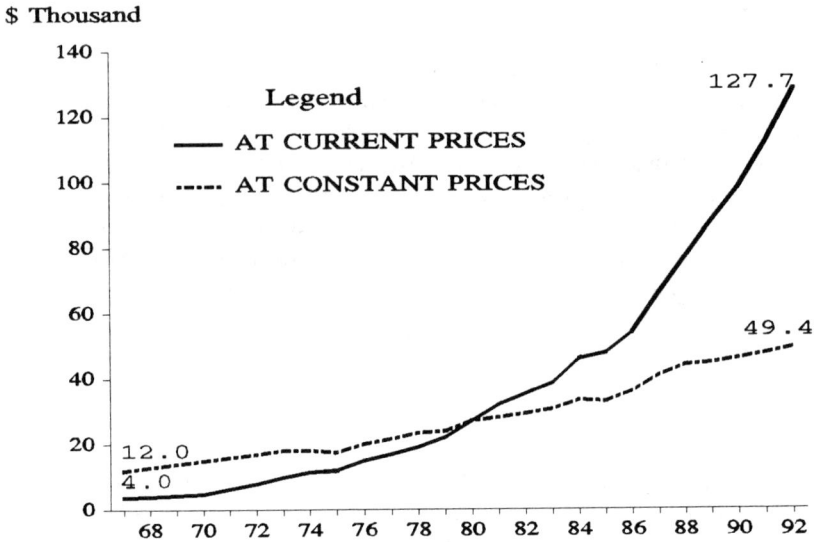

Figure 3.1   **Per capita domestic product at current market prices and constant (1980) market prices, 1967-92**

Source: Hong Kong Census and Statistics Department (1993a), p.14, chart 4.1.

This economic restructuring has had significant impact on the working class, especially on manual labourers or unskilled labourers, such as working class women. In recent years, many the labour intensive industries have migrated north into the Shenzhen Special Economic Zone and to the Pearl River Delta in China, just across the Hong Kong border. Therefore, it is increasingly difficult for manual workers to find jobs. For example, it is difficult for married women returning to work after their children have grown up or for lone mothers returning to work after divorce. Jobs in the factories where they used to work in the 1970s and 1980s are no longer widely available. It is even worse for those living in the new towns, where the major employment opportunities in the past were in factories.

The government proudly attributes this economic success mainly to its laissez-faire economic strategy, which involves minimal government provision of social services. Here I have to warn the readers that it is problematic to regard the Hong Kong Government as a 'laissez-faire' state. Many scholars have pointed out that the economic success of Hong Kong hinges on the state's involvement in many political and economic arenas (Schiffer, 1991; McLaughlin, 1993, pp.107-8; Henderson and Appelbaum, 1992; Castells, 1992). The social housing system, which housed 45 per cent of the population in Hong Kong, is an obvious example of massive government intervention.

28

It should be noted that government intervention and the economic boom has not led to substantial improvement of the social welfare system, basically it is still a 'residual welfare regime' (McLaughlin, 1993). Although government expenditures on housing and social welfare are rising gradually (Table 3.1), it is far from adequate in meeting the needs of the population. Total public expenditure has increased from about 15 per cent in 1970s to about 17 per cent in the 1980s and 1990s. This is still far from the standard of the OECD countries, in which the average 'social expenditure'[1] is 24.6 per cent of G.D.P. - ranging from the lowest 15 per cent of Spain to the highest 35.8 per cent of Belgium (OECD data as quoted in Cochrane, 1993, pp.243-4). Bearing in mind that the 'social services expenses' in Hong Kong is just about 40 per cent of the total public expenditure in the 1970s and the 1980s (Law, 1991, p.52), therefore our 'social expenditure' is still far behind that of the OECD countries.

Table 3.1
Gross domestic product, total public expenditure, and government expenditure on housing and social welfare (in HK$ Million), 1971-93

Year	G.D.P.*	Total public expenditure		Housing expenditure		Social welfare expenditure	
	HK$ M.	HK$ M.	% of GDP	HK$ M.	% of GDP	HK$ M.	% of GDP
71	20,320	2,939	14.5	179	0.9	55	0.3
76	47,226	6,591	14.0	218	0.5	358	0.8
81	165,346	27,778	16.8	2,672	1.6	1,185	0.7
86	300,818	47,931	15.9	5,579	1.9	2,554	0.8
91	642,930	108,422	16.9	12,577	2.0	6,913	1.1

Note:
* Gross domestic product at current market price.

Source: Hong Kong Government (various years), *Hong Kong*, HK: HK Government report of the year, 1971-94, Appendices.

From table 3.1, it seems that housing expenditure rose substantially from 0.9 per cent of G.D.P. in 1971 to 2 per cent in 1991, and social welfare expenditure rose from 0.3 per cent of G.D.P. to 1.1 per cent in the same period. However, official statistics can be misleading. For example, although the housing expenditure is increasing, under the new financial arrangement of the Housing Authority (to be discussed in further detail in the following section) the Authority has to pay the government 5 per cent interest per annum of the permanent capital injected and 50 per cent of the dividends from non-domestic operations (e.g. car parks, shops), and the government is entitled to appropriate the surplus of the Authority in selling Home Ownership flats. Under this arrangement, the Housing Authority is basically 'self sufficient' rather than receiving large amount of subsidies from the government. Another example is the expenses on social welfare and social security. Although there is an obvious increase in social security expenses, most of the expenses have to finance the needs of the increasing elderly population (see further discussion in later section of this chapter on problems of the social security system). In 1992/93, 65 per cent of the cases applying for Public Assistance are because of old age, while less than 6 per cent are because of lone parenthood (Hong Kong Census and Statistics Department, 1993b, p.251).

That is why we have to look at the housing and related social services in more detail in order to understand the problems in these systems. In the following sections I am going to reveal that individual experience in the housing, the employment and the social welfare system is not as encouraging as the statistics shows.

Housing in Hong Kong

The huge population and the scarcity of land are frequently mentioned in explaining the housing problems of Hong Kong (e.g. Wong, 1978; Pryor, 1983). Undoubtedly a population of 5.9 million crammed into an area of about 1,000 square kilometres will inevitably create substantial demand for land and housing, however, population concentration is not the only cause of housing problems in Hong Kong. Failure to solve housing problems is a consequence of ineffective state housing policies. This failure must be understood in the context of the political economy of Hong Kong, instead of blaming the population size which has been more or less predictable and under control.

In this section I am going to describe the general trend of housing policy development in Hong Kong, then we focus on some problems in the housing system that reinforce gender inequality.

Trends of housing policy development

At first glance, it seems contradictory that Hong Kong as a supposedly archetypal 'laissez-faire' capitalist state in the world is among the countries with the highest proportion of social housing. At present, about 45 per cent of the population in Hong Kong is living in social housing (see Appendix C for a list of various types of social housing). However, as I have pointed out in the last section, there is no 'non-interventionist' state as such in modern capitalism. Hong Kong government chooses what and when to intervene depending on the necessity of capitalist development and social and political pressures encountered. That is, massive intervention in housing in certain political and economic conjuncture can support the growth of capitalism. As Harloe (1981) pointed out, the massive development of social housing and its 'recommodification' is closely linked to the development of capitalism. This will be clearer if we look at the historical development of housing policy in Hong Kong.

Broadly speaking, the development of housing policy in Hong Kong can be divided into four stages according to the level of intervention or the role of the government (Castells et al., 1990). The first stage is the pre-1953 era, which can be called the non-interventionist stage. There was no social pressure or structural demand for government intervention. However, this non-intervention of government in housing and other social services left many social problems unsolved, such as the lack of housing for the working class, hygienic problems and law and order problems. With the massive influx of refugees from China in the 1950s, these problems deteriorated so rapidly that the government had to adopt a new housing policy.

The second stage is a period of ad hoc or unplanned intervention, extending from 1954 to 1972. Rapidly deteriorating urban conditions coupled with the economic boom paved the way for government intervention in housing. It was further precipitated by crisis in the form of the disastrous fire on Christmas eve 1953, which wiped out a highly congested squatter area in Shek Kei Mei, leaving 53,000 victims homeless. In response to the crisis, the government started to house the people in 'resettlement estates', low quality dwellings without basic facilities such as in-door kitchens, toilets or bathrooms. Although there were certain improvements in other types of social housing built later such as Housing Authority flats, Government Low Cost Housing and Housing Society flats, low quality was the predominate characteristic of housing in this era. However, the building programme was so massive that about 45 per cent of the population were moved to various types of public rental housing within less than 20 years.

The major rationale underlying this massive intervention in public housing was not humanitarian reasons to meet the housing needs of the working class, but because of economic considerations. From the very beginning, the government made it clear that squatters are resettled because they threaten economic prosperity.

More importantly, the government wanted the land. Keung (1985) has documented that the main concerns of the government in building Resettlement Estates massively are land resumption in the urban area for industrial and commercial use and migrating the working class to the urban periphery. This was made explicit by the government when rationalizing the massive Resettlement Estates building programme.

> ...because the community needs the land of which they are in illegal occupation. And the land is needed quickly (HK Commissioner for Resettlement, 1955, p.46).

31

The year 1972 marks the beginning of the third stage of housing policy development in Hong Kong, which can be termed the stage of planned state intervention. After 20 years of ad hoc, unplanned and uncoordinated development in various types of public housing programme, the government realized that this was an ineffective approach. Soon after the new Governor Murray MacLehose (a diplomat rather than a traditional colonial administrator) assumed duty in 1972, traditional short sighted colonial policies were completely reappraised.

There were three important reasons why the government adopted a new approach to housing policy. First, economic development in Hong Kong in the 1960s and the 1970s required the government to intervene to provide a higher quality and more stable labour force, essential for the continued growth of capitalism in that period. Second, the development of the urban area and its existing periphery was fully saturated, so the government had to relocate the population to remote new towns. Third, it was necessary to pacify the working class after a series of violent riots arising out of public discontent with the colonial government in the late 1960s. Obviously, improving housing services and other social welfare has had an important part to play in sustaining economic growth (see Castells et al., 1990 for more detailed discussion).

Housing policy at this stage was more systematically planned than that of the previous stages. Public housing adminstration was completely reorganized. A new Housing Authority was set up to coordinate all types of social housing, including public rental housing and the Home Ownership Scheme (which was launched in 1976). Undoubtedly, the quality of social housing improved to some extent, but government's financial commitment became more restricted. Before 1972, the government was responsible for building all types of social housing and rent was maintained at low levels with government subsidies. After 1972, the Housing Authority had to adopt a 'self balancing' budget, that is the income from rent had to be high enough to cover all maintenance and administration costs (see Ho, 1986, pp.339-46 for more detail).

That is why the rents of public housing have risen rapidly since then, and the housing burden on the working class has become heavier and heavier. Although there is a lack of systematic official data on public housing rent increases in this period (mid 1970s to mid 1980s), rent increases have become a major focus of conflict between residents and the government. This is especially true for the rents in newly completed flats, in which rents have increased particularly fast. As a housing action group, the Hong Kong People's Council on Public Housing Policy (1984, p.17), pointed out, compared to the year before, rent for newly completed public housing flats has increased by 15 per cent in 1980/81, 25 per cent in 1981/82, and 40 per cent in 1982/83. This rate of increase is obviously much higher than the average inflation of 10 per cent to 15 per cent in the early 1980s (Tang, 1992, p.310).

After the mid 1980s, housing policy in Hong Kong entered the fourth stage, the stage of privatization. In mid 1980s, the government thoroughly reviewed rent policy and subsidization policy for public housing, and subsequently launched the

'15 Year Long Term Housing Strategy' in 1986 (Hong Kong Housing Authority, 1987). In a nutshell, this strategy aims to privatize public housing and further reduce the government's financial commitments in housing. This strategy emphasizes reducing the provision of public rental housing while promoting home ownership (see fig. 3.2). Besides public rental housing and the Home Ownership Scheme, new forms of housing subsidies such as the Home Purchase Loan Scheme and the 'Sandwich Class' Home Purchase Loan Scheme (see Appendix C) were introduced to encourage the buying of new flats in the private market.

Subsidies for social housing have been further reduced after the new financial identity of the Housing Authority is established in 1988. That means, not only does the Housing Authority need to be self balanced in its budget to cover public housing maintenance and administration expenses, as in the 1970s, but it is also required to be 'self sufficient' to cover the capital expenses to build new social housing. The government is no more subsidizing the Housing Authority after injecting a lump sum of 'permanent capital', and the Authority has to raise funds for building new housing through rent collection and through the sale of Home Ownership flats. Under this arrangement the government has injected a total of HK$26,284.4 million (Hong Kong Housing Authority, 1994, p.131) as permanent capital for the Housing Authority, but at the same time the Housing Authority has to pay the government interest of 5 per cent per annum on the permanent capital and 50 per cent of the dividends arising from the Authority's non-domestic operations (e.g. shops, car parks) each year.[2] Most important of all, the surplus of the Authority on selling Home Ownership flats could be transferred back to the general revenue if the surplus is more than operational requirement. In 1994, the surplus of the Housing Authority is at HK$18,200 million, of which HK$9,500 million is considered as more than operational requirement. This 'more than required surplus' is expected to rise rapidly and will reach HK$17,000 million in 1997/98 (for more detail see Lau, 1994, pp.292-4). Under this financial arrangement, the government can claimed that it is subsidizing social housing heavily, while at the same time it can draw the money back gradually.

It is not my main concern here to explain why the state adopted this strategy of privatization in the 1980s, nor to develop theoretical explanations on state policy making in capitalist economy. There are numerous explanations on privatization such as 'recommodification of housing' by Harloe (1981), 'recapitalization of capitalism' by Millar (1978), and privatization as 'bureau-shaping strategy' by Dunleavy (1986). Some academics in Hong Kong even try to describe it as a political response of the British colonial government facing the transfer of sovereignty in 1997 (e.g. Cheung, 1988). Some, especially the Neo-Marxist, emphasize on the economic and political systemic functions of state policy making (e.g. O'Connor, 1973; Offe, 1984), while other critics emphasize on state as a partially autonomous actor and as structures in social policy making (Skocpol and Amenta, 1986; Skocpol, 1985).

Anyway, we have to leave the question of theoretical explanation here, and turn to look at how this ineffective housing strategy failed to solve the housing problems in Hong Kong, especially how this worsened the housing situation of lone mothers and women in new towns.

Housing problems

There are several housing problems arising from the present ineffective housing policy, which are closely related to my study: 1) privatization of public housing and marginalization of the poor; 2) discrimination against 'unconventional' families in the public housing system; 3) neglecting families with special housing needs.

Privatization of public housing The first problem that we are going to discuss is the privatization of public housing and marginalization of the poor in the housing system. Up to the present, there are not many detailed studies of the impact of the privatization of public housing on the poor in Hong Kong (see Chan, 1985). In Western countries, it is well documented that the privatization of public housing would lead to social polarization, marginalization of the poor, and residualization of social rented housing (Forrest and Murie, 1986, 1988b; Malpass, 1990; Willmot and Murie, 1988; Harloe, 1995, chapter 5).

In Hong Kong, one of the obvious consequences of adopting a privatization strategy is that the provision of public rental housing for low income groups has decreasing rapidly. According to the Long Term Housing Strategy of the Housing Authority, annual production of social housing will decrease gradually from 54,800 flats in the late 1980s to 45,600 flats in mid 1990s, and then further down to 30,400 flats in the late 1990s (figure 3.2). The most significant cut will be in public rental housing, which will decrease from 33,000 flats annually in the late 1980s to about 21,000 in mid 1990s, and then further down to about 17,000 in late 1990s.

With this drastic cut in public rental housing, it is becoming more difficult for low income families such as lone mothers families to get into public housing. In 1993, there were only 33,811 rental flats available for allocation. After taking care of those affected by redevelopment, clearance and land resumption projects, only 14,030 units were allocated to those on the waiting list, but there were 176,045 live applications in the waiting list (HK Housing Authority, 1993, p.38 & 114). With this slow rate of housing production, it will take more than 12 years to clear this waiting list even if no new applicants join. Since September 1990, new applications for public rental housing in the urban area have not been accepted because of the lack of supply. At present, the waiting time for public rental housing in urban area is at least 10 to 15 years. For housing outside the urban area, the average waiting time would be about 7 to 8 years. Of course, it would be much faster (about 2 to 3 years waiting time) if the applicants accept housing units in very remote new towns such as the newly developed Tin Shui Wai. The situation is expected to worsen with the gradual reduction of public rental housing provision (see fig.3.2). In our study, many lone mothers in urgent need of public housing had to find their own accommodation in the private market, or were

34

compelled to accept public housing units in very remote new towns (see discussion in Chapter 6).

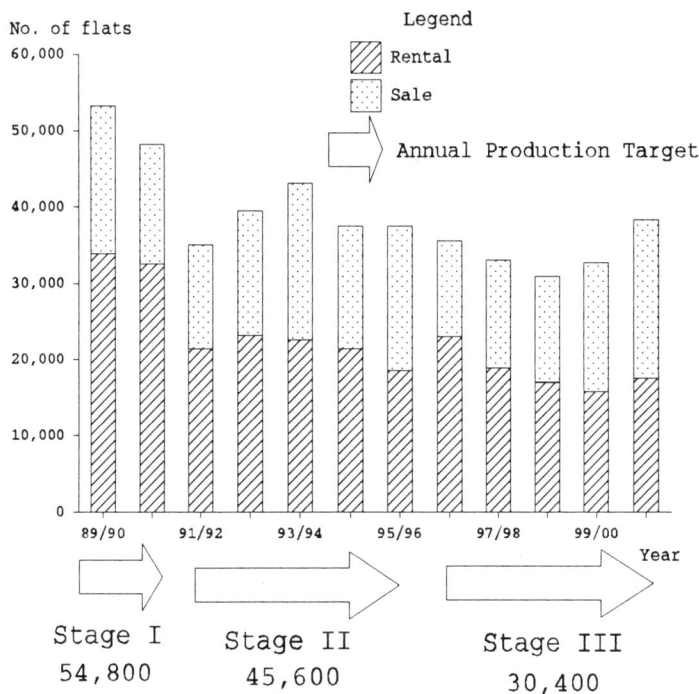

Figure 3.2   Social housing provision targets, as at 31 March 1991

Source: HK Housing Authority (1991), p.20.

Another threat from this privatization strategy is the rapid increase in rent for public housing. Since the Housing Authority adopted the Long Term Housing Strategy in 1986 it has to be 'self sufficient' - that is to generate sufficient income from rent of public rental housing and the sale of Home Ownership flats, not only to maintain existing housing stock, but also to build new social housing. Consequently rents have has to be raised drastically. In recent years, rent for newly built public housing is increasing more rapidly. According to Housing Authority Reports, typical rents for newly built public housing unit in 1986, 1991 and 1994 were HK$18.94, HK$26.95 and HK$41.74 respectively (Hong Kong Housing Authority, 1986, p.113; 1991, p.165; 1994, p.121). That is, rent increases averaged at about 9 per cent annually between 1986 and 1991, and about 15 per cent annually between 1991 and 1994. This increasing rate is higher than inflation. The average annual inflation in late 1980s was about 7 per cent, while

35

in the 1990s it was about 10 per cent (Tang, 1992, p.310). That means low income households in public rental housing are facing more and more financial difficulties.

As a result of this privatization policy, not only do public housing tenants suffer, but those living in private housing are also affected too. Since more and more people are compelled to turn to the private market due to the lack of supply and the rising rent of public housing, consequence of the private housing prices and rents are rising very rapidly. Figure 3.3 shows the changes in rental and price indices for small to medium (less than 100 square metres) private domestic housing units from 1986 to 1993. These small and medium flats account for 93 per cent of all private domestic housing stock. We can see that rent in 1993 is about two and a half times that of 1986. The situation for home buyers is much worse, housing prices in 1993 are nearly five times that of 1986. In 1993, the rent for a small or medium domestic unit in the urban area is about HK$200 per square metre, the selling price of such a unit is about HK$50,000 per square metres. That is, for a small flat of about 50 square metres, the rent will be HK$10,000 per month, or the selling price HK$2.5 million (HK Rating and Valuation Department, 1994, table 12, 13) which would incur a mortgage of about HK$18,000 per month with HK$750 thousands down payment. This trend of soaring price has continued to the end of 1993 and into early 1994. For most small and medium size new flats in the urban area, the price have already risen to well above HK$60,000 per square metre.

Obviously housing prices and rents are rising much faster than wages. According to official data, median monthly household income is HK$5,160 in 1986 and HK$9,964 in 1991 (Hong Kong Census and Statistics Department, 1992b, p.60). That is, wages have risen 1.9 times while housing prices have risen 3 times from 1986 to 1991. Although there is no more updated census data on household income than the 1991 figures, but the general trend of wage increase is about 10 per cent (Hong Kong Census and Statistics Department, 1993b, p.41) while housing prices increased by 30 per cent annually from early 1990s to 1993 (see fig.3.3). Relatively speaking, those who rent are slightly better because the average rate of rent increase is about 15 per cent (see fig.3.3) from 1986 to 1993. Yet, this is considerably higher than the average wage increase of about 10 per cent.

That is why the proportion of housing expense for families in Hong Kong is increasing rapidly in recent years. According to official data in 1993, the annual increase of the Consumer Price Index was 8.8 per cent. The housing expenses component is the item of highest increase (13.1 per cent), which contributes to 38 per cent of the rise in the Consumer Price Index (Hong Kong Census and Statistics Department, 1994, pp.4,7,10). The most recent household expenditure survey conducted by the Government in 1990 shows that on average, owner occupiers are paying as much as 32 per cent of their family income for mortgage, while those who rent a flat are paying 27 per cent of their income (Hong Kong Census and

Statistics Department, 1991, p.13). Judging from our earlier discussion, this proportion is expected to be further increased in 1993.

Price Indices

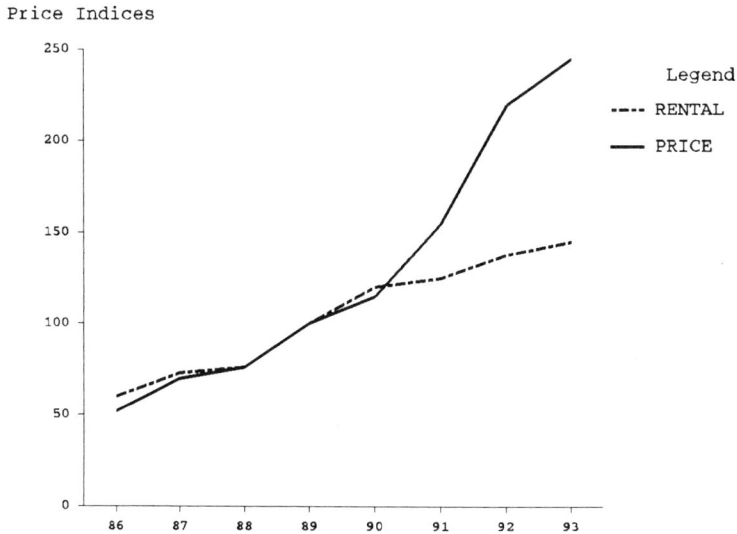

Figure 3.3   **Rental and price indices (based on 1989 prices) for small/medium private domestic housing units, 1986-93**

Sources: Hong Kong Rating and Valuation Department (1993), p.5.
               Hong Kong Rating and Valuation Department (1994), p.5.

Bearing in mind that this is only the average figures on wage and housing expenses. For those low income families who want to improve their living conditions by buying or renting a new flat in the private market, it is still a dream. There is not much hope of improvement other than applying for public housing. As we have seen earlier, with the gradual reduction of public rental housing provision (see fig.3.2), the hope of getting a public housing unit is diminishing.

Under this privatization strategy, in order to promote the home owning policy, the government is subsidizing those who are rich enough to buy, but at the same time cutting housing resources for the working class. For example, the newly introduced 'Sandwich Class' Home Purchase Loan Scheme[3] grants a HK$550,000 loan for middle income families to buy their own home in the private market; while many low income families are left struggling to survive in urban slums or are displaced to remote new towns. In this way, housing resources are gradually shifting from the low income groups to better off families, and the poverty gap in Hong Kong continues to widen.

One of the argument of the government in defending the Home Ownership Scheme and the Home Purchase Loan Scheme, is that these schemes help to 'filter' out low rent public housing for the needy. However, it should be noted that most of the flats recovered are from older housing estates. Although the Housing Authority does not produce any official data on the type or quality of the public housing recovered, it is obvious that those in newly built housing estates have less need to improve their environment through home ownership while those in older estates are more eager to buy. In this way, low income families, who need public housing, increasingly have to take up old and worn out flats. According to the Housing Authority, from 1993/94 to 1997/98, on the average there would be 35,800 public rental flats provided annually, of which 16,500 (i.e. 46 per cent) would be vacated flats mainly recovered in Home Ownership Scheme and Home Purchase Loan Scheme while the other 19,290 flats are newly built (Hong Kong Housing Authority, 1995, p.60). Of course, the major problem is not with this filtering system as such, but the cut in newly built public rental flats, which deprives the low income families of the chance to enjoy a better living environment. In chapter 6 we will see how these poor environment in old public housing estates failed to solve lone mothers housing problems.

Discrimination against 'unconventional' families   The second problem in our housing system concerning us here is discrimination against 'unconventional' families. In chapter 2, I have pointed out that housing policy is dominated by traditional 'familial ideology' and capitalist logic of 'minimum investment with maximum return'. Before 1985, families with two members or less did not qualify for public housing. The rationale from the Housing Authority was that this was more efficient use of housing resources, because larger families have greater housing needs, so they should be given priority. The problem with this rationale is that family form or size, instead of housing needs, becomes a determining factor of access to public housing. Many lone mother families are two-person families comprising of the mother and a child. According to census data in 1991, 57.9 per cent of the lone mothers are living with 1 child (Social Welfare Department, 1992, p.12). Similarly, the husband who leaves the family after divorce becomes a one-person family. In this way, the housing needs of lone parents (both male and female) and the absent partner are being neglected.

It was after several very vigorous protests from singleton and two-person families in 1985 that the Housing Authority promised to revise its policy. Yet progress has been extremely slow. Although singleton families and two-person families were allowed to submit applications for public housing, it was not until 1995 that housing units for these families was available. In 1993, amongst the 176,045 applicants in the waiting list for public housing, there were 23,970 singleton and 46,434 two-person families, that is these two groups account for 40 per cent of public housing applicants (HK Housing Authority, 1993, p.38). However, according to Mok's study (1993, p.120), the production of public housing units for small families is falling far behind demand. For example, it was predicted that in the coming five years 35,000 two person families will need to be rehoused in redevelopment and land resumption programmes. However, only 21,000 two-person units will be provided in this period. This is far from sufficient to rehouse those affected by redevelopment programme, not to mention taking care of those two-person family applicants on the waiting list.

Singleton and two-person families are not only being discriminated against in public rental housing, they are discriminated against in home purchasing schemes also. For example, two person families were not qualified to apply for the 'Sandwich Class' Home Purchase Loan Scheme at the beginning. It is under public pressure that the government has recently changed this policy. Still the government has stated clearly that two-person families and lone parent families have been assigned lower priority. In this fierce competition for limited housing resources, those families not conforming to the so called 'conventional' standard, that is two parents with at least one child, are being discriminated against or excluded. Even studies conducted from a classical economic perspective (Wong and Liu, 1988, p.3) have confirmed that small households in Hong Kong share less social housing resources.

Families with special housing needs The third problem of the housing system is that families with special housing needs are being neglected. Present public housing allocation policy is very problematic. A major proportion of the allocation is related to the compensation of those affected by redevelopment programmes, land clearance and resumption projects. If we scrutinize the allocation of public rental flats in 1993 (table 3.2), we can see that categories 2 and 3 are all of this nature. These categories amount to 40.5 per cent of the flats allocated, which is nearly as much as those being allocated through the waiting list. Most of these flats are considered as compensation and are not means tested. On the other hand, means tested waiting list applicants only comprised 41.5 per cent of the flats allocated.

More important, it should be noted that only 4.3 per cent of flats are allocated on compassionate grounds. In our housing allocation system, all other categories are not related to special social needs, except the priority given to elderly people applying for public housing. That is, most of those with special social needs such as the disabled, the chronically sick, low income families, and lone parent families have to compete for the extremely scarce resources of compassionate housing. Or else, they have to join the long waiting list as all other families do.

Technically, it is not too complicated to take into consideration the special social needs of public housing applicants. With modern computer technology, it is not difficult to give priority to certain groups with special needs. In fact, in recent years the Housing Department has implemented policies to give priority to the elderly and to those families taking care of the elderly. These applications have been speeded up by about 2 years.

Table 3.2
Allocation of public rental flats, 1993

	No. of flats	%
1) Waiting list	14,030	41.5
2) Redevelopment		
a) comprehensive redevelopment programme	8,910	26.4
b) major repairs	90	0.3
3) Clearance		
a) development	3,690	10.9
b) re-use of Temporary Housing Areas	980	2.9
4) Emergency	450	1.3
5) Junior civil servant/Pensioners	1,300	3.8
6) Compassionate	1,470	4.3
7) Transfer and relief of overcrowding	2,891	8.6
Total	33,811	100%

Source: Hong Kong Housing Authority (1993), p.114.

However, the Housing Department is reluctant to give priority to other families such as lone mother families. This is closely related to the traditional Chinese culture and patriarchal ideology. In Chinese culture, the elderly are very much respected. Although it is less so in modern society in Hong Kong, it is still well accepted that priority should be given to the elderly. On the other hand, lone mothers, especially those divorced from their husbands, are considered undeserving. Therefore, it is more difficult to force the government to face lone mother's housing needs squarely.

It should be clarified that although the Housing Department is moving in the right direction to give higher priority for elderly housing, this does not necessarily imply that the situation of the elderly (who are mostly women) is much better. On the one hand, the elderly population is increasing rapidly, for example, according to census the proportion of elderly population (those aged 60 or above) has increased from 7 per cent in 1981 to 13 per cent in 1991 (Hong Kong Census and Statistics Department, 1993c, pp.36-7). On the other hand, there are higher proportions of elderly not living with their children because of various reasons such as Westernization of family life or emigration of the younger generation. At present, there is still a lack of thorough research or official statistics to help us to understand the problem.[4] We need further research before we can draw any conclusions. This also reminds us that women's experience of housing varies significantly with different social backgrounds such as class, education, age or employment history. That is why we have to study the specific housing experience of women in specific social context, instead of over generalizing.

Moreover, housing policy does not operate alone to create gender inequality. It is closely related to other state policies. That is why throughout my analysis of women's experiences in new towns and lone mothers' housing experiences, I constantly refer to other social systems such as employment, social welfare, the family, education, etc. In order to help the reader to understand my analysis better, here I give a brief description of two of the more important systems I shall frequently refer to: the employment system and the social welfare system. Emphasis is placed on gender inequality in these systems, rather than presenting a comprehensive description of the systems.

Women and employment

As expected, government intervention in the employment system is extremely minimal, objectives such as gender equality and class equality have never been the concerns of the colonial government. With the rise of the women's movement in recent years in Hong Kong, the government is facing greater pressure to review its policy on minimizing gender inequality, especially the inequality of employment opportunities. In recent years, some women's groups have pressed the government to adopt the United Nation's Convention on the Elimination of All Forms of Discrimination Against Women (CEDAW). As a response to public pressure, in 1993 the government has published a consultative paper on equal opportunities for women (HK Government, 1993). Although the issue is still under debate, the general attitude in the green paper is that gender inequality in Hong Kong is not so serious and that women's employment opportunities are comparable to men's. This green paper tends to encourage a biased public perception that the situation is improving and that no change in present social policies or legislation is necessary.

If we look at the labour market situation, it is not that encouraging. In this section, I am going to focus on two aspects. Firstly, women's participation in the labour market, and secondly, gender segregation in employment.

Women's participation in the labour market

It is commonly believed that women's labour participation rate has increased over the years, and that gender inequality in employment opportunities is gradually decreasing. This assumption seems to be too optimistic and simplistic. Table 3.3 shows the labour force participation rate of males and females from 1961 to 1991. The labour participation rate for women has increased from about 40 per cent in the 1960s and 1970s to 50 per cent in the 1980s and 1990s. However, in the 1980s and 1990s women's participation rate is fluctuating and remains at about 50 per cent, instead of increasing continuously. Census data in recent years do not support the argument that women's labour participation will continue to rise to a comparable level of that of men.

Table 3.3
Labour force participation rate* of the male and female population
aged 15 and above, 1961-91

	1961	1971	1976	1981	1986	1991
Male	90.4	84.7	80.4	82.5	80.9	78.7
Female	36.8	42.8	43.6	49.5	51.2	49.5
Total	64.4	66.1	63.6	66.8	66.4	64.3

Note:
* Labour force participation rate is the proportion of economic active population in the whole population, expressed in percentage.

Source: *Census Main Reports*, (various years), as quoted in Association for the Advancement of Feminism (1993), p.7, table 1.

Besides the overall labour force participation rate, we also need to pay attention to variation between women of different backgrounds such as education and age. For example, younger women may have higher opportunities for employment while, middle aged and older women are being displaced from the labour market. Comparing the census data between 1991 and 1981 (figure 3.4), it is clear that the labour force participation rate for women aged 20 to 50 has increased, while the other age groups are decreasing. It is expected that the labour force participation rate for those aged below 20 will decrease because of the higher proportion of this age group in full time education. Labour force participation rate for women aged over 50-54 is decreasing possibly because of earlier retirement, or possibly they are being displaced from the labour market because of age discrimination. Evidence from my case studies on lone mothers (see chapter 5) and women in new towns (see chapter 8) also confirms the wide existence of this age discrimination.

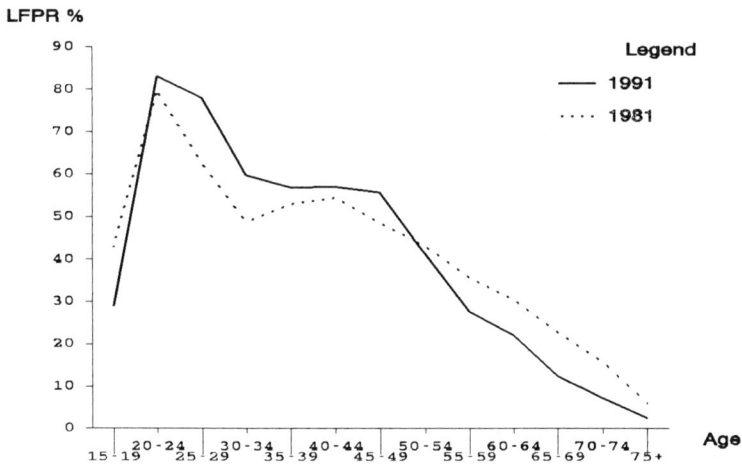

LFPR %

Figure 3.4   **Labour force participation rate (LFPR) by age for women aged 15 and above, 1981-91**

Source: Hong Kong Census and Statistic Department (1992b), p.52.

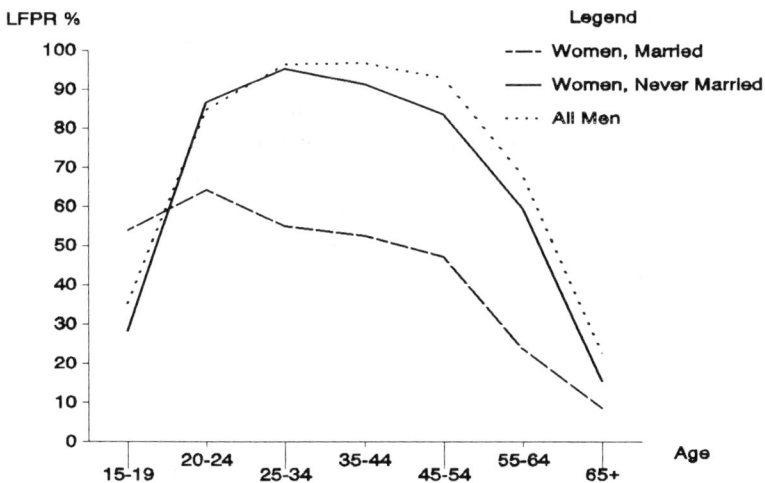

Figure 3.5   **Labour force participation rate by age, sex and marital status, 1991**

Source: Hong Kong Census and Statistics Department (1993c), p.90.

Marriage and commitment to child care is one of the major factors affecting women's participation in the labour market. In general, married women enjoy far less employment opportunities than their unmarried counterparts. In figure 3.5, I have tried to differentiate never married women from married women. It is apparent that labour participation rate for married women is much lower than for never married women. On the other hand, the labour participation patterns of never married women and all men are more or less the same. That is, if women are not affected by marriage and child caring duties, their levels of labour participation is more or less the same as that of men. At the same time, the impact of marriage and child caring on women's labour participation can be further amplified by being a lone parent or living in new towns, which will be further discussed in the following chapters.

Overall, although the labour force participation rate for women is increasing in general, we should be aware that there are great variations amongst women of different backgrounds according to age, marital status, education and class. I have shown that younger women enjoy better chances in the labour market, while middle aged and older women may face more difficulties or discrimination, this is especially true for the target groups of this study - lone mothers and married women in new towns.

Gender segregation in employment

Because of the lack of opportunities or discriminations in the labour market, even if women can find jobs, many of them occupy relatively low positions in the employment structure. In other words, there is obvious occupational segregation between males and females in the labour market, both horizontally and vertically.

First of all, let us look at the situation of horizontal segregation. In Hong Kong, men and women are clearly segregated in different occupations. Table 3.4 shows the distribution of occupations amongst the working population in the 1991 census.

Gender segregation is especially obvious in occupations such as clerical workers and craft and related workers. The percentage of females in clerical work is about 3.6 times that of males. On the other hand, craft and related work is largely reserved for men, the percentage of males in this category is nearly 5 times that of females. Similarly, women are assumed to lack leadership ability and skill necessary to be managers and administrators. Consequently, only 5 per cent of the working women are in managerial jobs, as compared to 12 per cent of men.

The Index of Segregation[5] is useful to indicate the degree of employment segregation. Based on the 9 categories of main occupational groups in the 1991 census (see table 3.4 and 3.5), the index of occupation segregation is 0.27. That is, 27 per cent of the male and female working population would have to interchange their occupations in order to maintain a balanced situation. At first glance, it seems that 27 per cent is not an extremely high figure. However, we should note that this segregation index is highly affected by the level of specification in classifying occupation groups. In general, the more detailed the

Table 3.4
Occupation of the working population by sex, 1991

Occupation	Male %	Female %	F%/M%
Management/Administration	11.79	4.90	0.42
Professional	4.06	3.00	0.74
Associate professional	9.73	11.26	1.16
Clerical	8.04	28.77	3.58
Services/Sale	13.69	12.49	0.91
Craft & related workers	20.89	4.44	0.21
Plant & machine operators/ assemblers	13.93	12.72	0.91
Elementary	16.87	21.72	1.29
Others	1.23	0.70	0.57
Total	100% N=1,686,366	100% N=1,028,737	

Source: Compiled from Hong Kong Census and Statistics Department (1992a), p.112.

Table 3.5
Index of segregation (I.S.) in employment, 1976-91

	1976	1981	1986	1991
I.S. based on main groups	0.10	0.10	0.15	0.27
Number of main groups	8	8	8	9
I.S. based on subgroups	0.49	0.49	0.51	0.39
Number of subgroups	154	147	78	30

Source: Chan and Ng (1994), p.153.

Table 3.6
Working population by occupation, sex and monthly income

Occupation	Sex	Monthly income from main employment (HK$)				
		Under 1,000	1,000- 1,999	2,000- 3,999	4,000- 5,999	6,000- 7,999
Managers & adminis- trators	M	7,831	--	6,263	15,801	21,805
	F	3,015	--	3,054	5,374	5,051
Profess- ionals	M	1,357	175	1,141	2,207	5,110
	F	515	62	441	1,355	2,668
Association profess- ionals	M	2,468	305	7,501	27,964	31,828
	F	2,266	727	10,144	23,855	19,688
Clerks	M	1,721	972	14,246	55,603	31,895
	F	4,906	2,985	44,361	139,248	60,735
Service & shop sales workers	M	5,840	6,479	29,790	68,278	56,285
	F	5,398	10,079	34,389	43,893	15,851
Craft & related Worker	M	15,968	8,960	55,599	110,834	94,094
	F	2,407	4,060	18,143	14,348	3,689
Plant & machine operators, assemblers	M	5,987	3,824	31,640	93,588	65,896
	F	8,166	14,313	68,276	33,166	4,230
Elementary occupations	M	10,925	11,947	91,357	112,629	35,762
	F	9,159	23,282	135,516	43,273	3,589
Others	M	2,012	2,522	4,320	3,018	2,627
	F	1,243	753	1,185	528	200
Total	M	54,109	35,184	241,857	489,922	345,302
	F	37,075	56,247	315,509	305,040	115,701
	T	91,184	91,431	557,366	794,962	461,003

8,000-9,999	10,000-14,999	15,000-19,999	20,000-29,999	30,000 and over	Unpaid family workers	Total
19,772	46,558	23,567	26,037	30,534	689	198,857
4,569	11,239	4,939	5,049	4,374	3,726	50,390
6,030	15,401	8,599	10,052	18,436	8	68,516
3,764	9,239	4,384	4,367	3,966	54	30,815
26,064	35,407	15,223	10,175	6,957	229	164,121
16,770	26,207	9,996	3,988	1,395	742	115,788
15,579	11,570	2,357	872	326	524	135,665
23,541	13,851	2,166	599	346	3,248	295,986
28,173	26,781	4,278	1,769	1,270	1,880	230,823
5,551	5,064	1,132	587	311	6,241	128,496
38,719	22,342	3,215	1,433	669	431	352,264
1,053	616	173	32	81	1,140	45,728
20,057	10,693	1,871	803	259	311	234,929
832	561	121	113	148	971	130,897
9,327	5,056	991	334	118	1,988	280,434
766	757	244	87	30	6,695	223,398
928	1,406	843	819	504	1,758	20,757
31	248	55	91	20	2,885	7,239
164,649	175,214	60,944	52,294	59,073	7,818	1,686,366
56,877	67,782	23,210	14,923	10,671	25,702	1,028,737
221,526	242,996	84,154	67,217	69,744	35,520	2,715,103

Source: Hong Kong Census and Statistics Department (1992a), pp.134-5.

classification the higher the level of segregation which could be revealed. If we recalculate the index of segregation based on more detailed occupational subgroups (totally 30 subgroups, see HK Census and Statistics Department, 1992a, pp.116-7), the index of segregation for 1991 would become 0.39, which is substantially higher.

Some people try to argue that gender segregation in employment is improving over the years. This seems to be too optimistic. If we look at the changes of employment segregation in the past 15 years, this is not the likely conclusion. In table 3.5, I have listed the index of segregation for various census years from 1976 to 1991. The index of segregation were calculated based on both occupational main groups and subgroups. However, the categorization of occupation has changed in the 1991 census. Therefore, data in 1991 are not strictly comparable with that in the previous years. Nonetheless, we can see that there is no obvious sign of reducing gender segregation in 1991 over the previous years. On the contrary, data in 1986 indicates a rapid increase as compared to the previous years. For the index based on main groups, it has risen from 0.1 in previous years to 0.15. For the index base on subgroups, although the number of subgroups in the census data available has been reduced to 78, the index is as high as 0.51. That is 51 per cent of male and female have to interchange their occupation in order to maintain a balance, which is an extremely high proportion. For the 1991 census, although the subgroups available to the public was further reduced to 30, the index is still as high as 0.39.

Besides the horizontal segregation in which males and females are being employed in gender stereotyped occupations, vertical segregation is also serious in Hong Kong. In other words, men tend to occupy higher ranks or get higher pay than women in the same occupation.

Let us look at the difference in wages between males and females for the various occupation groups in 1991 (table 3.6). Not only women are concentrated in low pay jobs (as shown in table 3.4), even within the same occupation high income men are far out-numbered women. On the contrary, within the same occupation, low income women out-numbered men. Considering all the working population together, the median income of women is only 70.8 per cent that of men (HK Census and Statistics Department, 1993c, p.96). There is considerable variation between different occupations. In general, in occupations which have a high proportion of women, such as clerical workers and associate professionals, the wage difference is less. The greatest gender different in wage is amongst the occupation with high proportion of man, such as administrative/managerial work, plant and machine operators/assemblers, craft and related workers.

Has the situation improved over time? I have calculated the ratio of median income of female to male working populations (table 3.7). The ratio in 1991 has increased slightly as compared to that in 1976, from 62.5 per cent to 70 per cent. However, it dropped in the 1980s, indicating that a continuous increase has not been happening as expected.

Table 3.7
Median monthly income ratio between females and males, 1976-91

	1976	1981	1986	1991
Median income ratio (F/M%)	62.5	64.7	69.9	70.8

Sources: HK Census and Statistics Department (1993c), p.96.

Other studies in this area have also indicated serious vertical segregation in employment. For example, a study by the Association for the Advancement of Feminism shows that occupations in the electronics industry have been highly segregated (table 3.8). Although female workers in the electronic industry outnumber males by more than 50 per cent, most of the females (92 per cent) are operative workers. On the other hand, a much higher proportion of males are craftsmen, technicians, or technologists.

Table 3.8
Distribution of employees by sex in electronic industry, 1988

	Male (%)	Female (%)
Technologist	13.62	0.33
Technician	35.49	2.04
Craftsmen	16.74	4.67
Operative	31.80	92.0
Unskilled	2.32	0.92
Total	100% N=39,159	100% N=61,172

Source: Vocational Training Council, 1988, *Manpower Survey*, as quoted in Association for the Advancement of Feminism (1993), p.20.

From the discussion in this section, we can see that employment opportunities for women are much less than that of men. However, this is only the overall picture. If we take into consideration other factors such as being a lone mother or living in remote new towns, this inequality could be sharper. We are going to look at the situation of women under these conditions in subsequent chapters (chapters 5 to 8).

Women and social welfare

Another significant factor contributing to women's disadvantageous housing position is the gender blind social welfare system. In this section we are going to focus on two service areas - child care service and the Public Assistance Scheme - which are particularly important to our analysis of housing problems of lone mothers and women living in new towns (Those who are interested to know more about the social welfare system in Hong Kong, please refer to McLaughlin, 1993; Chow, 1986).

Before we go into the detail of these two service areas, it is revealing to look at the two basic ideologies underpinning the social welfare system in Hong Kong - namely the patriarchal ideology and the laissez-faire capitalist ideology of 'minimal state intervention'. The government emphasized that social welfare should be only limited to 'those least able to help themselves', instead of developing a comprehensive welfare system. For example, in a review of the social security system in 1977, in a paper titled *Help For Those Least Able To Help Themselves*, the government proudly declared that:

> The most important conclusion of this review is that the present aim of social security policy - to help those who are least able to help themselves - is right (HK Government, 1977, p.1).

This is always the predominant approach even in the 1990s, although more implicitly expressed.

At the same time, our social welfare system is also underpinned by patriarchal ideology, which emphasizes the 'family as a unit'. For example, the objectives of family welfare and child care services are explicitly stated as: 'to preserve and strengthen the family as a unit' (HK Social Welfare Department, 1993, p.12).

The underlying implication of this emphasis on the 'family as a unit' is that the traditional family pattern and the division of labour amongst family members is an ideal model that should be perpetuated. Under this 'ideal model' women are expected to be responsible for child care and the care of all family members, while men are the breadwinners supporting the family financially.

In modern societies like Hong Kong, the social structure has changed so rapidly that this ideal model no longer reflects the reality. More and more women are participating in the labour market because of their own preferences or because of financial necessity. However, our social welfare system is not responding to these changes and continues to expect women to take up all the responsibilities of child care. In other words, women are deprived of the choice of participating in the labour market, or they are penalized with the 'double burden' of child care and work if they insist on doing that. This is especially obvious in the cases of lone mothers and women living in new towns, which I am going to analyze in this book.

Child care services in Hong Kong are extremely underdeveloped (table 3.9). Basically, there are two types of service,[6] day creche service and day nursery services. First, let us look at the service provision of day creche service. Day creche service is for infants below age two. Up to March 1993, there were only 947 places in 18 subsidized day creche centres, and 64 places in 1 non-profit making but not subsidized centre. With just over 1,000 places for a population of about 5.7 million (with 129,703 infants aged below 2 in the 1991 census). That is, only about one in 130, or less than 0.8 per cent, of the infants can get a place in these creches. With this scarce provision, it is only under very exceptional conditions that a family is qualified for the creche service. The family must be of very low income, not more than 133 per cent of the income limit for Public Assistance, and there must be special reasons why the parents cannot take care of the children, such as sickness. In this situation, many women who need creche service have to turn to privately run centres. According to the study of the Association of Advancement of Feminism (A.A.F., 1990, p.39), in 1989 there are altogether 305 places in the private creche service. The charge ranges from HK$1,700 to HK$2,200 per month, which is much more expensive than the subsidized service of HK$541 per month. Therefore, most working class lone mothers are unable to afford these private creche services.

Dominated by the belief that it is the duty of women to take care of their children, the development of creche services has literally been frozen. There has been no expansion of places since 1979. The government did not even bother to do any study on the needs for day creche services, and there is no planning standard and development planning for this service. In 1991, when the Social Welfare Department was drafting its future plans for the coming decade, it accepted the principle that the day creche service should be expanded (HK Social Welfare Department, 1991b). However, up to the present, there is still no clear indication of how this is to be done.

The second type of child care service is the day nursery, which is for children aged 2 to 6. In 1993, there were only 21,190 places in 193 subsidized non-government organization (NGO) centres, 973 places were in non-profit making centres without subsidy, 11,087 places in profit making private service centres (table 3.9). There are only 22,163 subsidized and non-profit making places for a population of 5.7 million in 1993 (with 359,615 children aged 2 to 6 in the 1991 census). That is, only about 6 per cent of the children aged 2 to 6 in the Hong Kong population can get a place in subsidized or non-profit making centres.

Most families (more than 94 per cent) have to solve the problem by themselves or turn to the expensive private service. According to the study of the Association for Advancement of Feminism (1990, pp.39-40), in 1989, subsidized nursery service charge about HK$800 per month,[7] the non-profit making ones charge about HK$700 to HK$1,200, while the private ones charge HK$1,200 to HK$2,000 per month. In the case of children who cannot get the subsidized service, private nursery services can be an extremely heavy burden for their families, especially for families with several young children.

Table 3.9
Provision of child care services as at 31 March 1993

	Planning ratio	Provision as at 31 March 1993	
Day creche (for age below 2)	not available	NGO Aided	947 places in 18 centres
		non-profit making	64 places in 1 centre
Day nursery (for age 2 to 6)	100 places to 20,000 population	NGO Aided	21,190 places in 193 centres
		non-profit making	973 places
		private	11,087 places

Source: Hong Kong Social Welfare Department (1993), chapter 4.

Table 3.10
Demand, provision and shortfall of day nursery service (in number of places) projected as at 31 March 1993

	Projection				
	93/94	94/95	95/96	96/97	97/98
Demand	28,842	29,036	29,217	29,383	29,544
Provision					
Social Welfare Department	113	113	113	113	113
NGO aided	22,590	23,990	25,390	26,790	28,190
Shortfall	6,139	4,933	3,714	2,480	1,241

Source: Hong Kong Social Welfare Department (1993), p.22.

Another point we should note is that the planning standard of the nursery service is extremely low, with a planning ratio of 100 places to 20,000 population. With a child population (aged 2 to 6) of 359,615 in the 1991 census, this means that less than 8 per cent of the children will be able to get subsidized nursery service even if this planning standard is met. Even worse, this planning ratio is only an ideal rather than the standard already achieved. Existing service is far from meeting this already very low standard (table 3.10). In the projection for 93/94, the provision is just about 79 per cent of the extremely underestimated 'demand'. Even with this extremely low planning ratio, this standard will not be met up to 97/98.

This extremely low level in child care service provision discourages women from participating in the labour market. Most women have to pay for expensive child care services in the private market if they want to get employment. However, for the low income working class women, there would be not much left in their wages after deducing this expensive charge. In other words, many low income women are deprived of the chance of getting employment because of the lack of child care service.

Public assistance

Another important area in the social welfare system concerning us in this book is the Public Assistance Scheme within the social security system, which is especially important for understanding the situation of lone mothers. Similar to other social welfare services, the ideology of 'minimal government intervention' is so prevalent that expenditure on Public Assistance is kept at an extremely low level. In 1992/93 the Public Assistance expenditure is at HK$1,409 million (HK Social Welfare Department, 1993, p.84), while the G.D.P. of Hong Kong is as high as HK$847,931 million in 1993 (see table 3.1). That is, Public Assistance expenditure is just about 0.17 per cent of the G.D.P.

Let us look at the provision of Public Assistance[8] in more detail. According to the Social Welfare Department, any family in which no members can get employment because of various reasons such as sickness or need to remain at home to look after young children can apply for Public Assistance (HK Social Welfare Department, 1993, p.184). This is a means tested, non-contributory benefit. Family with inadequate income can also apply, under the disregarded earning policy. As at March 1993, the first HK$225 of earnings is disregarded entirely and half of the next HK$900 of earnings is also disregarded. A maximum total of HK$675 in disregarded earning per month is allowed; and any earnings in excess of HK$1,125 are taken fully into account as assessable income (HK Social Welfare Department, 1993, p.193).

The basic scale rate of Public Assistance for 1993 is listed in table 3.11. In addition to these basic rates, these families are entitled to rental allowance of either the actual expense on rent or the highest rental allowance as listed in table 3.12, whichever is the less. For example, a lone mother family of three members is entitled to get HK$2,250 basic allowance and HK$1,718 rent allowance maximum, that is a total of HK$3,968 per month maximum.

Table 3.11
Basic scale rates for public assistance, as at 1 April 1993

	HK$ per month
For single person	900
For family:	
first to second eligible member	675 each
third to fourth eligible member	665 each
each additional eligible member	655

Source: Hong Kong Social Welfare Department (1993), p.190.

Table 3.12
Highest rent allowance, effective from 1 April 1992

	HK$ per month
For single person	743
Family:	
two members	1,215
three to four members	1,718
five members	2,063
six members or more	2,273

Source: Hong Kong Social Welfare Department (1993), p.193.

Is this an adequate subsidy? The benefit level is extremely low as compared with the median household income of about HK$12,000 per month for the Hong Kong population in 1993. For example, the three-person family entitled to receive HK$2,250 per month for the basic scale rate is getting just 19 per cent of the median household income of the general population.

The Social Welfare Department likes to put forward two counter arguments. The first argument is that families depending on Public Assistance are entitled to other allowances such as medical allowance, allowance for children's school activities, allowance for telephone charges, etc. However, in reality the procedures for claiming these allowances are very tedious and there are many conditions to be fulfilled before these families are entitled to claim. Therefore, it is exceptional, rather than typical, that lone mother families are able to get extra allowances other than the basic rate together with rent allowance. There are no official statistics on the take up rate of these special allowances or the expenditure on these allowance. If this is meant to be a significant part of the Public Assistance, the Social Welfare Department should publish relevant statistics. In fact, in my case studies, all the 8 lone parents who are on Public Assistance did not get any supplement other than the basic rate and rent allowance (see chapter 5). They are either not being informed of or being discouraged from applying for these allowances.

The second argument the Social Welfare Department often put forward is that the level of benefit is sufficient to cover all basic needs and necessities.[9] The level of benefit is calculated according to a weighting scale which covers various items such as food, fuel and light, clothing, transportation, etc. (see table 3.13). If we calculate the actual amount which a Public Assistance recipient gets per day, we can see that this is incredibly low.

Let us use a single person receiving Public Assistance as an example (table 3.13). In 1993, this person had only HK$22.5 for food, HK$1 for clothing, HK$1 for transportation and HK$1.2 for services per day. It is difficult to imagine what kind of clothing, transportation or services a person can get with such a low income. For example, in 1993, the cheapest public transport, that is by bus, costs about HK$2 to HK$3 for the shortest single trip. This subsidy is not even enough for a single trip using the cheapest transportation. Similarly, it is practically impossible for the service recipients to afford socially acceptable clothing with HK$1 per day or HK$30 per month, which includes everything from underwear to overcoats, from hats to shoes.

If we compare this expenditure pattern with ordinary singleton household of the Hong Kong population (table 3.13), we can see that Public Assistance families are in extreme poverty. In general, for the average singleton household, expenses on food is more than double that of the Public Assistance recipients; while the expenses on clothing, transportation and services in two days is more or less equal to that for the Public Assistance recipients in a month. Bear in mind that we are only making comparisons with average singleton households, not with the particularly high income groups. Moreover, we are comparing the expenses of average singleton households in 89/90 with that of the Public Assistance recipients in 1993 (see note b in table 3.13). Even without taking into account inflation over the past 3 years (which is about 30 per cent), the expenses of the Public Assistance recipients are still disproportionately small.

Another common defense made by the Social Welfare Department is that the level of benefit has increased rapidly over the years. But, this only reflects the rate of inflation and the increase in living standard of the whole society over the years. In fact, if we examine in more detail the rate of increase of Public Assistance benefit as compared to the median income of the population, it is apparent that Public Assistance recipients have become worse off, relatively speaking (table 3.14). In 1991, the basic rate of Public Assistance for a single person is 14.4 per cent of the median income for a working person. This ratio has fallen nearly 10 per cent as compared to that in 1976. That is, Public Assistance recipients are becoming relatively poorer and poorer because of the rapid rise in living standards.

Table 3.13

Actual amount of commodity and service allowances covered in public assistance (1993) as compared to expenses of the general population, for singleton households

Commodity/services	Public assistance singleton households		All singleton households[b]
	weights[a] (%)	HK$ per day	HK$ per day
Foodstuffs	75.13	22.5	53.6
Fuel & light	5.31	1.6	--
Clothing & footwear	3.45	1.0	16.5
Durable goods	1.55	0.5	--
Miscellaneous	7.43	2.2	--
Transport & vehicles	3.19	1.0	18.5
Services	3.93	1.2	16.5
Total	100%	30[c]	206.1

Notes:
a   This rating scale is effective from 89/90 (HK Social Welfare Department, 1993, p.191).
b   This is the daily household expenses of all singleton households in the general population, compiled from the 1989/90 Household Expenditure Survey (HK Census and Statistic Department, 1991, p.8) - the most current Household Expenditure Survey available in 1993 when data of this study were collected. The categories of expenditure and the weighting percentage for these households are different from those allocated to Public Assistance households, and some items cannot be compiled from the report, therefore are left blank.
c   Based on basic scale rates for singleton - HK$900 per month as at 1 April 1993 (see table 3.11), taking an average of 30 days per month.

Table 3.14
Level of public assistance 1976-91

	1976	1986	1991
Public assistance basic rate for single person (A)	HK$180	HK$510	HK$745
Median monthly income of working person (B)	HK$742	HK$2,573	HK$5,170
(A)/(B)	24.3%	19.8%	14.4%

Sources: HK Society of Social Security (1990), p.3.
HK Social Welfare Department (1991a), p.163.
HK Census and Statistics Department (1993a), p.13.

The situation can be even worse for women who have trouble with their marriage, but are not yet divorced. The social security system is underpinned by familial ideology which firmly believes that women in the family are taken care of by their husbands. Therefore, the family is regarded as an inseparable unit when applying for public assistance. However, if the husband is irresponsible and is not providing adequate financial support to the wife, which is quite common just before divorce, she is not entitled to apply for public assistance unless she is divorced formally. But, until now, there has been a strong taboo in Chinese societies against a woman divorcing her husband. In this manner, many women are excluded from welfare services even if they are in great need.

In general, we can see that Public Assistance is extremely inadequate in meeting the needs of low income families. At best, it can only keep service recipients surviving at subsistence level, but still effectively excludes them from normal social participation. At worst, it deprives some women of social assistance when they are in need, which consequently compels women to depend on men and the family.

Conclusion

This chapter illustrated how a structural approach, one which is informed by development in the sociology of knowledge and uses technical aids such as the index of segregation and graphical trend analysis, helps to reveal the institutionalized disadvantaged position of women. With gender inequality as our main theme for investigation, we can come to certain provisional conclusion after scrutinizing the housing system, the employment system and the social welfare system in Hong Kong. Discrimination in favour of men is entrenched within Hong Kong institutions. It is clear that social policy in Hong Kong is dominated by patriarchal ideology and the New Right ideology of minimal government intervention. In general, government intervention in social services is kept to a minimum, leaving all social problems to be dealt with by the individual and the family. For example, as I have pointed out in the discussion on social security services, government policy papers emphasized repeatedly that social security benefit is only for 'those least able to help themselves'.

Strictly speaking, the Hong Kong government is not 'non-interventionist' in all aspects as commonly believed. More exactly, the government actively intervenes to protect the interests of the capitalist enterprise, while keeping social services for low income families at a minimum level. That is why most social policies and laws in Hong Kong favour large corporations as well as modest capitalist entrepreneurs. Conversely, social services for low income groups are scarce, fragmented and unresponsive to social needs. The only exception is when government intervention in certain social services helps to foster economic growth or to restore social stability.

One exceptional example is the government's massive intervention in public housing in the 1960s and 1970s. The main purposes of this massive intervention were to obtain land for economic development and to relocate the population to provide a stable pool of labour for the labour intensive industries, instead of satisfying the housing needs of the population. When the economy of Hong Kong restructured drastically in the 1980s and 1990s, the government reverted its housing strategy from massive intervention to privatization, which helped to foster the growth of private housing market.

The consequence of this economically oriented housing policy is that many housing problems have been left unsolved. For example, privatization of public housing has widened the poverty gap; many low income families such as lone mother families are left on their own while housing resources have shifted to the better off; many 'unconventional' families such as singleton, two-person families and lone mother families have been discriminated against in the housing system; the needs of vulnerable groups such as the elderly, lone mothers, the disabled, the chronically sick, and low income families have been neglected in the public housing allocation system; low income families relocated to remote new towns are left on their own without adequate community services and facilities. In many cases, it is the women in the family who have to take up the extra burden or suffer the most discrimination.

Unlike the housing system, government intervention in the employment system and protection of workers from capitalist exploitation has always been minimal. The working class has been left on its own to struggle for survival in the exploitative labour market. Gender equality has never been the concern of government employment policies. Consequently, women are being discriminated against or have less opportunities in the job market. In turn, this lack of employment opportunities and the subsequent lack of financial resources further reinforces women's dependency on the family or on men, and thus strengthening patriarchal social practices.

Similarly, the government's intervention in social welfare has been minimal, and welfare policy is underpinned by traditional familial ideology. This is especially obvious in the child care service and the Public Assistance Scheme that we have discussed. Child care services are kept at an extremely minimal level because the government insists that it is the sole responsibility of the family (more exactly, the women in the family) to take care of the children. Without adequate support for child care services, many women are deprived of employment opportunities or other life chances. This is especially obvious for women living in new towns and women who are lone parents. Similarly, the minimal level of benefit for Public Assistance is ineffective in solving the problems of low income families. Many low income lone mothers are trapped in poverty by the social security system. Being affected by the ideology of 'family as a unit', women who are not taken care of by their husbands are not entitled to public assistance benefit unless they are formally divorced. In this sense, the social welfare system is not helping those in need. Instead, it is reinforcing traditional familial ideology and compelling women to depend on men and the family.

Minimal government intervention is not the key to economic success. It is only the government's rationalization for shedding its responsibility for solving social problems, and leaving the burden with individuals and their families. Coupled with patriarchal ideology, this public burden has effectively shifted to women, who are supposed to be the carers in the family.

In other words, the problems of women living in new towns or of low income lone mothers are not their individual problems. These problems are being constructed by our social systems. Our social policies, which draw on these dominating ideologies, are ineffective in solving these social problems. On the contrary, very often they reinforce existing gender inequalities.

However, the relationships between social policy and gender inequality are frequently neglected or being underplayed, even in academic spheres. This is partly due to the fact that most academic research in Hong Kong are dominated by male perspectives. Therefore, it is extremely important to pay attention to research approach as to gender studies, which we are going to discuss in the next chapter.

Notes

1. It is always problematic to compare social expenditure internationally because of the variation in definition of terms. In the OECD data social expenditure includes education, health and social security, while in Hong Kong 'social services expenditure' also includes housing expenditure in addition to the former three items.

2. In 1993/94, the Housing Authority is paying the government HK$1,286.5 million for interest on permanent capital and HK$863.6 million for dividends

on non-domestic operations (Hong Kong Housing Authority 1994:122), that is a total of HK$2,000 million.

3. 'Sandwich Class' is middle class family with household income between $20,000 to $40,000 per month (as at 1 April 1993). For more detail see Appendix C2.

4. A report of the Housing Authority estimated that in 1993 there will be 18,590 elderly in need of public housing in the following 5 years, but only 12,540 such flats will be provided in this period (Hong Kong Housing Authority, 1995, part II p.75). However, it is very doubtful whether this is an accurate estimation, and there is no clear explanation of how this estimation is made.

5. In this thesis we adopted an Index of Segregation (I.S.) to indicate the degree of segregation (see Treiman & Hartmann, 1981, chapter 2). The index is defined as:

$$I.S. = \frac{1}{2} \Sigma |X_i - Y_i|$$

where X_i =   percentage of males in the ith occupation category
           Y_i =   percentage of females in the ith occupation category
In other words, this index measures the percentage of males and females required to interchange their occupations in order to maintain a balance between male and female occupations. If the index is equal to 0 there is no occupation segregation, if the index is equal to 1 it indicates complete segregation.

6. Residential child care services in Hong Kong are mainly reserved for children who are not taken care by the family or children with behaviourial problems. Therefore, these services are not relevant to the discussion in this research.

7. There is a charge reduction policy for low income family using the subsidized nursery service. If after deducing the rent from their income, their disposable income is less that the Public Assistance income limit, they do not need to pay. Effective from March 1991, for every $100 in excess of the Public Assistance income limit (which is extremely low, see the following section on Public Assistance for more detail), they have to pay $15. This charge reduction is so stringent that it is rare to get this benefit.

8. Categorization of the Public Assistance Scheme has been re-organized starting from 1 July 1993, and the Public Assistance Scheme has been renamed the Comprehensive Social Security Assistance Scheme. Because the data for this study were collected in late 1992 and early 1993, we prefer to refer our

discussion to the old Public Assistance Scheme, which was more relevant to the experiences of the cases we interviewed. However, our analysis of the social security and the public assistance system is still valid because the level of benefits in the new 'Comprehensive Social Security Assistance Scheme' is as low as the old system. It is only recategorizing and renaming the system rather than improving benefits substantially.

9. This begs theoretical questions on the definition and measurement of poverty and deprivation, see Townsend (1993, chapter 2 and 4) for more detail.

4 Researching gender issues

Academics have played a significant role in trivializing women's issues. Many feminists have pointed out that most academic fields are dominated by men without gender consciousness, so that women's issues are excluded or marginalized in academic study (Oakley, 1989; Westkott, 1979). In Hong Kong the situation is even worse. Launching a feminist research like this study needs to face many challenging questions, especially those concerning 'objectivity' and 'reliability', not to mention limited funding and the lack of support. Hence, it is essential to deal with these methodological questions in more detail before we proceed to our data analysis.

The first part of this chapter focuses on the methodological issues in conducting feminist research, while the second focuses on the methodology of this study. It is demonstrated how the gender dimension can be reinstated in commonly researched phenomena - lone parents and new town problems.

Doing feminist research

Traditional 'mainstream' social research is very critical of feminist research for being biased toward women and 'nonobjective'. In Hong Kong, studies on women's problems are frequently dismissed as biased and unreliable. I want to point out that very often the problems lie not in these feminist researches, but more within 'mainstream' research itself.

Feminist critique of mainstream social research

Many feminists have criticized the limitations of traditional social research (Stanley and Wise, 1983, chapter 1; Reinharz, 1983; Abbott and Wallace, 1990, chapter 1; Eichler, 1988; Harding, 1987; Roberts, 1990; Stanley, 1990). The major problem with traditional research is that it reproduces patriarchal domination through defining problems and developing solutions from a male perspective. It tends to underplay or completely neglect women's issues. For example, in Hong Kong, although there are numerous studies on the problems of Tuen Mun New Town (e.g. Han, 1982; Chow, 1988), women's problems were never the concern of these researches.

There are several common criticisms of traditional approaches to social research (see Reinharz, 1983, pp.168-72 for detailed comparison between mainstream and feminist approaches). The first criticism is about male domination in social research and sociology in general (Oakley, 1989). Most mainstream sociological studies are gender blind; or the mainstream approach is more or less the male-stream approach. Before the 1970s, women's issues were very much underplayed in the academic sphere. In most sociological studies, women did not seem to exist at all. Or if she existed, she was only considered as part of her husband. For example in Goldthorpe's classical study of the affluent workers, women's class position is considered as equivalent to their husband's class location. That is why Goldthorpe's study attracted much criticism from feminists (for the debate see e.g. Goldthorpe, 1983, 1984 and the criticism by Stanworth, 1984).

In recent years, the situation within the academic sphere has improved a little. Gender issues are more visible in universities and colleges. However, there still exists the danger that women's issues are considered marginal. Women are simply added onto the mainstream curriculum as a deprived group or minority, without questioning the fundamental theoretical approach.

The second criticism of mainstream sociological research is the emphasis on 'scientific values' such as objectivity, validity and reliability. That means social research has to rely heavily on positivistic quantitative approaches, social surveys with probabilistic sampling methods, and statistical presentations of the results. Oakley (1990a, p.38) points out that this emphasis reflects the logic of masculinity. The emphasis on 'rationality' is a form of masculine culture, while women are considered as emotional and unreliable.

However, the research questions raised in many feminist researches aim to reveal more in-depth problems such as the life experience of women, ideological oppression of women, and the development of inequality in power between the two sexes. Obviously, quantitative approaches are not too particularly effective in these aspects. With strong emphasis on qualitative approaches, many feminist researches are criticized for lacking objectivity.

Feminists' counter argument is that traditional researchers emphasising objectivity are just pretending to be neutral and value free. It seems on the surface that they are just uncovering some 'objective truth' in our society. However, it is not difficult to see that every researcher must have her/his own value biases. And this must affect the research, no matter whether she/he is aware of it or not. In other words, even the most 'objective' social survey or 'neutral' statistics are value laden. The process of research, from choosing a research topic (or not choosing a certain topic), to what types of questions are included (or excluded) in the questionnaire, to what kind of data are presented (or not presented) and how they are presented, are all underpinned by some value judgement.

Another point is that traditional research, especially statistical methods, are no more 'true' than the case study approach. Social reality is multi-faceted. At best, traditional 'scientific' research is only one approach for seeing one side of reality. While in-depth case studies are another approach looking at different aspects of reality. They are no less 'true', if not better, than the 'scientific' approach (for more details of defending the feminist standpoint, see Stanley and Wise, 1983, pp.168-75). Therefore, instead of pretending to be neutral, it is better to acknowledge the subjectivity of the researcher, and be aware of his/her influences on the interviewees.

Closely related to the principle of objectivity, the third criticism of traditional research is the emphasis on emotional detachment from the interviewees. The researcher is supposed to be totally rational without emotional involvement. It is only with this neutrality that the researcher is able to see the 'objective facts' without bias. Moreover by emphasizing detachment from the interviewees, it is claimed that the researcher can avoid biasing the respondents and leading them to his/her own presumed conclusion.

This conception of 'objectivity' in interviews is self contradictory (Oakley, 1990a). The interviewer has to be friendly in order to gain cooperation of the interviewee, but at the same time he/she cannot be too friendly for fear of emotional involvement. The interviewer has to pretend to have no opinion. Especially, they are alerted to prevent the possibility of questions being asked back by the interviewees.

Feminists are critical of this 'emotional detachment'. This will treat the subject of study as a tool, or a data producing machine. Interviewing is also conceived as no more than a mechanical instrumental process of asking questions and recording the answers. This process depersonalizes and objectifies both interviewers and interviewees. Moreover, the traditional interview establishes a hierarchical relationship between interviewer and respondent. The interviewer becomes the superior who asks questions, and the interviewee becomes the subordinate who has to answer every question without asking back. Since it is one of the feminist concerns to fight against depersonalization of human relations and against the hierarchical gender relationships, obviously traditional 'scientific' interview technique is not recommended.

In criticizing the 'emotional detachment' of traditional research, feminists have to face the question whether they need to be 'objective'. Before answering this question, we should noted that there are two aspects of the concept 'objectivity' (Eichler, 1988, p.11-12; Fee, 1983, p.9-27). On one side, it emphasizes the openness of the researcher to perceiving different aspects of a social incident and to different kind of explanations for social phenomena. This is the part most feminists would like to uphold in their researches. Ironically, many mainstream researchers, while emphasising 'objectivity', are blind to the gender dimension of their research. Another aspect of 'objectivity' is the emphasis on detachment and the pretence of being value free. This is the part feminists reject.

Besides its gender blindness, traditional quantitative methods are also ineffective in exploring some feminist issues. For example, the structured questionnaire, especially the close ended type, forces the interviewees to choose a stance which does not exactly reflect the complexity of life. Another problem is that the snapshot approach of a social survey does not get information on the process of how certain social culture and social relationships have developed over time. Therefore, quantitative surveys are not very effective for exploring subjective feelings or experiences in social life.

Especially in research on women issues, it is difficult to explore what women really think because their answers are often obscured by patriarchal ideology. For example, when you ask a woman whether she likes to do housework, most probably she will answer yes. It is because she has internalized unconsciously the gender role of being a career. She may even think that in being a housewife she is in a more advantageous position than her husband who needs to work in the factory. However, accepting such roles does not mean that she is happy. That is why we have to probe into her underlying feelings, instead of getting a simple answer of 'yes or no', 'satisfied or not satisfied'. Therefore, these researches tend to use in-depth case studies, and borrow methodological ideas from ethnography and ethnomethodology. In addition to women studies, ethnographic approaches are also gaining popularity in the study of housing problems (see Franklin, 1990). This trend in research indicates that qualitative studies of women's housing problems may help to reveal problems not apparent in quantitative studies (such as Brion and Tinker, 1980).

What is feminist research?

Besides criticizing traditional positivist approaches to research, what are the feminists trying to uphold in their researches? Is there a feminist approach to research as such? If so, how is it different from mainstream ones?

Some feminists prefer to adopt qualitative approaches like in-depth case studies, ethnography and ethnomethodology.[1] Ethnographical methods emphasize the natural experience of everyday life as it is. Usually, the researcher starts with no assumption or theory about the social phenomenon he/she is going to observe, and tries to report things as they happen as completely as possible. Of course, as the research develops, the researcher may come up with some explanation or theory for his/her observation. Ethnomethodology as a research methodology emphasizes on the importance of analyzing everyday life experience, it is the study of the ways in which people create and construct their way of life. The focus is how a person comes to perceive a particular situation, and how this perception influences their subsequent actions. In other words, ethnomethodology concentrates on the unwritten rules that make everyday social activity orderly, and tries to express these taken for granted rules explicitly.

These approaches have several strengths. First, by focusing on interactions between individuals we can develop more in-depth understandings of the operation of our society, which may be easily missed in the overall picture given by quantitative analysis. Second, it allows more space for different explanations of social problems to develop instead of adopting traditional ideologies unconsciously. Third, these approaches are able to reflect the contextual meaning of the social situation to the respondents as it is, instead of forcing them to adopt the researcher's framework as in the close ended questionnaire of a social survey. Fourth, these are more effective for studying a continuous social processes, especially the formation of cultural rules, than the snapshot approach entailed in survey methods.

These approaches have important implications for feminist research because gender blind ideology is usually implicit and obscured by taken for granted values. Women are engaged in their gender roles without consciousness of underlying ideology. For example the role of being a housewife seems to be so natural that a woman will rarely query why she is doing this from day to day. The power of ethnomethodological approach in feminist research is that it can help us to uncover the veil of women's common sense perceptions of the situation, how these perceptions are developed and how they affect their actions.

However, feminist research is not simply a matter of using ethnography or ethnomethodology. More than that, Eichler has tried to develop a 'non-sexist research method' and has proposed detailed guidelines for this approach (1988, pp. 129-65). There are several basic principles in this feminist research method, which I am also trying to adopt in my study as far as possible.

First, women as the central issue. The simplest answer to the question 'what is feminist research?' is that gender dimension is considered to be the central issue in the research. Of course, there is no need to say that these researches have a vision of improving the situation for women. Here researchers are explicitly committed to minimizing gender inequality in contrast to the traditional emphasis on so called 'neutrality'. That is why in my study one of the explicit aims is to minimize gender inequality.

Second, the need for emotional involvement. Rejecting the emphasis on emotional detachment in traditional positive research, feminists such as Oakley (1990a, pp.44-51) and Stanley and Wise (1983, pp.160-5) have argued that research should build on friendly relationships with the interviewees. The interviewee in a research should not be treated as simply a data producing machine. Instead, the interviewer should try to engage in a dialogue with the interviewee on equal grounds, answering questions asked back and responding to the interviewee's need, rather than conducting a mechanistic one way question and answer session. Therefore, in the interviews in my study, I do not follow the interview guidelines rigidly in 'question and answer' mode. More often, I respond to the interviewees' interests and main concerns. By doing so, we can establish a more trusting relationship with the interviewees, which is essential for revealing their in-depth feeling and experience. After the interviews, many interviewees in my study reflected that they felt just like they were talking to an old friend instead of being 'interviewed' literally. Some women even admitted that they were revealing some feelings and opinions which were unknown to their husbands.

Third, reflexivity. Researchers should be aware of their power over the interviewees. It is not only that interviewing tends to embedded within a hierarchial relationship, but also that it authorizes the researcher to have control over the data collected. Therefore, the researchers must be very aware of abusing this power and of doing harm to the interviewees. Feminists are fighting against hierarchical power relationships in patriarchal society. They are trying to replace dominating and possessive human relationships with the more equal relations of 'sisterhood' and cooperation. Therefore, feminists have to be very alert to the need to establish equal relationships in interviews, and their research should be geared toward minimizing gender inequality instead of making use of the interviewees for personal benefit. That is why in my interviews I repeatedly clarified that I, the academic researcher, am no more 'superior' than the respondents. I have an interesting experience of talking to a respondent for one hour after the interview, on whether professionals such as researchers and social workers can really benefit the working class.

Fourth, empowering women in the research. Being conscious of the power issues has led some feminists to propose that women should be empowered to do research on themselves, instead of being researched as an object by an outsider. No doubt this is an stimulating idea, although it is obvious that there will be numerous difficulties in doing so. Of course, not many researchers will be able to achieve this objective. But, at least feminist research should be conceived of as an empowering process in which women are helped to develop more in-depth understanding of their situation (Oakley, 1990a, p.50). In other words, feminist research can be considered as a praxis for social change (Lather, 1988, pp.570-1). So, in my interviews, I was also conscious of supporting and encouraging the interviewees to fight for their own rights whenever appropriate.

By criticizing the underlying values of traditional research, I do not mean that feminist research is perfect. On the contrary, there are still many unresolved contradictions in feminist approaches to research. Stacey (1988) has pointed out the danger of ethnography exploiting women in the process of interviewing and publishing the products of the research. The relationship between researcher and interviewee is an unequal power relationship, which exists independent of whether the researcher is conscious or unconscious of this power dimension. Feminists face the same danger of abusing this power as researchers using positivist methods. Ribbens (1989) has also pointed out that interviewing women is an unnatural situation (also see Oakley, 1990a). There are inherent contradictions between being a feminist who emphasizes equality and being a researcher who is granted the power to manipulate. This issue further leads to the question of whether it is possible to have feminist research methodology as such. Can the contradiction between feminist principles and research be resolved successfully? Since these questions are beyond the scope of this book, I am not going to pursue them any further (those who are interested please see Abbott and Wallace, 1991, pp.205 and Harding, 1987).

Concluding the discussion in this section, we can see that traditional positivist and quantitative research methods have considerable limitations for studying women's issues. Therefore my study basically relies on in-depth case studies. Having said that, we should not rule out quantitative method completely. The simple distinction between qualitative and quantitative method does not capture the essence of the problem (Hammersley, 1992, chapter 9). The problem of traditional social research is not the use of quantitative methods as such. It is the gender blindness of the researchers that causes the problems. If we reject quantitative methods completely, it will limit the scope of study in feminist researches and exclude some important questions to be asked about gender inequality (Roberts, 1990, p.XX, and Oakley, 1990b). I think both qualitative and quantitative methods can be employed in feminist studies. They deal with different research questions. For example, quantitative approaches are more effective for answering questions such as how many women are in such situations, while qualitative method are more effective in exploring women's feelings and experiences in a certain situation. Since this research mainly focus on how gender inequality is being constructed in the housing system and how women experience this inequality, I mainly rely on qualitative methods. However, I also supplement my analysis with quantitative data such as official statistics and relevant surveys. This approach is more readily apparent if we look at the research methodology of this study in the following section.

Research methodology

The main concern of this research is to explore how women's housing problems are constructed in our social system on the one hand, and how their housing situation and their living environment affects their life chances on the other hand. That is, the subjective experience of women in the housing system is the main focus of this study. This is difficult to be measured by quantitative methods, and usually cannot be adequately reflected in structured questionnaire surveys. In-depth case studies are more suitable for this research concern.

In my case studies, I explicitly adopted a feminist approach, which emphasized revealing women's experience of subordination in the family and in society at large. Special attention was paid to building up trustful relationships with interviewees. I were able to engage the respondents in sharing their experiences frankly, instead of simply questioning them and recording answers. Frequently, I engaged in friendly dialogue, responding to questions from interviewees, giving information and advice on access to social services, education for children and child care services, or encouraging women to break through traditional constraints. Briefly, I considered the interview as an empowering process rather than a simple data producing exercise.

At the same time, we do not rule out quantitative data completely. Qualitative data in the case studies are supplemented with analysis of census and other statistical data, as well as with documentation of government reports and related academic studies.

Needless to say I cannot cover every aspect of women's housing experience in a single study. I have focused on two target groups in this study: lone mothers and women living in new towns. In chapter 1, I have explained the significance of choosing these two target groups, therefore, the rationales are not reiterated here. All interviews for the cases and of the informants were done between August 1992 and August 1993

Lone mothers

For the study of lone mothers, data were collected from two major sources. One is an in-depth case study of 20 lone parents. The other source is the secondary data analysis of a small scale survey on housing problems of lone parent families in Hong Kong, conducted by me in 1992 under the auspices of the Department of Applied Social Studies of the Hong Kong Polytechnic (Chan, 1993).

For the in-depth case studies, 20 lone parents (17 female and 3 male) were interviewed. Amongst these cases, 10 were selected from the respondents in the small scale questionnaire survey that I conducted in 1992 (Chan, 1993). Respondents to the survey were asked to indicate whether they would like to attend further in-depth interviews. The response was very good. More than 20 lone parents indicated interest in further interviews. I chose 10 cases amongst these respondents. Another 10 cases were introduced by social service agencies, women's organizations, and earlier respondents in the case studies. This brought the total number of cases interviewed up to 20.

Amongst these 20 cases, I have tried to maintain a balanced proportion with respect to several important background variables. The most important three variables are: 1) living in public housing or in private housing; 2) separated from spouse for short period (less than 2 years) or for long period of time (more than 2 years); 3) being employed full time/part time or having no employment (depending on Public Assistance).

By drawing the samples from both private and public housing, we can study women's housing experiences in various types of dwellings. The length of time separated from the husband also significantly influences lone mother's housing experiences. Those just separated are most probably in a crisis situation, they need to deal with numerous pressing problems. Those separated for a longer period have better chance of having settled down, and they can reflect on their experiences more systematically. Finally, the employment status of lone mothers is an important indication of their financial ability to solve their housing problems. That is why it is essential to control these three variables in order to obtain a wide spectrum of housing experiences.

Most of the respondents come from the lower middle or working class. The causes of lone parenthood are mainly separation/divorce, only 3 interviewees were widowed. Widows were given lower priority in the selection of samples because as compared to the separated and divorced, their housing problems seem to be less serious and urgent. Focusing on the most vulnerable and needy groups is more effective for showing the shortcoming of present policies and services. In the case studies, many of the respondents have even suffered from domestic violence and abuse before they divorced. In addition, I have also interviewed 3 lone fathers for comparison, which helps to reveal gender differences in lone parenthood.

For a summary of the backgrounds of individual respondents, please refer to Appendix B1. Names of persons and some easily identified places are changed for confidentiality. Common Chinese names are assigned to the 20 respondents in alphabetical order from A to T. These given names have no relation with their real names.

Please refer to appendix A1 for the interview guidelines employed. However, these are only broad areas for discussion in the interviews, instead of a structured questionnaire. The interviews are rather free flowing and open ended, allowing plenty of space for respondents to elaborate on issues of concern for them. All interviews were taped and then transcribed. The interviews lasted for about one and a half hours each.

The analysis of lone mothers' housing problems is supplemented with secondary data analysis of a small scale questionnaire survey conducted by me in 1992 (Chan, 1993), under the auspices of the Department of Applied Social Studies of Hong Kong Polytechnic. Since official statistics and systematic research on lone mothers' in Hong Kong is extremely scarce, this is the most comprehensive and current set of data available on the housing problems of lone mothers. The methodology employed is structured questionnaire survey. It aims to explore general housing needs, access to housing and the general housing conditions of lone parent families. The target of the study was lone parents who are service recipients in social service agencies and women organizations. Sampling was non-random. Social services agencies and women organizations were contacted by mail and followed up by phone, to solicit support in distributing questionnaires. A quota of 100 respondents was set because of resource limitations, those who replied earliest were accepted. Finally, 98 lone parents from 13 organizations were successfully interviewed. Amongst the respondents 88 were lone mothers and 10 were lone fathers.

Although this is not a representative sample of all lone mothers in Hong Kong, it reflects some significant housing problems for working class lone mothers. The respondents were referred by different social services agencies and came from various districts in Hong Kong. From the background of the respondents, we can see that this sample is comparable to past studies (e.g. Young, 1985; H.K.F.W.S. and Law, 1991) on lone parents in Hong Kong.[2] Another important point is that the situation of lone mothers varies greatly with different factors such as class, ethnicity, age, working experience, education, number of children, whether widowed or divorced, etc., therefore data focusing on particular groups - in this case working class lone mothers who need to seek help from social welfare agencies - can be more illuminating than using aggregated data of the general situation of lone mothers.

Women in new towns

In the second part of my study, women in Tuen Mun new town is chosen as the target of analysis because it is one of the most typical illustration of how women's interests have been neglected in urban development. Tuen Mun is one of the new towns with the worst housing and community problems (see chapter 7 for more detail). By choosing a crucial problematic new town, we can demonstrate more clearly the impact of the housing system on gender inequality. Another interesting point of choosing Tuen Mun is that although there are numerous studies on problems in this new town (e.g. Han, 1982; Chow, 1988), women's problems are rarely mentioned in these studies. Therefore I choose this target of study to illustrate how the gender dimension can be reinstated in social research.

The data on women in new towns mainly comes from in-depth case studies of 21 women and 5 couples (interviewing both husband and wife) living in Tuen Mun and Yuen Long new town. Snow ball sampling methods were employed to draw up the list of respondents. Finally, 10 women were introduced by social service agencies in Tuen Mun, and the other 11 were introduced by friends and the women interviewed earlier. All the women interviewed were also asked to invite their husbands for interview. At the end, 5 men accepted the invitations and were interviewed. A few men were included in this study to serve as comparison between males and females.

In this quota sampling process, there are two important background variables - the type of housing (public/private, rental/ownership) and employment status - I have considered to select respondents in order to maintain a balanced sample (see Appendix B2). Amongst the 21 female interviewees, 10 were living in public rental housing and 11 were living in private housing, including 8 in private ownership and 5 in rural village housing. By looking at women in various types of housing, we can see that gender inequality exists widely instead of just being confined to particular accommodation such as public housing. Concerning employment status, 10 of the women had full time and part time jobs at the time of interview while the other 11 were full time housewives or unemployed (Appendix B2). This sampling helps to show that problems do not only affect full time housewives in Tuen Mun New Town. Both women with or without employment are affected, albeit in different ways.

Ten of the women had household income above HK$10,000 per month (the median household income of the Hong Kong population in 1992), while 11 women were below the population median. Judging from their income level (Appendix B2), this sampling can be considered as mainly reflecting the experience of women in lower or lower middle income families in Tuen Mun.

On average, most women have lived in the New Town for 10 years, which corresponds with the peak period of development in Tuen Mun. Most women are middle aged with primary or lower secondary education. All women are married and have to take care of children. The norm was having 2 children (14 cases), but it was not rare to have 3 or more children (6 cases). With the heavy burden of child care, it is not surprising to see that women in new towns suffered greatly. Please refer to appendix B2 for further detail on the background of the respondents.

Similarly to the study on lone mothers, the interview was free flowing, attending to the respondents' main concerns instead of adhering strictly to the guidelines (see Appendix A2 for the guideline). The interview was taped to facilitate transcription, and each interview lasted about one and half hours. In those cases when both husband and wife were interviewed, they were interviewed separately so that each one was free to express their views without interference.

The case analysis is also supplemented with documentation of relevant statistics and research on new towns. Unlike the situation of lone mothers, quantitative data on new towns, especially the Tuen Mun new town, are more readily available (e.g. Tuen Mun District Board, 1990; Han, 1982; Chow, 1988). There is no need to conduct another quantitative survey on problems in Tuen Mun new town. I have made use of existing statistics and research, where appropriate, to reinforce my arguments.

Finally, I have also interviewed 5 informants, including one social worker in a shelter for battered women and 4 housing officers working in various districts and different types of public housing. See Appendix B3 for a summary of the backgrounds of the informants. This provides further information on related housing policies and practice concerning both lone mothers and women living in new towns.

Conclusion

This chapter challenges the traditional approach to research, that emphasizes positive and quantitative methodology. These traditional researches are gender biased instead of being 'neutral' and 'objective' as they claimed to be.

My argument is that we must adopt a feminist approach in doing research in order to understand better women's problems in the housing system. This approach includes principles such as explicit concern for gender equality, emotional involvement and reflexivity of the researcher, and the empowerment of women in the research process.

It should be noted that feminist researches do not necessarily exclude quantitative methods. The problems of traditional researches lay in their gender bias orientation, not the methodology as such.

In fact, my research emphasizes both on quantitative and qualitative data, and on analysis at both the structural level and the level of everyday social interactions.

That is why it is essential to integrate a comprehensive statistical and graphical analysis of the structural constraints on women (as in Chapter 3) with an in-depth analysis of women's subjective experience in the housing system, which we are going to discuss in the following chapters (Chapter 5 to 8).

Notes

1. We are not going to describe these methods in detail, this is not our main concern here. Please refer to basic text such as Yin (1993), Fetterman (1989), Hammersley and Atkinson (1990), Hammersley (1992), and McNeill (1985) for further detail.

2. Since the secondary data analysis of this questionnaire survey only constitute a minor part of our analysis, we are not going into detail of comparing the background of respondents with that of other researches on lone mothers in Hong Kong. Those who are interested, please refer to the research report (Chan, 1993).

Part Two

HOUSING EXPERIENCES
OF LONE MOTHERS

5 Restraining lone mothers' problem solving ability

In the previous chapters I have repeatedly emphasized that women's housing problems are not caused by their own deficiency, they are constructed by our social system. How are these problems constructed? In this part of the book (chapter 5 and 6) we are going to look at the housing experiences of lone mothers. Chapter 5 demonstrates how various social policies and social practices increase the burden on lone mothers and restrain lone mothers' ability to tackle their problems, instead of helping them to solve their problems. Chapter 6 focuses on lone mothers' experiences of various types of housing.

This chapter starts by giving some basic background information about lone mothers in Hong Kong, which is essential for understanding the following discussion in the Hong Kong context. Then, we are going to focus on four important factors that limit lone mothers' problem solving ability: 1) limited access to child care services coupled with the mothering role has created tremendous difficulties for lone mothers taking care of young children; 2) discrimination within the employment system reduces women's financial ability and independence; 3) the inadequate social security system traps lone mothers in poverty; and 4) social stigma and discrimination against lone mothers in the wider social context further limits their chances to solve their problems.

Lone mothers in Hong Kong

Since lone mothers' problems are overlooked, official statistics and research on lone mothers in general are extremely scarce. No official census data on lone parents are published. The only official statistics available is a brief report by the Social Welfare Department (H.K.S.W.D., 1992), which presents some patchy information estimated from the 1991 population Census. At present, there has been little substantial academic research studies on lone parents (e.g. Young, 1985; H.K.F.W.S. and Law, 1991; H.K.C.F.S.C., 1986). However, their focus is more on intra-family relationships, and it is not surprising that gender issues are completely neglected.

The lack of statistics and research on lone mothers is not because these problems do not exist. Very often they are underestimated or even not defined as problems. For example, the Social Welfare Department report claimed that in 1991 only 34,538 families (that is, about 2.2 per cent of all families) in Hong Kong are single parent families (H.K.S.W.D., 1992, p.1). Obviously, this is an extreme underestimation. One reason for this underestimation is that the definition of a lone mother is very limited. For example, it only includes those with children aged 18 or below, and who are formally divorced or separated. In reality, because of the strong social stigmatization of lone mothers in a Chinese society like Hong Kong, many women are reluctant to file an application for divorce even if their husbands have deserted the family. Similarly, many lone mothers with children aged above 18, but still in full time education are being excluded from the definition. Unlike some Western countries where support for young people who are in full time education or who are living independently of their parents is more easily available, in Hong Kong children are more dependent on their parents, especially when they are still in full time education.

Even in an earlier Labour Force Survey conducted by the government (as quoted in Young, 1985, p.2), it is estimated that 3.3 per cent of the families in Hong Kong are headed by lone parents, and 8.2 per cent of the families are not classified as lone parent households but with a father or mother not living in the household because of various reasons such as staying in hospital, prison or other institutions, living in Mainland China or living aboard, or not legally divorced. Obviously, the existing classification is problematic, many of these 8.2 per cent should also be classified as lone parent families.

It may be helpful to compare with statistics in Britain. Data in *Social Trend* indicated that in 1991 over 18 per cent of families with dependent children are lone parent families, and of these over 17 per cent are headed by lone mothers and just over 1 per cent are headed by lone fathers (Central Statistical Office, 1994, p.36). Although the proportion of lone parent families in Hong Kong may not be as high as that of Britain, it is very unlikely to be as low as that estimated by the Social Welfare Department in 1991.

Contrary to the unreliable official statistics in Hong Kong, there are various indications that the problems of lone parent families are becoming more serious. According to a large scale social indicator survey in 1988, there are 6.6 per cent lone parent families in Hong Kong (Lee, 1991, p.42). This seems to be more credible than the estimation of 2.2 per cent. Moreover, the divorce rate is increasing more rapidly. According to the census data, the number of divorce decrees has risen from 809 cases in 1976 to 6295 cases in 1991, that is an increase of nearly 8 times over 15 years (table 5.1).

Another alarming indicator of the problem is that the age of lone parents, especially lone mothers, is decreasing. The median age of lone mothers has decreased from 44.3 in 1986 to 40.8 in 1991 (table 5.2). This reflects that more people become lone parents because of divorce or separation instead of widowhood, and people get divorced earlier than before. At the same time, we need to aware that young lone mothers usually face more difficulties than older ones.

Table 5.1
Divorce statistics 1976-91

	1976	1981	1986	1991
Petitions filed	1,054	2,811	5,339	7,287
Divorce decrees	809	2,060	4,257	6,295

Source: Hong Kong Census and Statistics Department (1986b), p.19; and (1993b), p.20.

Table 5.2
Age of lone parents in Hong Kong, 1986 and 1991

Age	Lone mothers (%)		Lone fathers (%)	
	1986	1991	1986	1991
15-29	5.3	5.0	6.4	5.5
30-39	29.2	38.8	29.0	29.5
40-49	32.6	37.8	30.2	37.7
50 and over	32.9	18.9	34.4	27.3
Median age	44.3	40.8	44.4	42.9

Source: Hong Kong Social Welfare Department (1992), p.15.

Judging from this evidence, it is not difficult to see that lone mothers' problems are becoming more serious. How do lone mothers cope with their problems? Many people assume that existing social services and lone mothers' own supportive networks are adequate for solving their problems. How far is this true? Let us look at lone mothers' experience of child caring, of employment, of the social security system, and at discrimination against lone mothers in the wider social context.

Child caring: who cares?

First of all, let us look at the situation of child care burdens on lone mothers. In chapter 3, I have pointed out that child caring services are extremely lacking in Hong Kong. In general, this affects most women in Hong Kong, lone mothers are no exception. In most cases, the predicament of lone mothers is worse than their counterparts in two-parent families because they have to take up the child care burden all alone.

Child care burden on lone mothers

Child care burdens mostly fall on women after a marriage break down. That is, most of the lone parent families are headed by females. In the questionnaire survey conducted by me in 1992 (Chan, 1993), amongst the 98 lone parents interviewed, 88 (about 90 per cent) were female and only 10 are male. In Hong Kong, there are no official statistics on the sex proportion of one parent headed families. However, many important studies on lone mother families in Hong Kong have indicated that the proportion of female head is about 80 per cent to 90 per cent (Young, 1985; H.K.F.W.S. and Law, 1991; H.K.C.F.S.C., 1986).

In that survey, amongst the 88 lone mothers interviewed, most of them (92 per cent) had children aged 15 or less. The number of children ranged from one to three, with an average of 1.44 children per family. A significant proportion (29.5%) of lone mothers even had children aged 6 or less. The need to take care of children, especially young children, creates tremendous housing difficulties. For example, families with young children are generally not welcome in private tenements (see chapter 6).

Moreover, there are obvious differences between male and female lone parents in the accessibility of child care service (see table 5.3). Amongst the 88 lone mothers interviewed in the survey, 73.9 per cent had to take care of the children all on their own, without support from other relatives or social services. On the other hand, for the 9 lone fathers, the situation was better. Four lone fathers had to take care of the children all by themselves, while 5 had some other relatives (mostly their mothers) to help, had employed domestic helpers, or had placed the children in welfare institutions. In the case studies, all the three lone fathers I interviewed had been able to get child care support either privately or in public services.

Lone fathers have more access to help partly because they can purchase private services with their better financial resources as compared with their female counterparts. Another reason is that patriarchal ideology assumes that child care is not a man's duty, so they can obtain subsidized child care services or get help from other relatives more easily than lone mothers. For example, Mr Siu, a lone father I interviewed was able to get help from the neighbour to look after his three children after his wife died. Of course, this is not to deny that there are still very insufficient child care services for lone fathers. As I have pointed out in chapter 3, child care services in Hong Kong are extremely lacking.

Table 5.3
Sex and pattern of child caring

	Male	Female
On their own	4	65 (79.3%)
With helps from others[a]	5	17 (20.7%)
Total	9[b]	82 (100%)

Notes:
a   This include all those with helps from parents and other relatives, those employing domestic helpers, those placing their children full time in welfare institution.
b   The total number of lone fathers is too small that percentage is not calculated.

It is assumed that women should be responsible for child care, therefore, it is much more difficult for lone mothers to get help from other sources, unless they have sufficient income to employ domestic workers or pay for private child care services.

Among the lone mothers interviewed, many complained that it is difficult for them to get subsidized child care services if they have full time employment. For example, at the beginning of a separation from her husband, Ms Pang has approached the Social Security Office to get financial assistance and subsidized child care services. At that time, she was working, but with very low income of about HK$4,000 per month (but this was already above the very stringent Public Assistance level). The Social Security Officer told Ms Pang that her situation was not too bad:

> You are quite O.K., you don't need public assistance or child care services. If you want to go to work, it is easy, you take the child to the nursery before you go to work, you can take it home after work. You see, its your responsibility to take care of your child. (Ms Pang)

This officer has neglected the fact that private nurseries are very expensive, especially in comparison with Ms Pang's low income. And, in practice it is extremely difficult, if not impossible, for Ms Pang to find a job with suitable working hours at a location that enables her to take her child to and from the nursery.

Ms Gon is another example of difficulties faced in child caring. Although her income was not too bad as compared to other cases in this study (in fact, it was one of the highest), she still found difficulties in arranging child care services for her son. She was a senior clerk working in a Bank, with salary of HK$8,000 per month. As expected, she could not get any subsidized child care services, so she had to rely on a private nursery. The nursery closed at 5:30 p.m., but she had to work until 7:00 p.m. regularly, and sometimes even up to 8:00 p.m. Therefore she had to pay HK$1,000 per month to employ a child minder to take her son back from the nursery, and look after him until she came back from work. However, since perhaps she did not pay her child minder enough, they kept changing frequently.

> I feel that my son is just like a ball, being kicked from place to place. In these three years, we have employed five child minders. It is impossible for my son to adjust to these rapid changes, he has become uncooperative, naughty, jumping around all the time. (Ms Gon)

Many people may believe that lone mothers can solve their child care problems by receiving maintenance from their ex-husbands. This belief is erroneous, especially for most working class lone mothers. In table 5.6, we can see that only 14.8 per cent of the lone mothers in my survey were receiving maintenance from ex-husbands. Moreover, the level of maintenance was extremely low, with median income of HK$3,000 per month only, which was not much better than the social security benefit. Anyway, this is not a reliable, stable and adequate source of income for most working class lone mothers.

Child caring limits employment opportunities

Besides creating extra physical and psychological burdens on lone mothers, child caring duties also limit women's employment opportunities and career development. In Britain, it is well documented that the availability of day care services greatly affects lone mothers' income and employment opportunities (Hardey and Glover, 1991). In my survey, we can see that those lone mothers who need to look after the children all by themselves are less likely to have full time jobs (table 5.4). Only 36.5 per cent of the lone mothers can keep a full time job under this circumstances, while 63.5 per cent cannot work full time or has no employment at all. On the contrary, those who can get help in child caring are more likely to work, 14 out of 15 of these lone mothers are able to work full time, while only 1 works part time or has no employment at all.

Table 5.4
Employment and child caring pattern for lone mothers

	On their own	With helps[a]
Full time job	23 (36.5%)	14
Part time/ no job	40 (63.5%)	1
Total	63 (100%)	15[b]

Notes:
a   This includes all those with help from parents and other relatives, those employing domestic helpers, those placing their children full time in welfare institutions (see table 5.3 for comparison between male and female).
b   Total number of lone mothers with helps in child caring is too small, so percentages are not calculated.

The influence of child caring duty on employment is more clearly revealed by my case studies. For the lone mothers interviewed, almost all of those who did not have a job indicated that it was because of the burden of child care. Otherwise, they would prefer to work. For example, Ms Lee, with two children aged 4 and 7, was on Public Assistance. She was unable to go out to work because of taking care of her children.

I like to go out to work, I like to be independent, but, I also worry that I cannot take good care of my children. If I go out to work, I have to leave my children at home by themselves. But then, I would be very worried about them. It would be much better if the government could provide child care service for us. (Ms Lee)

But since Ms Lee had no employment at the moment, she was expected to take care of the children by herself. So, she was not eligible for subsidized child care services. The problem is that if Ms Lee get a job, most probably she would still not be eligible for subsidized child care services, because her income from employment would easily exceed the income limit for any child care subsidies. In Hong Kong, subsidized child care services are so scarce that it is mainly reserved for those extremely low incomes or those on Public Assistance, and also unable to take care of the children by themselves because of sickness or other family problems (see chapter 3).

For those who have got employment, quite often, child caring duty limits their opportunities for career development. Ms Pang has been a civil servant for nearly ten years, working as Office Assistant in a government department. Normally, she could sit promotion examinations which if she passed would qualify her for promotion.

> After I divorced, I had to give up sitting these promotion examinations, it is too difficult for me to take these examinations and take care of my child at the same time. Now, I want to have a more stable life, I need more time with my daughter. I won't fancy a promotion any more. (Ms Pang)

This is a very typical example in which lone mothers have to give up their promotion opportunities because of the increasing child care burden after divorce.

Why lone mothers care

Obviously it is very unfair for lone mothers to take up most of the burden of child caring without support. Then, why do lone mothers accept this arrangement? Or, to what extent do they accept this?

It is not surprising that most women accept responsibility for child caring, given the dominant patriarchal culture in our society. In fact, it seems uncontentious that the mother should be granted custody of the children after divorce, unless she is deemed unsuitable to take care of the children due to health or social reasons.

Being influenced by the ideology of 'women as carers', many lone mothers interviewed believed that their children were far better with them than with their fathers. Even though they might face great financial difficulties, they would still try their best to keep their children. For example, Ms Gon admitted that her son might be better off financially if he was living with his father. She had thought of leaving her 7 year old son to her ex-husband, because it was extremely difficult for her to take care of the child. However, she believed that her ex-husband would not take as good care of their son as she did. Most probably, he would just leave the child to the grandmother, whose child rearing method was extremely outdated. She insisted that her son would have better quality of care by staying with her even though she was poorer. Therefore, no matter how difficult it was, she would take up this child care responsibility. This reflects a very common attitude amongst lone mothers.

Although most lone mothers accepted that child caring is their responsibility, it is an over simplification to conclude that they are satisfied with the present situation or that they enjoy this arrangement. Lone mothers' subjective feelings vary greatly between individuals.

Not all lone parents enjoy child caring or housework. For example, Ms Bao felt very bored in taking care of her one year old baby.

> I really don't like to stay at home the whole day looking at the baby, she is too young, she knows nothing, just crying or laughing the whole day. I feel very bored, and feel strong pressure on me. (Ms Bao)

However, the ideology of 'women as carers' is so dominant that no other voices can be heard. Negative feelings like Ms Bao's are frequently taboo, suppressed, or not heard even if expressed.

Moreover, the over emphasis on the ideology of 'women as carers' also provides excuses for men to shed their responsibility for child care after divorce. Of course, it is in no doubt that through socialization most mothers are more concerned about caring for children. But, at the same time, this becomes an excuse for perpetuating the unequal distribution of responsibility between males and females after divorce.

Similarly, the emphasis on women's child care obligations also helps the state to shed its responsibility for providing child care and related social services. This echoes the dominant ideology of laissez-faire capitalism in Hong Kong, in which state intervention in social welfare is kept to a minimum (please refer to chapter 3 for discussion on the lack of child care services and the inadequate social security benefits in Hong Kong).

It is interesting to compare the mentality of lone mothers with lone fathers regarding the care of children. Although all the lone fathers interviewed accepted that it is also their responsibility to take care of the children, all of them emphasized that they were compelled to take up the roles of carer only because there is no other alternative. On the other hand, all the lone mothers interviewed unanimously pointed out that child caring is their primary concern.

From the above discussion, we can conclude that lone mothers are in an unfavourable position regarding child caring duty. Usually, they have to take up all the child care burden without adequate support. This inequality is reinforced by the patriarchal ideology of 'women as carers'. With this heavy burden of child care, lone mothers' competitiveness in the labour market and the housing market is greatly reduced, and lone mothers' problem solving ability is very much hampered.

Discrimination in employment

Now, let us turn to the employment system to look at how lone mothers are marginalized, subordinated or excluded. Without equal opportunities in employment, lone mothers' ability to solve their problems are very much restricted.

This section starts by examining the lack of employment opportunities for lone mothers. Then it goes on to look at how employers' discriminatory attitude limits lone mothers' employment opportunities and career development. Finally, we explore lone mothers' conception of work, in order to understand how lone mothers disadvantageous position in employment is being socially constructed, and how far they accept this inequality in employment.

In general, women are less competitive than men in the labour market (see chapter 3 on women and employment in Hong Kong), this is also true for lone mothers as compared with their male counterparts. Most of the lone fathers (8 out of 10) interviewed in my questionnaire survey had full time employment, while only 47.1 per cent of the 86 lone mothers had full time jobs (table 5.5).

Table 5.5
Employment status

Employment status	Lone fathers	Lone mothers
Full time job	8	41 (47.1%)
Part time job	0	7 (8.1%)
Outworker	1	3 (3.5%)
Full time housework	1	33 (38.4%)
Cannot work because of sickness	0	2 (2.3%)
Total	10*	86 (100%)

Note:
* Number of lone fathers is too small, percentage is not calculated.

By saying that lone fathers have better employment opportunities than their female counterparts, it is not to imply that there is no discrimination against lone fathers. Both male and female lone parents are susceptible to employment discrimination. As a lone father Mr Tang has pointed out that his employer was quite doubtful of his ability to take care of his family and his job at the same time, especially at the early stage of his divorce. However, as time went by, he demonstrated that his performance was no worse than other colleagues. He felt that his employer accepted him gradually.

However, being a lone parent and being a woman at the same time can make things worse. Even before divorce, women have less opportunities for employment because of various reasons such as child care commitments, lack of education opportunities, discontinuity of career due to pregnancy and discrimination in the employment system (see chapter 3). After divorce, the situation worsens because lone mothers have to take up the burden of child caring all on their own. This affects their choice of employment, working hours and location of work, to a great extent.

The case of Ms Gon is very representative. She was a Senior Clerk working in a bank, which was a very demanding post. She had to work until 7:00 p.m. or 8:00 p.m. regularly. With these working hours, she faced great difficulties in taking care of her 7 year old son. At last, she had to ask her boss to transfer her to work with regular office hours, from 9:00 am. to 5:30 p.m. Although her boss granted her a transfer, this affected the assessment of her performance substantially, which in turn affected her promotion prospects. She thought that this was very unfair to her because the transfer of her work involved only an adjustment of working hours and the nature of the work, it did not mean than she was doing less than before or was less committed. Although before she applied for transfer, she was well aware of this negative effect, it seemed that she had no choice other than to accept the reality.

Of course, we cannot say that all lone mothers inevitably have problems in employment. There are variations in access to employment with according to various factors such as class, ethnicity, age, and working experience. In general, in my case studies, the 10 lone mothers who were able to find jobs were those with better education (usually secondary education), younger in age, coming from middle or lower middle income families before divorce, and having long employment history. On the other hand those more likely to depend on Public Assistance were those with lower education (usually primary), coming from working class families before divorce, with not much working experience, or older in age.

Employers' attitudes and discrimination in work

Frequently lone mothers were unable to find jobs not because they lacked working ability, but rather because they were marginalized or excluded from the job market. We have seen in the previous section how child care duty constrains their employment choices. Now, we turn to how employers, or the employment system in general, discriminates against lone mothers.

Many employers are quite reluctant to employ lone parents. For example, Ms Fung's interview for a job vividly illustrates employers' attitudes. Most probably Ms Fung failed to get the job she was applying for simply because she was a lone mother.

> After he found out that I was a lone parent, he asked me how many children I'd got. I told him that I had two. He immediately asked how I was going to take care of the children. I tried hard to explain the arrangement, but he didn't seem to be convinced. At last, he concluded the interview by saying: 'you should go home to take care of the children, how can you work under these circumstances'. (Ms Fung)

Another form of discrimination is that employers are quite reluctant to promote lone mother employees. Ms Oi was a Departmental Secretary in a quasi-government organization. She was over qualified for the present post; given her qualification she should be promoted to a higher grade. But she has failed several times when applying for promotion. This is her experience of promotion interviews.

> One of the problems they were concerned about most was how I could take care of my child without affecting my work. Questions such as: 'how do you take care of your child', 'does your son exhibit any deviant behaviour', 'what would you do if he is sick', 'do you need to leave the office early', etc., could constitute more than one third of the interview. This is nonsense. When they kept on asking these questions, I know that was it, no chance this time. (Ms Oi)

These employers' attitude is underpinned by two very common ideologies. First, this reflects the profit orientation of the capitalist logic. The employers are afraid that lone parents may affect their business because they think that lone parents frequently need to sacrifice their work to take care of the family. This seems to imply that lone parents will not be good employees. Second, this also reflects the belief that women's primary role is within the family. Especially in critical situations which demand greater concern for children, such as in lone parenthood, women are expected to focus all their attention on the family.

Obviously, these misconceptions are not well grounded. As Ms Oi has pointed out, many lone parents are as committed to their jobs as the other employees. She rarely needed to leave her job unfinished to take care of family problems. In fact, because she had heavier burdens in taking care of the family, she used to plan her schedule well so that she could fit in various tasks. It is problematic to assume that family commitment and work commitment are mutually exclusive.

Moreover, it seems that society has double standards. Lone parents not only need to fulfil their job requirements, but they have to work better in order to convince their boss that they are committed to the job. Ms Oi pointed out that people seemed to be more tolerant for other colleagues to take time off for family affairs, but were more sceptical for lone mothers in the same situation. Once, Ms Oi's son was sick, and she needed to take time off.

> In those few weeks I had to take leave for a few days to take my son to see the doctor, I knew that my supervisor and colleagues were talking at my back. I felt very bad indeed. I was not leaving my job behind for anybody, I had everything arranged properly before I left. I was not taking leave regularly, just a few hours off. But they still think that lone mothers are sacrificing their jobs. On the contrary, many women working in our office have to take time off regularly to take care of their children. They are two-parent families, so what, their husbands are not taking care of the children. So, they also have to leave their jobs behind. (Ms Oi)

Ms Oi is certainly right to point out the absurdity of this double standard. Lone mothers may not be very different from their colleagues, but they are stereotyped, stigmatized, and scapegoated. This contributes to the marginalization or exclusion of lone mothers from the labour market.

On the other hand, we find that some employers take advantage of lone mothers, because they know that it is difficult for the lone mothers to find jobs. Because of limitations such as working hours, working location, lack of specific skills, and lack of working experiences, together with the discrimination against lone mothers in the labour market, the choices for lone mothers are quite limited. Therefore, some employers pay very low wages to lone mothers, defer their promotion, or are over demanding about their performance, because they know that it is difficult for lone mothers to quit the job.

For example, Ms Ng who was working in a market stall thought that her boss was exploiting her. Ridiculously, her boss, a very mean middle age woman, always claimed that she was very sympathetic of Ms Ng's situation and trying to help her by giving her this 'good' job. Her boss frequently says that:

> ... you have to work here, if I do not employ you, you can never find a job as good as this, it is near your home... You cannot make ends meet with your husband's maintenance, only HK$5,000... (Ms Ng)

However, Ms Ng was only earning about HK$3,000 per month in this job, which was far below the average for jobs of similar nature. Ms Ng's boss was mean in paying her, but very demanding. However, Ms Ng admitted that it was not easy for her to get another job, and money was really important to her at this stage, otherwise she would have quit the job already.

Some lone mothers may even face the extra hazard of sexual harassment at work if they disclose that they have been divorced. Ms Chan was in such a situation.

> In my work place, I don't dare tell my colleagues that I am a lone mother, because the men there are very vulgar. They frequently try to sexually harass female colleagues, especially those they consider unprotected, even old women are no exception. Once the boss even tried to harass me in the presence of his wife. If they knew that I am divorced, I would be very vulnerable, so it is hazardous to let them know. (Ms Chan)

Discrimination and exploitation in employment can take other complex forms, especially when they interact with other dimensions such as ethnicity and age. For example, lone mothers who are new immigrants from China are one of the groups discriminated against the most. All the new immigrant lone mothers, except Ms Quan, interviewed in the case studies did not have employment. Ms Quan had fewer problems in finding a job partly because she was well educated (post secondary level), and partly because she came from GuangZhou (a metropolitan city very close to Hong Kong) which enabled her to integrate into Hong Kong more easily.

Even with all these favourable conditions, Ms Quan was unable to escape from discrimination. She was a Merchandiser in a trading firm, she was discriminated against as a lone mother and a new immigrant.

> My salary is very low indeed as compared to jobs of similar nature, and compared to my colleagues. The secretary, who is doing much less work than me - just typing - is getting as much as I do. But I have to do everything, going out to negotiate with buyers, checking the quality of the products, preparing all the documents, etc. They say that I come from China, my English is not good, so I have to get less pay. I think it is very unfair. But what can I do? I need this job desperately, I need the money for my son. They know that I can't quit the job. (Ms Quan)

Another form of discrimination in employment concerns women's age. This is also closely related to the economic restructuring in Hong Kong we have discussed in chapter 3. Employment opportunities in manufacturing industry are diminishing rapidly, while there are more vacancies for service jobs. However, many service sector jobs are only open to young women, while lone mothers in their middle age are being excluded. Ms Quan neatly described the present situation:

> Hong Kong is a very strange society, if you are over thirty, if you are not young and beautiful, it is difficult to find a job. (Ms Quan)

Even Ms Fung who is only aged 26 had experienced discrimination in this aspect, when she was applying for a job in a cake shop.

> I had applied for a job in a cake shop, they said that the age limits were 18 to 23. I thought that 26 was not too old for that, so I went for it. But they said that I was too old, I could not do the job. I was very angry, I was not much older - just 3 years - I didn't understand why I couldn't sell cakes. (Ms Fung)

Of course, Ms Fung has good reason to be angry. Clearly, this is a form of age and sex discrimination. This type of age discrimination mainly applies to women's employment, not men's. It seems to imply that women have to be young and beautiful in order to do their jobs well. However, many lone mothers are well above 30 when they divorce. The average age for lone mothers in the case studies is 37.6. Before they divorced, many lone mothers had left the labour market and had spent several years at home taking care of their children. By the time they left their husbands they were regarded as too old for better paid jobs in the service sector.

That is, lone mothers find difficulties in getting jobs not only because of heavy child care burdens, but they are also discriminated against in the labour market.

Very often, they cannot get the jobs or the pay justified by their skill level, or, they have less chance of getting promotion. Many lone mothers can only gain access to low waged and unstable employment such as cleaning, care taking, domestic helping, etc. This unfavourable labour position reduces their financial resources for solving housing and other related problems.

Lone mothers' conception of work

Some people have tried to argue that lone mothers are not excluded from the labour market, they choose to stay home to look after their children. In this section, we turn to look at lone mothers' own concept of work. Do they prefer to go out to work, or do they prefer to stay at home?

In my case studies, most of the lone mothers clearly indicated that they prefer to go out to work. Although in the previous section, I have pointed out that all lone mothers accept that child caring is their primary responsibility, this does not mean that lone mothers do not like to have employment. On the contrary, most of those who do not have employment say that they want to go out to work. But the lack of child caring services and lack of employment opportunities discourage them.

Some lone mothers prefer to have employment because of financial necessity. Lone mothers have to take up new roles as breadwinners for the family after they divorce. Therefore employment becomes more important to them than ever.

> I like to go out to work, I don't like to do the housework. Maybe I like to have more money ...money is very important for us, especially for a lone parent family... I can buy my children the things they want, as far as possible. You know, I don't mean that we have to be extravagant, I just don't want my children to feel that they are deprived and poor... My son is attending computer class, my daughter going to piano class, I employ private tutors to help my children with their homework, I can afford all these. I don't want to be looked down upon by others because we are lone parent family. I have to show that my children are as good as the others. (Ms Ng)

Here, we can see that Ms Ng is very conscious of her role as a breadwinner. In this respect, she is quite similar to a man, who is judged by his ability to provide financial support to his family.

But money is not the only reason for working. Many women point out that it will be too boring, or they will feel useless if they do not work.

> There is not much difference financially if I quit this full time job and apply for Public Assistance, and then do some part time jobs... But if I stopped working, I'd feel that I am useless, you have to stay at home all day, doing nothing. Although I feel very tired after my work, it makes me feel more comfortable, more productive, I am not too old, it is better to have a job. (Ms Quan)

This job is very precious to me, it gives me self confidence, satisfaction, in addition to the daily necessities such as food, clothing, and employing a Philippine maid. It is really important. (Ms Oi)

Many lone mothers are torn between the role of being carer for the family and breadwinner. Sometimes, it may seem contradictory that the same person tells you that she regards child caring to be of primary importance; and at the same time she tells you that she likes to work, and that she feel useless if she is not working. But, this is the reality. Patriarchal ideology emphasizes that women should take good care of their children. On the other hand, capitalist ideology judges a breadwinner by the ability he/she earns for the family. Lone mothers have to take up both burdens.

It is interesting to compare the mentality of lone mothers with that of lone fathers. Lone fathers rarely consider giving up their jobs to take care of the children. In the capitalist world, men are judged by their ability to work, and their achievement in their careers. That is why the lone fathers I have interviewed, Mr Siu and Mr Tang emphasized repeatedly that they will keep on working as far as possible, and that it is unusual for a man to stay home to take care of the children.

The only exception is Mr Rod, who gave up his job to take care of the 3 children since his wife died about 2 years ago. This is because he was already 56 years old then, and was expected to be displaced sooner or later even if he did not opt for early retirement. Moreover, he was a manual worker just earning about HK$4,000 per month, which was not very different from the social security benefit for his family. In this case, Mr Rod is being displaced from the capitalist labour market because of his old age and the lack of marketable skills. Quitting the job is only a practical financial consideration rather than a means to improve the quality of child care.

There are different social expectations and job opportunities for lone mothers and lone fathers. Their own conceptions of work and child caring also differ. Consequently, most lone fathers are able to keep their jobs, while many lone mothers are unable to work or unable to get fair pay in their jobs.

In conclusion for this section, we can see that employment opportunities for lone mothers are very scarce. Lone mothers are discriminated against, marginalized, subordinated and exploited in the labour market. It is not that they do not want to work, but that there is inadequate support available to release their burden of child care and there are scarce opportunities in the labour market. Obviously, access to employment makes a lot of difference for lone mothers in helping to solve their housing and other related problems.

The ineffective social security system

The previous two sections have shown that limited access to child care services and a lack of employment opportunities are creating many difficulties for lone mothers.

Now we turn to examine the effectiveness of the social security system at helping lone mothers to solve these problems.

This section starts by looking at the extent of lone mothers' dependency on Public Assistance, and at the level of benefit they get. Is it adequate for helping lone mothers to solve their problems? Secondly, we will examine the attitude of social security officers and social workers, and show how this reinforces dominant ideologies, instead of helping lone mothers to solve their problems. Finally, we examine lone mothers' own conception of social welfare. How do they feel about depending on social security? How do they feel about the present social welfare system?

Trapped in poverty: problems of the social security system

It is a common sense assumption that most lone mothers are adequately taken care of by the social security system if they cannot get sufficient maintenance from their ex-husband. If this is true, then lone mothers should not face significant financial difficulties. This assumption seems to be over optimistic (see my analysis of the social welfare system and Public Assistance in Chapter 3). Although detailed studies or statistics on the financial circumstances of lone mothers are lacking in Hong Kong, in Western countries it is well documented that lone mothers are one of the groups suffering most from poverty and social deprivation (e.g. see OECD, 1990; Marsden, 1973; Townsend, 1979; Millar, 1987; Millar and Bradshaw, 1987; Bradshaw and Millar, 1993).

If we look at the sources and level of income of lone mother families in my questionnaire survey (table 5.6), the situation in Hong Kong appears discouraging. As pointed out earlier in this chapter, usually maintenance is too low or too unreliable to be an adequate source of income to support the children. Depending on social security is not much better.

Among the lone mothers interviewed in the survey, 29.5 per cent receive social security. However, the level of this income is extremely low, with median income of HK$2,325 per month only (table 5.6), that is about HK$802 per capita, which is only about 25 per cent that of the general population. No wonder most lone mothers prefer to earn their own living through employment instead of depending on social security, unless they are in a desperate situation.

The level of benefit is so low that it is only just sufficient to maintain subsistence. For example, a lone father Mr Rod had to support three children age 11, 10 and 7 on a social security benefit of HK$3,800 per month. A lone mother Ms Ell was receiving Social Security benefit of HK$2,600 for herself and her three year old son.

> I have to buy the cheapest food available in the market. We can't afford things like fresh fish or chicken... My children often complain that the meals are boring, and we are having more or less the same thing all the time. But I really can't do anything about it, we cannot afford better things... (Mr Rod)

I try to give everything to my baby first, food, clothing, etc. Then there is not much left behind. Sometimes, I don't even have enough to eat... (Ms Ell)

Table 5.6
Sources and level of income of lone mothers

Source	Those having income from this source (%)	Median monthly income[b]
Employment	53.4	HK$5,000
Social security	29.5	HK$2,325
Maintenance	14.8	HK$3,000
Others[a]	6.8	HK$3,000
Total family income	All families (N=88)	HK$4,500[c]

Notes:
a   'Others' includes income from children's employment, letting a room to other tenants, helps from relatives, etc.
b   'Median monthly income' for a particular income source is calculated based only on those families having such source of income.
c   For comparison, the median household income in Hong Kong in 1992 is about HK$11,000, average family size is 3.4 (i.e. HK$3,235 per capita). The average family size for this survey sample is 2.9, therefore median household income per capita is HK$1,551.

Ability to subsist does not mean that these families are out of poverty. Townsend (1993, chapter 2, 4) has long been arguing that in modern societies it is problematic to define poverty in terms of subsistence. Instead, poverty and social deprivation are relative concepts. People are in poverty if they lack the resources to achieve normal social activities. This social deprivation is extremely common, or inevitable, amongst Public Assistance recipients in Hong Kong.

Public Assistance is very low indeed, it is just sufficient for food, we don't have other things, no amusement, no outings, no other social activities, we have to stay home all the time in order to save money. (Ms Kam)

Obviously, many Public Assistance recipients, like Ms Kam and her children, are isolated from society, because of their low income. They are deprived of the opportunity to participate in normal social activities. In this way, it is extremely difficult for lone mother families to establish normal social life after divorce.

Another problem with the social security system is that it does not encourage lone mothers to work. Practically all lone mothers with employment are not entitled to any social benefit. This is because the income limit for most social benefit is so low that income from any employment would exceed these limits. As I have pointed out in chapter 3 on the social security system in Hong Kong, although there is a disregarded income policy, the maximum disregarded earning for a family receiving public assistance is only HK$675 per month in 1993. This is only about 5 per cent of the median household income of Hong Kong population.

Similarly, there is no consideration of the need for child care services, after school services for children, child minders, or housing services on compassionate ground for working lone mothers. Nor is there any concern to provide services to help lone mothers to find jobs, such as job placement and retraining. The welfare system totally neglects lone mothers' need for help to stay in the labour market. They are simply left on their own to struggle for survival in a labour market which tends to discriminate against them.

Ms Oi has many grievances in this respect. When she became a lone mother her salary was quite low but still above the Public Assistance level, and she was desperately in need of child care services and housing services, but she could not get any help from the government.

> It seems that the government is not encouraging us to work. If I am working, I am not entitled to any benefit, no compassionate housing, no child care service, no financial assistance, etc. Sometimes, I really want to give up my work, maybe that's the only way to get some service. (Ms Oi)

For those who are lucky enough to find jobs, it does not mean that they are lifted out of poverty. From table 5.6, we can see that 53.4 per cent of the lone mothers in my survey have their own employment, but the median income from employment is only HK$5,000. Unlike two-parent families which can supplement their household income by having a second earner, which is quite common in Hong Kong,[1] lone mother families can only rely on a single earner. Consequently, lone mother families are among the groups with the lowest household income.

In this manner, many lone mothers are trapped in poverty. If they depend on Public Assistance, they are in extreme poverty. Public Assistance benefit only just 20 per cent of the general household income. The subsidy for a child is just HK$675 in 1993, which is insufficient even to pay for private child care services (ranging from HK$800 to HK$1,700 per month, see chapter 3 for more detail). On the other hand, if they try to get a job, they have to face discrimination and lack of opportunity in the labour market, together with the lack of support for working lone mothers from our social welfare system. Under this situation, many lone mothers are unable to earn enough to support child care services and decent housing.

Now let us look at the attitude of the social security officers and social workers who are supposed to serve the needs of lone mothers. By examining their attitude, we can reveal the ideologies underpinning their practices, and thus understand better how gender inequality is being reinforced in our welfare system.

As I have pointed out in chapter 2, in general, there are two major ideologies dominating our social system, patriarchal ideology and laissez-faire capitalist ideology. Patriarchal ideology emphasizes familism which stresses a woman's duty as carer and preserve of the unity of the 'conventional' family system. Laissez-faire capitalist ideology emphasizes the need to have minimal government intervention in social welfare and to leave problems to the individual and the family. These two ideologies interact to reinforce women's subordination and dependency on the family.

A typical example is Ms Quan. Once, she was beaten up by her husband and was so seriously injured that she was admitted to hospital. After she was discharged from hospital, she went to see a social worker and asked for help in divorcing her husband. This was the 'professional' advice she got from the social worker.

> She told me that marriage is for life, I should not think of divorce, I am not trying hard enough to save my marriage. I should go back to my husband, try harder to mend my broken home with love, caring, endurance, forgiveness, patience,... (Ms Quan)

This kind of conservative attitude is not uncommon in Hong Kong. Familism is so dominant and unchallenged that for some social workers, it is a sin to break up the family for any reason, even for cases of extreme domestic violence. No wonder some feminists have raised the issue of developing 'anti-discriminatory' or feminist approaches to social work (Langan and Day, 1992; Dominelli and Mcleod, 1981). In this case, Ms Quan was blamed for not being patient enough even though her life was threatened by her violent husband. Obviously, the 'professional' advice of going back to her violent husband was more concerned about reinforcing the 'conventional' family system than about helping the clients.

A 'blaming the victim' approach is extremely common in the social security system. Lone mothers are not considered to be victims of family changes. More often, they are blamed for being too lazy, for not working hard enough to solve their own problems, or for over dependency on social benefits. Ms Deng was accused of being lazy and over dependent when she was trying to apply for compassionate housing.

> The Social Security Officer told me to rent a cheaper place, and to go out to find a job. She said that she knew a lone mother who had got three jobs, one in the morning, one in the afternoon, and one in the evening. That person was

earning about HK$10,000 per month, and was able to buy a flat. It seemed to be that it is very easy to do that. When I mentioned my need to take care of my daughter [age 6], the officer even suggested that I leave my child at home on her own, with no need to pay for child care service... They seemed to accuse me of not working hard enough, and implied that I should not depend on Public Assistance. (Ms Deng)

In this case, it is obvious that there is insufficient support to enable Ms Deng to go out to work, not that she does not want to work. The suggestions of the social security officer are unrealistic and ridiculous. It is irresponsible to leave a child of 6 years old on her own and go out to work, especially in the appalling living conditions in which Ms Deng finds herself. In many Western countries, it is an offence to leave a young child unattended at home. But this social security officer even suggested it as a solution to a child care problem.

Sometimes, even in urgent situations, lone mothers' needs are not entertained. Instead, they have been accused of being too greedy. Ms Quan tells of her unhappy encounter with a social security officer.

Once I really had no money, I had only a few dollars left in my pocket. It was not even enough to cook a meal for my son [age 7]. So, I bought bread with HK$2 and shared it with my son. Then I decided that we should go to the social security office to ask the officer to dispatch the benefit payment for the next month in advance. But when she saw me eating the bread with my son, she said very scornfully: 'you don't have money? how come you can buy bread, don't dream of getting more money from us' I was really very angry. What a government department! Even if I begged on the street, I think I would get a few dollars. This is worse than begging. (Ms Quan)

Here, it should be noted that our social security system is quite self contradictory. On the one hand, it is expected that lone mothers should go to work as far as possible. On the other hand, very few supportive services such as child care, housing, job placement and retraining, are provided to encourage women to work. Consequently, lone mothers are trapped in the system, and are blamed or penalized because they have a commitment to take care of their children.

Lone mothers' conception of social security and welfare

It is also interesting to look at how lone mothers themselves see the social welfare system. Why are they so complacent about this ineffective welfare system?

Like most citizens in Hong Kong, many lone mothers are greatly influenced by the ideology of minimal government intervention. That is, to certain extent, they also accept that family problems should be solved by the individual instead of relying on the state. Unlike many Western countries where citizenship rights are considered fundamental, in Hong Kong rights to welfare are not well established.

Therefore, terms such as charity, mercy, pity and sympathy are frequently used to refer to the welfare they get. Ms Ng's dialogue with her son reflected this mentality.

> I have thought about it [applying for Public Assistance], I have discussed with my son [a Form 5 secondary school student], he said that we should not opt for Public Assistance because we are not the poorest, we can still work, we should not depend on the government. So I keep working. (Ms Ng)

Here, obviously you can see that Ms Ng and her son perceived Public Assistance not as a citizenship right, but as charity from the government. They are trying to avoid this stigma as far as possible.

Stigmatization and humiliation when applying are major deterrents against lone mothers seeking help.

> The workers there seem very impatient, their faces always look straight and black. It makes me feel very inferior, so I avoid going to them as far as possible. (Ms Ell)

Although some lone mothers know that it may help to speed up the process if they keep putting pressure on the officers, many lone mothers are quite reluctant to do so partly because they feel that they are asking for something extra instead of upholding their welfare right. Another reason is that Chinese cultural practice tends to avoid conflict. Therefore, they feel bad if they pressurize the officers.

> I know that we can fight for a better deal if we are not satisfied, but I feel too apologetic to push the social security officer so hard. Maybe my sister is right in saying that I should not put too much pressure on the officer, otherwise it may cause negative effects. (Ms Ell)

Given these conceptions, no wonder that many lone mothers are very complacent about this ineffective social security system. Very often, frustrated by the system, lone mothers have to rely on their own means to solve their problems.

Concluding this section, I have shown that the level of social security benefit is far from adequate to solve lone mothers' problems. On average, social security recipients only receive about 20 per cent as much as the general household median income. Lone mothers are trapped in poverty with this ineffective social security system. On the one hand, our social welfare system does not provide adequate support for lone mothers. Besides the low level of benefit, there is a lack of support services such as child care, employment placement, and compassionate housing; and the level of disregarded income for Public Assistance recipients is too low to be an incentive to work. On the other hand, lone mothers are blamed for over dependency on social welfare and reluctance to get employment. Our social security system reflects and reinforces the dominant patriarchal ideology and the laissez-faire capitalist ideology of minimal government intervention in social welfare. Consequently, lone mothers are penalized for their commitment to the care of their children, and penalized for not depending on their husbands.

Widespread social discrimination

In the above sections, we have seen evidence of the discrimination against lone mothers in significant social systems such as employment and social welfare. In this section we will widen our analysis by looking at the discrimination against lone mothers in society as a whole. We start with looking at how lone mother families are stigmatized, labelled, discriminated against and excluded from normal social life. Then we look at lone mothers' conception of their own identity: how they perceive their label, and how they react to social stigmatization.

Social stigma of lone parent families

Our society is so dominated by familial ideology that only 'conventional' two-parent families are considered normal. Frequently, lone parent families are labelled abnormal and problematic. Discrimination can come from any quarter such as their friends, parents, relatives, their children's teacher, their children's schoolmates, neighbours, employers, social workers, or landlords/landladies.

This is Ms Chan's experience of discrimination. Her son has some good friends at school, and she gradually made friends with their mothers too.

> Once, the mother of one of my child's classmates approached me, asking me to work as part time child minder for her child. I didn't want to deceive her, I told her that I am a lone mother. She immediately withdrew her request. And since then she had avoided contacting me. She also doesn't allow her child to play with my son any more. It is a pity, they are good friends. (Ms Chan)

This seems to imply that if a woman fails to keep her husband, she is not suitable to be a child carer, and that lone mother families are problematic families. In the case studies, we have learnt that it is very common that many parents in 'conventional' families to forbid their children to associate with children from lone parent families.

Discrimination is not directed at lone mothers only, children in lone parent families suffers too. Ms Ng told us how her child is discriminated against by his schoolmates. The force of this discrimination is so strong that even children are socialized to adopt such an attitude at an early age.

> Once, I heard my son quarrelling with his friends, they had beaten him up, mocking him for having no father ... (Ms Ng)

This also reflects that fatherless children are considered unprotected. In a patriarchal society women and children are considered to be property of men, they are under the protection of men (husband/father) in the family. Therefore, a fatherless family is one without protection.

Ms Kam is another typical example. She was very unhappy about her neighbours, she thought that they were looking down upon her because she did not have a husband at home. The neighbours always complained about her son being naughty. They labelled and penalized her son whenever there were quarrels between the children, because he was unprotected by a father.

Discrimination does not only come from layman such as friends, relatives and neighbours, sometimes professionals such as teachers and social workers are no exception. Patriarchal ideology is so deeply rooted in society that even some practitioners in the 'helping professions' are unaware of this discrimination. Ms Au was discriminated against by her son's teacher.

> Some of the teachers seemed to look down upon us. After I told him [one of her son's teacher] that I am a lone mother, he said to me: 'Ah, no wonder your children are so naughty, I know, children from lone parent families are assumed to behaving like that.' After that, this teacher just gave up my child, he didn't bother about what he is doing, he was not trying to help him any more. (Ms Au)

It is commonly believed that children in lone parent families are more problematic, they are labelled as rebellious, naughty, uncooperative and delinquent. For example, one of the most influential studies on juvenile delinquency in Hong Kong attributed the major cause of the problem to broken families (Ng, 1985, pp.244-45). This echoed the classical debate on 'culture of poverty' (Lewis, 1968) or the more updated debate on 'underclass' (Murray, 1984; 1990). Theses arguments tend to reduce complicated social problems to individual inadequacy, and neglect the structural constraints and the social process structuring the problems of the lower income families. It is not my major concern here to rebut this conservative explanation of the problem of poverty (see more detailed discussion in Alcock, 1993; Oppenheim, 1990; Katz, 1993), however, in this research I have found that this labelling of lone parent families is not well grounded.

Lone parent families are not necessarily unsuitable for child rearing. In many cases, lone mothers revealed that the parent child relationship and the behaviourial problems of children improved significantly after divorce. Ms Ng, Ms Deng and many other lone mothers had such experiences:

> My child is better behaved than before. He was unhappy in the past, he liked to go out, wandering around and fighting with other children, because in that period we didn't have much time and energy to take care of him. But now it is far better. (Ms Ng)

It has become better for my daughter after we divorced. Previously, my daughter seldom talked, she was always sitting silently at home, doing nothing. But now she seems much happier, she talks much more than before, and is playing more happily. (Ms Deng)

Obviously, the lone parent family is a normal pattern for raising children. The difficulties lone mothers encountered in taking care of their children, such as lack of child care services, lack of financial resources, stigmatization by friends and relatives, are largely constructed by our social system. They are not inherent in the nature of lone mothers families.

In this research, I have noticed that discrimination against lone parent families varies according to the background of the family and the cause of lone parenthood. For example, the widowed are socially acceptable, while the divorced are considered immoral. The widowed do not feel that they are discriminated against because of their marital status. It is not considered as their fault, it is only misfortune. Ms Oi and Mr Rod, both widowed, share similar feelings on the issue of discrimination against lone mothers.

I don't feel too much of a problem, may be because I am lone parent because my husband died, not because of divorce. It is not my fault, as long as I take good care of my child, I don't think they will look down on me. (Ms Oi)

I don't feel that there is any obvious discrimination because I am a lone parent. In my case my wife passed away, it is not a separation or a divorce. (Mr Rod)

On the other hand, lone parenthood resulting from divorce is more likely to result in discrimination, as in the cases I have described above. Quite often, even in cases involving family violence, women are blamed for the divorce from their husbands.

The situation can be worse if there are other 'undesirable' factors, such as being new immigrants. A new immigrant lone mother Ms Quan, told us her experience of dealing with the Legal Aid Department. When she asked for help in divorce, one of the officers asked her bluntly: 'did you marry your husband for love? or...'. She felt very humiliated. The question seemed to imply that all new immigrant women marry just to get the right of abode in Hong Kong.

Lone mother' conception of being a lone parent

Some lone mothers are adversely affected by these negative attitudes towards lone parent families. In fact, as members of society themselves, many lone mothers find it difficult to resist adopting the dominant familial ideology themselves.

In many cases, women have gone to great lengths to avoid becoming a lone parent. For example, Ms Quan had been battered by her husband for some years before she divorced. She was still young (age 32) with good education (post-secondary), and it was quite possible for her to be on her own without her husband, but she was very reluctant to leave. One of the major reasons was of her child's status.

> I worried about my child, I hoped that he could grow up in a two-parent family, I thought that would be better for him. But now I know that it isn't, I made a wrong decision then. (Ms Pang)

The belief that 'two parents are better than one' is so dominant that even when Ms Quan was facing serious domestic violence, she still preferred to stay. After she had broken through this ideological control, it was not difficult for her to see that a one parent family could be a happy family too.

Another lone mother, Ms Man, had tried to maintain a 'two-parent' model even after the divorce. Ms Man disliked intensely being labelled as lone parent family. She repeatedly stressed that a lone parent family was not a happy family, and that she did not want her children to grow up with a single parent. At the beginning of the separation, Ms Man insisted on living near her husband so that her daughter could see her father frequently. Unfortunately, this did not work out and the father seldom came to visit the daughter. On the contrary, when Ms Man met her ex-husband in the community (which they did quite often because they were living so close) he was very cool, cynical and scornful. That made her feel very depressed.

In this case, it can be seen that Ms Man cannot accept that a lone parent family can be a normal family. She tried to maintain a two-parent model for her daughter, instead of developing a new pattern of normal life within a lone parent family. This painful attempt was doomed to fail.

Some lone mothers tried to cope with the situation by isolating themselves. They tried to avoid conflict and escape from stigmatization by isolating themselves from friends and relatives. For example, Ms Hong, aged 45 with five children, worried about being looked down upon by her friends and relatives. After isolating herself she found difficulty in re-establishing normal social life.

> Maybe I am lacking confidence after divorce, I really can't explain why. I try to avoid contacting friends and relatives, because I worry that they may look down upon me...I seldom have contact with the neighbours, I go out to work in the morning, and after work I just stay at home. (Ms Hong)

Some lone mothers cope by telling lies to cover up their marital status. Ms Au is one of these typical cases.

> We are afraid that others may look down upon us if they knew that we are a lone parent family. So I just tell my neighbours that my husband is working in China, he comes back only once or twice every year. My children are telling the same lie to their classmates at school. Usually, we avoid answering questions about our husband/father directly. (Ms Au)

Sometimes lone mothers are compelled to tell lies because lone mothers are discriminated against in the labour market and the housing market. Frequently, this is the only way they can get a job or rent a room in the private housing market (see chapter 6).

These coping strategies are not conducive for lone mothers to become reintegrated into normal social life. However, in many ways our society compels lone mothers to adopt these unsatisfactory strategies.

Of course, not all lone mothers reject their identity as lone parents. Especially many younger and better educated lone mothers, some gradually break through the labelling and discrimination in our social system. Ms Gon, aged 32 with secondary education and an employment earning HK$8,000 per month, is such a case.

> I don't know whether some people discriminate against us, or I don't mind at all. Before I divorced, I wrestled for a long time about whether I should leave my husband. But after I made the decision, I felt very relaxed. Now, I am really very busy, going to work, taking care of my child. I have no time to care about what other people are saying about me. (Ms Gon)

Ms Gon was lucky in the sense that many of her friends, relatives, and child's teachers were very supportive. Although she was quite reluctant to leave her husband at the beginning, very soon she was able to re-establish her new life.

> I think the most important is that you can accept your own identity. If you take it as a normal life style, you can be a model for your children. I always tell my son that this is normal, some families are just like that. It may be better for all of us to be this way. He seems to understand and accept it. He is happy, healthy, and does not behave differently from other children. (Ms Gon)

Ms Pang is another example of someone who can overcome this stigmatization. She was aged 32 with lower secondary education, earning HK$8,000 per month.

> At the beginning, it was very difficult to overcome the psychological pressure. I was very worried about how other people may judge me, and sometimes very suspicious of others. Once I'd attended a talk for lone parents, I realized that we had to accept ourselves. We have done nothing wrong. So if you accept yourself, other people will accept you. I keep telling my daughter about this... My daughter is much better now, she is becoming tougher, more independent, happier than before... I really feel sorry for my daughter that I didn't divorce earlier. Maybe I was too weak and indecisive at that time. It may have been much better if I had decided to divorce earlier. Through these changes, I feel that I am growing up, growing stronger; so is my daughter. I am very satisfied with our present situation. (Ms Pang)

It is good to see that some lone parents are able to overcome negative stereotyping and can gradually rebuild a normal social life. However, this is still limited to a few lone mothers who are relatively better educated, younger, and with better jobs.

From the discussion in this section, we have seen how lone parent families are labelled abnormal and problematic, and are thus marginalized them, making it more difficult to integrate into normal social life, and more difficult to solve their problems. Our society is so dominated by familial ideology that many people regard the 'conventional' nuclear family as the only normal family pattern. Any pattern deviating from this norm, such as the lone parent family, is considered problematic. Women who have divorced from their husbands are considered loose women, immoral, wicked, or not performing their duties properly. Furthermore, women and children in lone parent families are considered to be unprotected by men. They are more susceptible to harassment. We need to re-affirm that the lone parent family is a normal family pattern, they should not be discriminated against or excluded.

Conclusion

After in-depth analysis, it is obvious that most problems of lone mother families are not inherent in the nature of such families. Instead, it is the result of discrimination against lone mothers in our society. On the one hand, women have to assume most of the duties in child caring after the divorce. On the other hand, child care service, which is an essential support for lone mothers, is in severe shortage. This reduces lone mothers' chances of getting employment. Moreover, lone mothers are discriminated against, subordinated and marginalized in the labour market. Together with other sources of discrimination such as from neighbours, friends, relatives, children's teachers and social welfare officers, lone mothers have to face numerous problems.

These problems are not only constructed by our social structure and in social institutions such as the social welfare system and the employment system, it is also reinforced through everyday social interactions. Many lone mothers become frustrated, lack of confidence, isolated or over reactive to criticism. This further reinforces the taken for granted assumption that lone parent families are problematic families, and creates further difficulties for lone mothers to rebuild a new life. Given this background, it is not difficult to understand why lone mothers have to face so many hurdles in solving their housing problems, of which we are going to discuss in more detail in the following chapter.

Note

1. In 1991, the average number of working members per family in Hong Kong was 1.7, but the average household size was only 3.4 (Hong Kong Census and Statistic Department, 1993c, pp.62 & 56). This indicates that two-earner families are quite common.

6 Marginalizing lone mother families

In the last chapter we saw how lone mothers' problems are socially constructed and how there are outside restrictions on lone mothers' problem solving resources. Therefore, it is not surprising to see that lone mothers have great difficulty in solving their housing problems. Let us now examine the problems lone mothers face in different types of housing, how they attempt to solve their problems and whether these solutions are effective.

The first section of this chapter focuses on the housing needs of lone mothers. It points out that many lone mothers have to move out of their matrimonial home, and have to move around frequently because of they lack sufficient resources to secure stable accommodation. The second section focuses on lone mothers' experience in the private housing market. The third section concerns our public housing system, especially the policy of compassionate housing for lone mothers and lone mothers' access to other types of public housing such as public rental housing, the Home Ownership Scheme, and the Home Purchase Loan Scheme. The fourth section is a brief discussion about living with friends and relatives, and living in temporary shelters for battered wives as possible solutions to lone mothers' housing problems.

Women on the move

In Hong Kong, it is generally believed that since most women have to take care of the children, they are entitled to remain in the matrimonial home after separation. If this was true, lone mothers would not face very serious housing problems. However, this is not the case. On the contrary, many lone mothers have to move out of their matrimonial home after divorce and many of them even have to move around frequently because of their difficulties in securing appropriate accommodation.

Many housing officers I have interviewed insisted that there should be no serious housing problems for lone mothers because they were entitled to stay put if they were taking care of the children. When asked whether there was any service gap in the provision of housing for lone mothers, a typical response was:

> Generally speaking, there shouldn't be any problem. According to existing housing regulations, if a divorced woman gets the custody of the children, she is entitled to stay in the matrimonial home. So, there shouldn't be any housing problem. (Mr Ming, a housing officer)

This is simplistic assumption. Whether or not the lone mother needs to move out of the matrimonial home varies greatly according to their background, such as the cause of lone parenthood (divorce or widowhood), whether family violence is involved, class background, education, and ethnicity. After further in-depth probing, even the above mentioned housing officer, Mr Ming, admitted that the situation is more complicated in practice. Nonetheless, this problem is neglected to such an extent that there are no detailed studies or official statistics on lone mothers' house moving patterns (for a discussion of the situation in the UK see e.g. Sullivan, 1986; Crow and Hardey, 1991; Bradshaw and Millar, 1993, chapter 8).

One of the major factors governing the need to move out of the matrimonial home is the cause of lone parenthood, that is whether the mother is separated/divorced or widowed. It seems that widowed lone mothers are more likely to remain in their matrimonial home. In my questionnaire survey, among the 17 widowed women interviewed, only 2 needed to move out, while the other 15 could stay put (table 6.1). On the other hand, among the separated and divorced only 21.4 per cent have stayed put, while the other 78.6 per cent have moved out. Therefore, in my subsequent case studies greater emphasis is placed on the divorced lone mothers, for whom housing needs are more acute.

Table 6.1
Marital status and moving out of the matrimonial home

	Separated/divorced	Widowed
Move out	55 (78.6%)	2 (11.8%)
Stay put	15 (21.4%)	15 (88.2%)
Total	70 (100%)	17 (100%)

Of course, there are also some variations among the widowed. In general, those living in public housing do not need to move out after the death of spouse. On the other hand, widowed lone parents in home ownership flats or private rental housing may need to move out because of insufficient financial resources to support the mortgage or to pay the rent. Or, sometimes even if the lone mother is able to support the mortgage, the bank is reluctant to continue to provide the mortgage loan. For example, Ms Oi has to sell her house after her husband died partly because the bank refused to finance the mortgage for her as a lone mother. Many studies in Western countries have pointed out that banks discriminate against women, especially lone mothers, in supporting mortgages. This results in lower proportions of female home owners as compared to males (Watson, 1988, pp.39-55; Morris and Winn, 1990, pp.117-22; Sexty, 1990, pp.27-8).

Divorced lone mothers avoid housing problems only if their husbands agree to move out voluntarily after the separation, leaving the house for them and their children. However, not many divorce cases are straightforward like this. Prevention of problems depends very much on the consciousness and the good will of the ex-husband in supporting the lone mother and the children. However, our social structure does not have any mechanisms to guarantee that a divorce works out as smoothly as that. On the contrary, the patriarchal system is biased toward males, so that little can be done even if the husband is irresponsible and uncooperative.

Situations in which the lone mother has to move out are typically cases involving family violence. In such cases, the lone mother has virtually no chance of staying in the matrimonial home. The main concern of lone mothers in this situation is to find an escape haven from the violent husband rather than fighting for the right to stay in the home. For example, Ms Quan was battered by her husband several times. Once, this was so serious that she was admitted to the hospital and stayed for 8 days. After she was discharged from the hospital, she decided to leave her husband.

> I had no place to go, I didn't know what to do. I went to a community centre asking for help. They didn't know what to do either. They were just about to go on a family camp for two days, so I went with them. In the camp, I met two social workers, they'd heard about Harmony House [a shelter for battered women run by a voluntary agency] so they helped me to get in touch with Harmony House. (Ms Quan)

This is quite typical of situations when a battered woman has to leave her violent husband. In such circumstances, there is no way that the woman can stay in the matrimonial home. There is neither an effective state agency nor a mediating service to attribute between the separating couple or to protect the battered women from further violence.

In addition to physical abuse, another reason for women not being able to stay in their matrimonial home is psychological pressure. Ms Gon divorced her husband after about 4 years, because he had a mistress. After she knew about her husband's affair, she quarrelled with him frequently. Although her husband did not batter her, she had to leave because she could not bear the psychological pressure any more.

I knew that it is difficult to find an accommodation, I had tried several times without success. But I really couldn't stand it any longer. My parents said that I looked like a lunatic at that time. It really hurt too much, I nearly broke down. So I decided to move out, regardless of how difficult it was to find a place to stay. (Ms Gon)

Obviously, those lone mothers who need to move out of the matrimonial home face great difficulties. Quite often, it is extremely difficult for them to find suitable accommodation because of their limited financial means, their lack of opportunity in the labour market and lack of child care support.

Moving around frequently

Given all these difficulties, it is very common among lone mother to move around frequently. This is especially true of those lone mothers who have had to move out of the matrimonial home.

Table 6.2
Frequency of house moving for lone mothers

Number of house moves	Those needing to move out of the matrimonial home	Those who stay put
No move	--	25 (83.3%)
Once	16 (28.1%)	5 (16.7%)
Twice	24 (42.1%)	0
Three or more	17 (29.8%)	0
Total	57 (100%)	30 (100%)

In my questionnaire survey, amongst the 87 lone mothers interviewed 62 (71.3 per cent) had to move at least once after they separated from their husband. The situation for those who needed to leave the matrimonial home after separation was even worse. Amongst the 57 lone mothers who needed to leave the matrimonial home, only 28.1 per cent settled down in the first place they got; 42.1 per cent had

110

to move twice, and 29.8 per cent had to move three times or more (table 6.2). In the worst case, a lone mother had lived in 7 different places after separation from her husband. Obviously, with this pattern of frequent moves, it is extremely difficult for lone mother families to settle down and start a new life.

Some of the most common reasons for moving were: threat of sexual harassment, repossession of the dwelling by landlords/landladies, changing job, health problems arising from a poor living environment, moving out from the parents' place because of difficulties in living together, etc.

Ms Quan's case is a very typical illustration. She had lived in 7 different places within one year, before she was granted a compassionate public housing unit. Let us look at her story in more detail:

Ms Quan was aged 32 and taking care of a son aged 7. She had divorced about three years ago. The first place she lived in was the Harmony House, which is the only temporary shelter for battered women in Hong Kong run by a voluntary agency. The maximum length of stay in this shelter is three months. The second place she lived in was Tsuen Wan, renting a room in an over congested flat, sharing with several households. She had to leave this place not because of the over crowded conditions, but because she was facing the threat of sexual harassment from the landlord. Then she moved into the third place, also renting a small room. This time she had found a place in the Kwai Chung industrial area, where the air was extremely polluted. Before long, her son suffered from serious bronchitis. So she had to move to the fourth place. This time she managed to find a cheaper place, but it was in Yaumatei which was a notorious red light district with a high crime rate. In this place, again she was sexually harassed by male co-tenants. So she had to move again, to the fifth place. This time she was once again renting a room in an urban slum, quite near to the previous one. But after three months, the landlord expelled her, saying that he had to reserve the room for a relative coming from Mainland China. So she moved to the sixth place. One of her friends had an empty flat in a public housing estate in Kwun Tong, which was about to be demolished for redevelopment. She became an illegal tenant in her friend's flat. The situation there was again very appalling, there was a high crime rate in the area. Most of the former tenants in these high rise blocks had moved out, some of the empty flats were occupied illegally by triad society members and had been turned into drug trafficking centres. Drug dealing and fighting among the gangsters was the usual way of life on this estate. After she had stayed there for three months, the demolition work commenced. Therefore she had to move to the seventh place. This time she moved to live with a friend's mother. This 'aunt' was quite sympathetic toward her situation, but she was living with other family members and really could not help too much. The most she could do was to let Ms Quan and her son sleep on a spare bed space in her flat. Because of the overcrowded conditions in the flat, Ms Quan had to be very cautious in order to avoid causing inconvenience to her 'aunt's' family. Ms Quan did not cook in the kitchen. Literally, she had to leave the flat early in the morning (at 8:00 a.m.) and return only at night (after 9:00 p.m.).

After a hectic year of moving around, finally the Social Welfare Department was convinced that she had genuine needs for public housing on compassionate grounds. At last, she was granted a public housing unit, and settled in her home after one year of 'wandering'.

It has been very chaotic, I have moved seven times in a year, everything is so confusing, all mixed up. I feel so muddled that I really don't remember too much of what has happened in the year. I just feel that I have been homeless, and only after I got a public housing unit did I feel that I had settled down. (Ms Quan)

This illustrates the general problem for women - it is they, not their former male partners, who are expected to find solutions to housing problems and make adjustments. However, with limited financial resources and overwhelming social constraints, it is extremely difficult for lone mothers to solve their housing problems and secure stable accommodation. Therefore moving around frequently becomes a way of life for many lone mothers, especially those in the early stages of divorce.

Lone mothers in private housing

For those lone mothers who have to find their own accommodation after separation, a significant proportion has to turn to private rented housing. Can they solve their housing problems through the private market? In the first part of this section, we examine lone mothers' difficulties in gaining access to decent accommodation, and how they are discriminated against in the private housing system. The second part of this section examines typical private housing conditions for lone mothers.

Access to private housing

Hong Kong is a place notorious for its high price and expensive rents in private housing (see chapter 3, especially figure 3.3). With limited financial ability, it is extremely difficult for the lone mothers to find decent accommodation in the expensive private housing sector in Hong Kong. According to the Household Expenditure Survey (HK Census and Statistics Department, 1991, p.12), among those living in private housing, on average 33 per cent of household expenses is spent on housing, which amounts to HK$4,229 per month in 89/90. Based on these figures, a reasonable estimate of the average housing expenses for a family in private housing in 91/92 should have been about HK$5,000 per month. This far exceeded the financial resources of most of the lone mothers interviewed.

Among the lone mothers in my survey, the average monthly housing expenses were HK$1,674, about 32.3 per cent of their average income (table 6.3). Both their average income and their average housing expenses were far below that of the total population. In other words, their financial resources for securing accommodation in the private market were extremely limited.

Table 6.3
Monthly housing expense and income for lone mothers
in different types of housing

Housing type	Housing expense* (HK$)	Income (HK$)	Expense/income ratio (%)
Public rental	1,280	5,084	25.2
Owner occupier	3,009	8,592	35.0
Private rental (whole flat)	5,040	9,875	51.0
Private rental (room/cubicle)	1,574	2,976	52.9
Temporary housing	690	2,900	23.8
Housing provided by employer	1,200	6,500	18.5
Temporary shelter by welfare agency	0	2,839	0
Living with friends/relatives	1,140	5,400	21.1
Total	1,674 N=87 missing=1	5,179 N=81 missing=7	32.3

Note:
* Housing expenses including rent, rate, and estate management fees, if any.

The picture is much clearer when we focus our attention on lone mothers in private rental housing, whether renting a whole flat or renting a room (table 6.3). Among lone mothers renting a whole flat, housing expenses were HK$5,040, a figure comparable to that in the Household Expenditure Survey. However, the average monthly income of this group of lone mothers was only HK$9,875. In other words, they were spending 51 per cent of their income on housing. The situation for lone mothers renting a room in private housing was even worse. On average, they were spending HK$1,574 per month on housing, but had an average income of only HK$2,976 per month. That is, they were paying 52.9 per cent of their income for housing. With their low level of income and high housing expenses, their disposable income after meeting housing costs was extremely small.

Among low income households or those relying on Public Assistance, the situation was much worse. Although Public Assistance recipients are entitled to rent subsidy, the subsidy is so low that it is impossible for them to rent decent accommodation. In 1993, the housing subsidy for a two-person family was HK$1,215, and for a three- or four-person family it was HK$1,718 per month. This was far below the average rates of about HK$5,000 for renting a private flat. With this low level of subsidy, lone mothers on Public Assistance could only rent a room in very congested slums For example, Ms Quan was on Public Assistance about two years ago with a rent subsidy of about HK$800 per month.

> You can't expect too much with such a low subsidy, if it is a decent place, they will not let it to you. They have a lot of restrictions, they don't accept children, you are not allowed to cook, they ask you what is your occupation, where is your husband, how do you pay for the rent, etc. Therefore I have no choice except to live in places like Yaumatei [an urban slum, red light district]. (Ms Quan)

The fact that lone mothers are unwelcome by landlords/landladies also reflects the patriarchal assumption that a woman should depend on her husband, or that the main financial resources for women is from their husbands. Ms Deng's experience clearly demonstrates this point. Once, a landlord refused to rent a room to her because he was afraid that she had no money to pay the rent since she had no husband. Although Ms Deng had explained clearly that she got rent subsidy from the Public Assistance Scheme, this was considered less reliable than financial support from husband. (In reality, support from Public Assistance could be more stable and reliable than that from an irresponsible husband). Ms Deng's case reflects that there is a common belief that women have to depend on their husband.

Another reason why landlords/landladies are reluctant to let rooms to lone mothers is because they believe that women outside 'conventional' marriages are 'problematic'. Ms Jone's experience is very illustrative. She had covered up her lone parenthood status when she rented her accommodation. However, later, after the landlady discovered that Ms Jone was a lone mother, she became very sceptical.

the landlady was very critical of me after she found out that I am divorced. Whenever I talked to other male residents in the flat, she looked very sceptical... suspecting that I was trying to seduce them. (Ms Jone)

Ms Jone's landlady seems to assume that a divorced woman is a loose woman, or that there must be something wrong with a woman who has failed to keep her husband. The discrimination arising from this dominant ideology has created further difficulty for lone mothers trying to solve their housing problems.

Faced with such discrimination, it is no wonder that some lone mothers have to make up stories to cover up their marital status in order to get a dwelling. This is what Ms Bao did to solve her problem after she had been rejected by landlords and landladies several times:

At last, I have to tell lies. I just said that my husband is a seaman, and he is away from Hong Kong at the moment. (Ms Bao)

In order to get accommodation, many lone mothers are compelled to conceal their identity as lone mothers. This social interaction reinforces the feeling that divorced women are abnormal and that lone parents are problematic for society.

Lone mothers are also discriminated against because they have young children. Families with young children are most unwelcome in private rented housing. However, we have seen in the previous chapter that almost all the lone mothers interviewed had to take care of young children. In other words, lone mothers are penalized because they are committed to taking care of the children. For example, Ms Ip was extremely frustrated after being rejected by many landlords/landladies because she had two children aged 8 and 10.

It is extremely difficult for me, I have two children. I have tried lots of places, but the landlords refused me because they don't like to have children in their flats. Some landlords accept children, but don't allow me to cook. This makes it impossible for the children. (Ms Ip)

In this section, we have seen that it is extremely difficult for low income lone mothers to find accommodation in private housing because of the expensive rent. Moreover, lone mothers are discriminated because they are considered problematic by our dominant patriarchal ideology. Or, sometimes women are penalized by and excluded from the private market because of their commitment to child care.

Housing conditions in private housing

For those lone mothers who are able to find accommodation in private housing, it is not surprising that they have to face lots of problems in living in these low rent dwellings. Some of the common problems are over congestion and limited living space, difficulties in taking care of children, health problems, threat of sexual harassment and safety, conflicts in the sharing of household facilities, etc. I am not going to repeat some of the problems that I have elaborated before, such as costly rent (see the previous section) and discrimination against lone mothers by the neighbours (see chapter 5).

The first problem we are going to deal with is the over congested conditions of these dwellings. The most typical dwelling a lone mother can get is a small cubicle of about 50 sq. ft., with a non-permanent partition, and quite often without a window. These dwellings are mostly in congested slum areas in run down high rise blocks. Some of the older blocks do not have elevators, even though they are eight or nine storeys high. Usually they have to share a flat of about 500 sq.ft. with three to four other households (a total of 10 to 15 persons), sharing one kitchen and one toilet/shower room in the flat.

For example, Ms Jone was living with her 9 year old daughter, renting a room of about 60 sq.ft., sharing a flat of about 500 sq.ft. with 4 households. Literally, she had to do everything on the bed.

> The room is very small indeed, we don't have enough space for a small dinning table. So, we have to eat on our bed. The room is just big enough for a bed and a small wardrobe. We have to do everything on our bed. (Ms Jone)

Living in such an environment poses great difficulties for lone mothers in taking care of the children. Ms Fung was living in an extremely congested flat, with two daughters aged 10 and 6. She had to share a flat of about 700 sq.ft. with 20 persons in 10 different households. Her room was only about 70 sq.ft., and there was no other place such as a sitting room where they could go. They were just confined in the room all day.

> It creates difficulties for taking care of the children. They are bored and become annoyed easily, and so am I. But I cannot scold them or discipline them too strictly, because it would be too noisy and disturbing to other tenants. The children know about this, therefore they are naughtier. If you have your own home, it is much better and easier. (Ms Fung)

This over congested environment does not only increase the burden of child care, it also reduces the chance of getting help or support from other relatives such as parents. Their environment is so congested that it is difficult to ask relatives to come to the flat to help to look after the children as other women do.

A further consequence is that this may reduce their chance of getting employment. I have already pointed out in the previous chapter that the heavy burden of child care and lack of child care services or support from relatives are major reasons that inhibit lone mothers from getting employment.

Other problems in such living environments are the threat of sexual harassment and other physical danger for the women and their children. Ms Quan had faced the threat of sexual harassment from her landlord in one of the places she lived.

After I lived there for several months, I found that there was something wrong with the landlord. He was a single old man. At first, he frequently came to ask me to help him with this or that. I realized that he had wicked intentions. He often said things like: 'you are so young and without a husband, it's a pity'. But I pretended that I didn't understand. Later, he even said explicitly that he wanted to have sex with me. If I accepted this, I wouldn't need to pay the rent. If I didn't accept, he wouldn't allow me to stay in the flat any longer. I couldn't stand him any more, so I moved out. (Ms Quan)

Ms Au was harassed by a tenant in her flat. Before she was granted a compassionate public housing unit, she was renting a private room, sharing a flat with several households. Two of the male tenants there were very vulgar. They tried to harass her several times.

One night I was washing clothes in the kitchen, it was quite late, about 10 p.m. The man came in and took off his trousers, he took everything off including his underwear. I was so frightened that I raced back to my room immediately, leaving the clothes behind... Sometimes, he called out loudly outside my room, asking me to go to sleep in his room at night, saying things like: 'it is wasteful for a women like you to be without a man'. I was extremely worried that he may attack me one day. (Ms Au)

Lone mothers are more likely to become the target of harassment because it is believed that women without husbands are unprotected. The lone mothers themselves are also very aware of this, which greatly impedes their daily activities. For example, Ms Ell, who is facing the threat of sexual harassment, has to lock herself up literally in her room most of the time.

I try to stay in my own room as far as possible. If I know that someone is outside, I won't go out unless it is absolutely necessary....I am very aware that I don't have a husband at home. So I try to avoid conflict as far as possible. (Ms Ell)

The sharing of household facilities is another major problems in these dwellings. If we take a look at the sharing of household facilities and appliances in these dwellings, we can see the difficulties of the situation for lone mothers.

In the questionnaire survey, I explored the extent for which basic household facilities were shared. The situation was worst in 'marginal households' such as those renting a room/cubicle in private housing, living in Temporary Housing Areas and squatter huts, living temporarily with friends and relatives, and living

117

in temporary shelters provided by welfare agencies (table 6.4). In the sample, there were altogether 32 lone mothers (that is 36.4 per cent of all lone mothers interviewed) living in these types of housing conditions.

Table 6.4
Sharing of household facilities and appliances for marginal households

Facilities/appliances	Sole use	Shared	Not available	Total
Toilet	2	29	1	32
Kitchen	5	22	4	30
Sitting room	2	11	17	30
Refrigerator	12	10	19	31
Television	14	8	9	31
Washing machine	6	8	16	30
Telephone	11	19	2	32

Such facilities or household appliances are very basic in present day Hong Kong. A household without them is existing in extreme poverty because people are unable to keep food fresh without a refrigerator, unable to wash clothes regularly without a washing machine and access to outside clothes drying facilities, unable to access to social information without a television, or unable to communicate easily with relatives and friends without a telephone. For these marginal households, 29 have to share a toilet and 22 have to share a kitchen. Some households did not even have these basic facilities within the area of the flats. A sitting room becomes a luxury, only 2 families had a sitting room to themselves, 11 had to share and 17 simply had none. That is, for most families, they had to stay in their small cubicle most of the time, just like confinement to prison.

As for the other basic household appliances such as a refrigerator and a television, only 12 and 14 respectively of these marginal households had one for their sole use. A washing machine becomes a luxury, only 6 of the lone mothers had one for their sole use. In Hong Kong a telephone has already become a basic necessity for social contact. However, 19 of the lone mother families had to share with other households and 2 families could not even gain access to one.

The sharing of facilities and household appliances in an over congested environment causes conflicts between the co-tenants. This creates more difficulties for lone mothers. These difficulties are further exacerbated by the ideology that lone mothers are unprotected by men and that they are one of the most powerless groups in the fierce competition for scarce resources. For example, Ms Au had to reschedule her daily activities substantially in order to avoid conflict.

> Every evening, I have to wait until everybody in the flat has finished using the toilet before I can use it. For the kitchen, I have to cook as early as possible, before any one comes back. I always have to be in a hurry, just in case somebody may need to use the kitchen or the toilet. (Ms Au)

From the discussion in this section, we can see that most lone mothers, with limited financial resources and faced with discrimination against them in the private housing market, find it extremely difficult to obtain decent accommodation. Quite often, they have to accept very appalling living conditions in slum areas. This not only creates further difficulties for them in taking care of the children, but also exposes them to harassment. To certain extent, we can say that living in these appalling dwellings creates housing problems for lone mothers. Even if they can find a place to stay in the competitive private housing market, very often it is the beginning of a series of problems rather than a solution to their housing needs.

Lone mothers in public housing

Since it is difficult for low income lone mothers to solve their housing problems in the private market, public housing provides the only hope of obtaining reliable or basic accommodation. However, the public housing system provides little encouragement. Lone mothers can apply for public housing on compassionate grounds, or they can apply for public rented housing, Home Ownership flats or the Home Purchase Loan Scheme through normal channels. But all these services are ineffective for solving lone mothers' housing problems.

In this section, we start with looking at the accessibility of public housing on compassionate grounds, since this is one of the major sources of public housing for lone mothers. We also examine the difficulties for lone mothers of applying for other types of social housing such as public rented housing, the Home Ownership Scheme, and the Home Purchase Loan Scheme (see Appendix C for a list of social housing service in Hong Kong). Finally, we explore the housing conditions of lone mothers in public housing.

Access to compassionate housing[1]

Applying for public housing on compassionate grounds is one of the major strategies used by low income lone mothers to solve their housing problems. Among the 85 lone mothers interviewed in my survey, 46 (that is 54.1 per cent of the 85) had applied for compassionate housing. However, the results were very disappointing, only 13 (15.3 per cent of the 85) had so far had such housing granted, while 27 (31.8 per cent of the 85) had been rejected and 6 applications (7 per cent of the 85) were still in process (see figure 6.1). The success rate was extremely low.

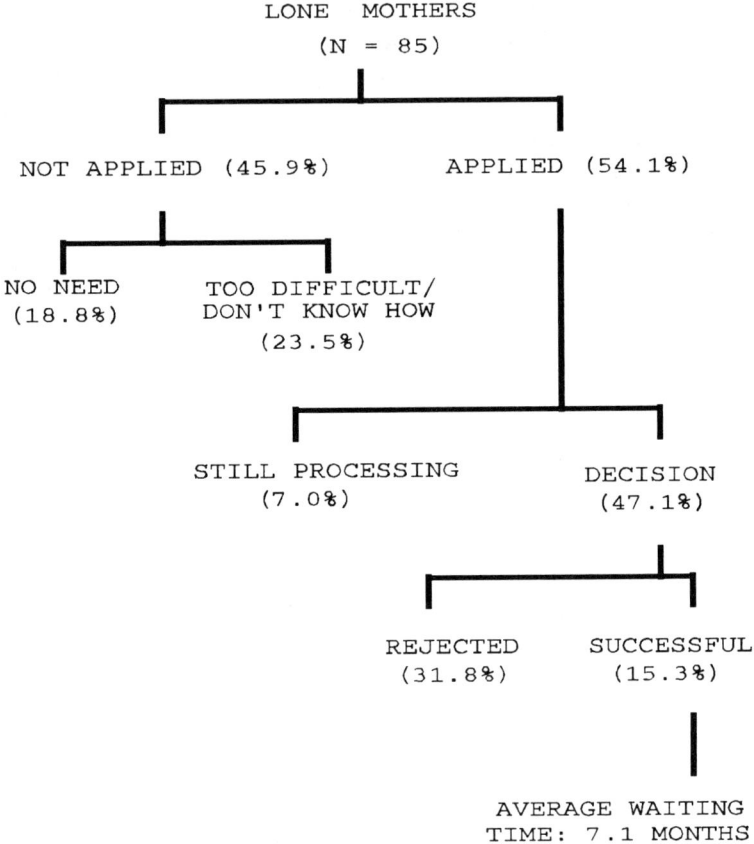

LONE   MOTHERS
(N = 85)

NOT APPLIED (45.9%)   APPLIED (54.1%)

NO NEED   TOO DIFFICULT/
(18.8%)   DON'T KNOW HOW
                 (23.5%)

STILL PROCESSING   DECISION
     (7.0%)   (47.1%)

REJECTED   SUCCESSFUL
(31.8%)   (15.3%)

AVERAGE WAITING
TIME: 7.1 MONTHS

Figure 6.1   Compassionate housing filter

Moreover, even if the lone mothers were entitled to apply for compassionate housing, they still had to wait for a long time before they could get the service. Among the lone mothers interviewed, the average waiting time for those eventually successful was 7.1 months. The quickest one waited for 2 months, while the slowest one waited for 12 months. Obviously waiting for 7.1 months on the average is too long to solve lone mothers' pressing problems.

Given all these problems, many lone parents were effectively discouraged from applying, 39 (45.9 per cent of the 85) lone mothers did not apply. Amongst them, only 16 (18.8 per cent of the 85) said that they had sufficient resources to solve their own problems or that they were already living in public housing, such that they did not need the service. On the other hand, 20 (23.5 per cent of the 85) pointed out that the procedure for applying was too complicated and the criteria were too stringent, so much so that they had to give up; or that they did not know what 'compassionate housing' was or how to apply for it.

To summarize the situation, I have constructed a diagram, which may be called the 'compassionate housing filter', to illustrate this process (figure 6.1). Lone mothers are being discouraged, excluded or disqualified, leaving only a very small proportion to pass through the filter. Obviously, compassionate housing is not providing an effective service to meet lone mothers' housing needs.

One of the major problems in the compassionate housing service is that the Social Welfare Department has set up very stringent criteria. For example, Ms Jone had tried to apply for compassionate housing after she left her violent husband. She hoped to get a public housing unit so that she could live with all her four children. At present, she can only afford to rent a room in an urban slum to live with her youngest daughter aged 9. The Housing Department gave her many reasons why she was not qualified:

> The Housing Department said that I was not qualified for compassionate housing because I am the household head of the public housing unit, that means I should have a place to stay already. Another reason is that they had to wait until all the court procedures for divorce were completed, to make sure that I could get the custody of the children before they could consider any further service. They also said that I was working and since I am not on Public Assistance, they couldn't grant me compassionate housing. (Ms Jone)

Although Ms Jone was officially the household head of the public housing unit before she left her violent husband, it was impossible for her to go back to her public housing flat. However, the housing Department used this as a reason to disqualify her application. This rationale seems ridiculous, but is frequently used by the Housing Department. I am going to elaborate on this point in the next section on access to public rental housing.

Another rationale for rejecting Ms Jone's application was that they have to wait until all the court procedures for divorce have been completed. This is another very inconsiderate policy. Court procedures for divorce can take months or even years, depending on whether the husband is cooperative. It is illogical to leave lone mothers and their children homeless until the court procedures are completed. This policy has been under strong attack from women's groups and lone mothers organizations in recent years.

In reaction to these criticisms, starting from July 1991, the government launched a trial programme of 'conditional offer of tenancy' to lone parents with children who are going through the legal procedures for divorce. After launching this trial programme for one year, the government declared that they were now taking good care of lone parents. This is because official records show that in the first year, out of the 158 lone parent families applied, 101 families were granted compassionate housing. That is a success rate of about 64 per cent.

Definitely, having a policy of 'conditional offer of tenancy' is better than none. However, it still leaves many questions unanswered, such as whether the stringent criteria are relaxed or not. With so many stringent criteria, many lone mothers may be discouraged from applying. The fact that the number of applications is as low as 158 may be taken as a sign of this. With the rapidly rising divorce rate in Hong Kong, the number of applications for divorce filed in 1991 reached 7,287 (HK Census and Statistics Department, 1993b, p.20), not including those separated without filing a formal application. It is quite incredible that only 158 lone parents (that is only about 2 per cent of the number of applications for divorce) have expressed the need for housing by submitting an application. Most probably, many lone parents were filtered out by the 'compassionate housing filter'.

Coming back to Ms Jone's case, the third reason for rejecting her application is that she was working. That means she had income above Public Assistance level. The income of Ms Jone, when she applied for compassionate housing, was only about HK$3,000, which was not much higher than Public Assistance level. But, with this low income it is impossible for Ms Jone to find decent accommodation in the private housing market.

The criteria for compassionate housing are so harsh that even many lone mothers depending on social security do not qualify. Lone mothers applying for compassionate housing have to prove that they have genuine needs for housing. 'Genuine needs' depends on the interpretation of the social security officer or the housing officer. Sometimes, it is so strictly interpreted that virtually anyone who can find a shelter, no matter how awful, is considered to be alright. In many cases, lone mothers depending on social security benefit, living in congested rundown slums, are not regarded as having 'genuine' needs.

For example, Ms Hong is living with her 17 year old daughter in a 80 sq.ft. cubicle, sharing a tenement with several other households, of which all are men. They felt threatened and asked for compassionate rehousing. But this was not a sufficient reason.

> Once, we went to see the social worker. She said that the place where we are living is acceptable, it is safe enough, and nothing has happened so far. My daughter became very angry, she challenged the social worker whether some one has to get hurt before we are qualified. (Ms Hong)

A lone mother Ms Au had experienced sexual harassment in her appalling dwelling. After that, she complained to the Social Welfare Department, and requested compassionate housing. But after waiting for several months without hearing anything from the Social Welfare Department, she went to the Department to check progress.

The social worker was very rude, she told me not to be too demanding. She said that I am already very 'lucky' because I had experienced sexual harassment. Otherwise, I would not be qualified. (Ms Au)

Such a welfare system is completely ironical. You have to get hurt, otherwise you are not qualified. Finally, Ms Au still had to wait for nearly one year before her application for compassionate housing was granted.

The strict attitude of the social security officers and housing officers reflects two basic underlying ideologies. The first is the laissez-faire capitalist ideology of the minimal provision of social welfare. Under this philosophy, the criteria for compassionate housing should be as stringent as possible in order to minimize over dependency on the government. The second underlying ideology is the patriarchal assumption that women should depend on their husbands. A woman unable to keep her husband is regarded as failing her duty, which is their own fault. So, they should go back to ask their husbands for support, not the government.

The housing officer handling Ms Deng's case clearly reflects these ideologies. Ms Deng had to take care of her daughter aged 6, so she depended on Public Assistance. When she applied for compassionate housing, she was being accused of abusing the system.

The Officer accused me of abusing the system. She said that: 'you always think that you can get a compassionate housing after divorce. This assumption is wrong. Compassionate housing is reserved for the extremely needy such as the very old, the sick, and those who really cannot work'... For my situation, they said that I am still young, I can go out to work, or I can ask my ex-husband for support, so I don't have urgent need for compassionate housing. (Ms Deng)

These ideologies completely neglect the structural constraints on the lone mothers. Therefore, the compassionate housing policy arising from this conceptual basis is self contradictory. Ms Quan is right to point out this contradiction in our housing policy.

It is very unfair to us. If you have income over Public Assistance level [about HK$1,500 per month for a two-person family, see table 3.11 for detail], you are not qualified. Why don't they use the income limit for public housing.[2] Then, we can continue our job while we are applying for compassionate housing. Now, we have to quit the job and depend on Public Assistance. It seems that the government is forcing us to depend on Public Assistance. It is a stupid policy, and not only increases the government's burden, but also makes the lone mothers feel inferior, dependent, and useless. (Ms Quan)

The contradiction is that on the one hand, lone mothers are expected to be on their own, to get employment and not to depend on the government. On the other

123

hand, inadequate housing services fail to support the lone mother in her efforts to continue to work. They are forced to give up their work and to depend on public assistance in order to get a compassionate housing unit. Many lone mothers have to do this because they have no other way to solve their housing problems.

Access to other social housing

Besides compassionate housing, there are other ways to gain access to social housing - such as applying for public rental housing, the Home Ownership Scheme, or the Home Purchase Loan Scheme. However, these housing service are not effective in solving lone mothers' problems. In these housing services lone mothers' needs are largely neglected or lone mothers are being discriminated against.

Let us start by looking at access to public rental housing. If lone mothers are not eligible for compassionate housing, they have two different channels for access to public housing. First, those already living in public rental housing before divorce can apply for transfer to another flat if they have to leave their matrimonial home. Second those living in private housing can apply for public housing in the normal way and join the waiting list.

For the first situation, lone mothers and their children can apply for transfer to other public housing unit, if they cannot stay in the matrimonial home for sound reasons. However, this is a grey area in which policy is not clearly spelled out. In most cases, the need for transfer depends on the interpretation of the housing officers involved. Being dominated by patriarchal ideologies and bureaucratic considerations, most housing officers are reluctant to support this kind of transfer.

Ms Jone is a typical example of someone trapped in this situation. She had been battered by her husband, and had applied for divorce. The court had already granted the divorce and Ms Jone had the right of custody of the children. Normally, it is expected that her husband should move out of the matrimonial home and leave it for the wife and the children. But, her husband refused to move out. She dared not move back, because her husband would have beaten her if she went back. When she approached the housing estate office asking for a transfer to another housing estate, the housing officer said that she was not qualified for a transfer. The rationale was that she should move back to her matrimonial home and convince her husband to move out. This was considered as an internal family affair, nothing to do with the Housing Department.

I could not contact the housing officer handling Ms Jone's case, however, when I brought up this case for discussion in my interviews with housing officers, most of the officers expressed similar views. This is a clear illustration of gender blind administration.

> If the husband is reluctant to move out, there is not much we can do. After all, it is their internal family affair, they have to decide who is going to stay in the flat. If they cannot come to a mutual agreement, we cannot let the

women take over the flat, we shall not intervene to help either party. (Ms Fun, a housing officer)

Of course, we are not suggesting to evict the divorced husbands by force. Neither party should be punished in a divorce. The situation would be much simpler if the Housing Department could provide adequate housing for both the lone mother and the divorced husband, if they have housing needs. However, being dominated by the belief of minimal intervention in social services, the state is reluctant to provide extra resources to support families in trouble. Consequently, they antagonize the husband and wife in the fierce competition for housing resources.

However the emphasis on treating family problems as private affairs completely neglects the fact that power between male and female in the family is unequal. In this case, the wife is powerless to 'convince' the husband to move out. Pushing the problem back to the family punishes the lone mothers and their children. That is why many lone mothers, like Ms Jone, have to take up the burden of finding new accommodation for their children after divorce.

In the second situation, in which lone mothers are not sitting tenants before they divorced, they can only gain access to public rental housing by joining the normal waiting list. However, this fails to attend to the immediate needs of lone mothers in a crisis situation. At present, the waiting list is so long that one has to wait for several years to get a flat. Although some lone mothers applied for public rental housing in this way, they considered it as a remote and long term solution rather than an immediate answer to their housing problems.

The application may be speeded up a little if the lone mothers accept housing units in very remote new towns. By doing this, sometimes they can get a public housing flat within two years. However, living in remote new towns may cause other problems, such as child care, which we are going to discuss in the following section on 'Condition in Public Housing'. On the other hand, those who want to get a flat in the urban area, which is sometimes essential for lone mothers needing help from their relatives, usually have to wait for more than ten years. Unfortunately, after December 1990 the Housing Department no longer accepts applications for housing in the urban area because public housing units in urban area are so scarce. That is, all new applicants must go to the new towns.

Another problem with the process for applying for public housing is that it discriminates against 'unconventional families' such as the small family with one or two persons (see the discussion in chapter 3). Quite a number of lone parent families are two-person families consisting of a parent and a child. Until recent years, one or two person families did not qualify for public housing. The Housing Department insisted that larger families (with three members or above) should be given higher priority. At the end of 1992, there were 23,970 single persons and 46,434 two-person families on the waiting list for public housing, which was about 40 per cent of the total live applications (HK Housing Authority, 1993, p.38). It is estimated that it is impossible for two-person families on the waiting list to be allocated housing units before 1995 (Mok, 1993, p.120). Therefore, in practical terms joining the waiting list is not a solution to lone mothers' urgent housing problems.

Let us now turn to look at the situation of home owners. Trouble in getting transfers and discrimination against 'unconventional' families does not only happen in public rental housing, it is also the case with the Home Ownership Scheme and the Home Purchase Loan Scheme provided by the government.

Those lone mothers who were living in Home Ownership flats before divorce, may also face problems in transferring their tenancy to public housing units after they leave their husbands. As with cases in public rental housing, the Housing Department likes to argue that these lone mothers already have the right of tenancy in their Home Ownership flats. So, they should not entitled to 'double benefit' by getting compassionate housing or transferring to a public housing unit after their divorce.

Ms Fung is a typical example. Before she divorced her husband, she was a home owner under the government Home Ownership Scheme. After separation, she got nothing from her husband, no maintenance or any share of the Home Ownership flat. Because she was threatened by violence from her husband, it is virtually impossible for her to negotiate with her husband and fight for her share of the family wealth. She had to depend on Public Assistance, renting a room in an urban slum. She had applied for transfer to a public housing flat, or a compassionate housing unit. The Housing Department rejected her application on the ground that she was a home owner. Although she declared that she had given up the share of her house, the Housing Department still rejected her application. She was pushed around between the Housing Department and the Social Welfare Department for several months. Only after numerous complaints and petitions was she granted a compassionate housing unit - more than one year after she started asking for it.

From Ms Fung's case, we can see that not only is the Housing Department bureaucratic and inconsiderate, literally, they force lone mothers to give up their right to share property with their ex-husbands. Before she can get a compassionate housing unit, Ms Fung has to sign a document in the Housing Department agreeing to give up her right to the flat she owned jointly with her husband. Ms Fung showed no hesitation in giving up her right because it was the only way she would secure stable accommodation. In this way, the housing system reinforces men's privilege.

We can see that this transfer of wealth is extremely unfair to lone mothers. The distribution and transfer of housing wealth to males from females reinforces gender inequality. This is especially true in Hong Kong where housing prices are extremely high. Even a government Home Ownership flat can be worth about 1.5 million Hong Kong Dollars, not to mention private housing worth several millions dollars. Access to such housing resources makes a great difference to one's life chances (Hamnett, 1991; Smith, 1990; Forrest and Murie, 1988b). In Ms Fung's case, her ex-husband remained a middle income home owner, while she and her two children became among the poorest and needed to depend on Public Assistance. Our housing system creates or reinforces this unequal distribution of housing resources instead of helping lone mothers to get a fair share. Ironically, many housing officers and social security officers are accusing lone mothers of being greedy when they request Public Assistance and compassionate housing in such circumstances.

Another problem for lone mothers' seeking Home Ownership flats is the discrimination against one-person and two-person families, similar to the situation in public rental housing that we have discussed. At present, the Home Ownership Scheme, the Home Purchase Loan Scheme, and the newly introduced Sandwich Class Home Purchase Scheme still explicitly favouring the 'conventional' family, which is defined as two parents with at least one dependent child (see Appendix C for more detail of these schemes). By adopting such policies, opportunities for lone parent families and other 'unconventional' families to solve their problems are further reduced.

No wonder some of the lone mothers were very unsatisfied when the government introduced the new Home Purchase Loan Scheme to help the middle income 'sandwich class', while lone mothers with more urgent housing problems were left on their own without adequate support. For example, Ms Pang complained that those with income like hers are forgotten by our housing system. She was earning HK$8,050 per month, which just exceeded the public housing income limit of HK$8,000 for two-person family. So she was not qualified to apply for public housing with her daughter. On the other hand, the Home Ownership Scheme for lower middle income families (with income exceeding public housing limit, but less than HK$20,000 per month) was too expensive for her to buy. Her frustration at being trapped in this policy gap is understandable.

> The government's housing policy is ridiculous, they have huge subsidies for those well off 'sandwich class' to buy their own flats, these families are earning HK$20,000 to HK$40,000 per month. But, see what we have, no one seems to care about us. The government is taking care of the better off sandwich class but not the 'lower sandwich class' like us. (Ms Pang)

As we can see from the above discussion, both public rental housing and home ownership housing discriminate against lone mothers or neglect their needs. Lone mothers' accessibility to these housing resources is very limited. And frequently, the pattern of inequality between male and female is reinforced.

Problems in public housing

As I have pointed out in previous sections, many low income lone mother families are unable to secure stable accommodation unless they are allocated a public housing unit. Relatively speaking, living in public housing is far better than in the over congested slum in private housing. However, this does not mean that as long as the lone mother can get a public housing unit, everything is solved. As some lone mothers have pointed out, it is not that the public housing unit they have got is perfect, it is rather that they have experienced the extremely appalling living environment in private housing and have become very complacent.

> I am very easily satisfied, I'll be satisfied with any flat they give me, any one will do. I have been living in more worse places before. Actually, this flat has got a lot of problems, for example there is no water to flush the toilet. Anyway, it is better than having no place to stay. (Ms Quan)

Lone mothers still have to face a lot of problems even when they have got their public housing flats. Usually, lone mothers are offered the worst choice of public housing unit. Because they are desperately in need of a shelter, they have to accept the offer even though it may not be appropriate accommodation for them.

One common problem is that they are allocated housing units far away from their established social support network, quite often in remote new towns. Although this solves their urgent needs for shelter, it dismantles their social support network. Their relatives, who are living in the city centre, cannot come very often to help them to take care of the children. In this way, they are isolated and left on their own. This increases the burden on child care and reduces their opportunity for employment. These are common problems for women who are moving to new towns even if they are in two-parent families (see chapter 7 and 8), but lone mother are affected more seriously. They require more support for child care or they rely more on getting employment to solve their financial problems. But frequently, lone mothers have to accept the offers because of lack of choice.

> Yesterday, the Housing Department asked me whether I am interested in moving to Tin Shui Wai [a very remote, newly developed new town]. If I don't accept that offer, there will be no place for me in the near future. Of course, I have to accept the offer, I really need accommodation urgently. Without stable accommodation, I am facing a lot of problems at present, such as children's education, personal safety, etc... I know that it is difficult to find a job there. Salaries are less than in the urban area, even if you can get a job. But I have no choice. (Ms Lee)

Another problem with public housing is that sometimes women are allocated flats too near their violent ex-husbands. Ms Ip left her violent husband, taking with her two children aged 10 and 8. Last year, she was granted a compassionate housing unit very near her ex-husband's place, which she rejected. In fact, when she applied for compassionate housing, she emphasized that she did not want to live near her ex-husband because of the threat of violence. However, her request was not entertained, or not even noted. After she turned down the first offer, it took another two to three months before she was offered another flat in Yuen Long (a very remote new town). This time she really could not wait any longer, she had to accept the offer.

> This is a new housing estate, everything is new, the place is quite good, but many facilities are still lacking. In particular, the traffic is very bad indeed, this estate is very far away, I became very isolated from my friends and relatives. It is too far away to travel to the city centre. (Ms Ip)

Here we can see that Ms Ip is being forced to accept a move to a remote new town. This is not a real choice, but rather a choice of the lesser evil.

Another problem is that compassionate housing units allocated to lone mothers are usually located in the worst parts of the housing estate, such as next to the garbage collection station, or are badly worn out units which are beyond repair. Such poor housing conditions can affect the health and safety of lone mothers and their children. It is not surprising to see that women in these poor living environments have comparatively more health problems (see Payne, 1991, pp.130-7, 178-85 for the UK situation and Leung 1993 for the Hong Kong situation).

All these problems show that our public housing policy has no special consideration for the needs of lone mothers. Even if the lone mothers were eligible for a public housing unit, they were allocated the worst choice. Again, this reflects the dominating ideology that lone mothers are not regarded as a 'deserving' group. At the same time, it is a matter of administrative convenience to allocate the worst housing to groups with the least bargaining power. Therefore, lone mothers requesting specific housing locations are often not entertained.

For example, when Ms Fung was granted a compassionate housing unit in Shatin (in the New Territories) which is very far away from her mother who was living in the Southern part of Hong Kong Island, she rejected the offer. She planned to rely on her mother to take care of her two children aged 4 and 10, so that she could go to work after she got this public housing unit. She was condemned by the housing officer of being too greedy.

> They scolded me, accusing me of being too greedy and too choosey. But it is impossible for me to live in Shatin, I have to live near my mother, otherwise no one helps me to take care of my children. (Ms Fung)

In deciding where to live, a lone mother has to consider various factors such as the social support network, child care support, schools for children, safety in the community, job opportunities, etc. (see Anderson-Khleif, 1981). Unless these factors were considered, housing services will be ineffective for solving their problems. No wonder, some lone mothers are deterred from applying for public housing because of the lack of choice of location.

Concluding from the discussion in this section, although compassionate housing and other types of social housing are very important for the solution of lone mothers' housing problems, the availability of these services is very limited. The 'compassionate housing filter' screens out most lone mothers in need of housing services rather than solving their housing problems. Not only are lone mothers' needs very much neglected by the public housing system, sometimes existing housing policy and practice even discriminate against lone mothers and reinforces gender inequalities in access to housing resources. For example, two-person families (many lone mother families are two-person families) have little chance of getting public housing units; frequently female home owners are forced to give up their rights to share property before they are allowed to apply for public housing. Those who are lucky enough to get a public housing unit do not have their problems solved completely. Public housing services and choices fail to response to lone mothers' needs. In most cases, lone mothers' request to live near their relatives for better social support are not entertained. That is why sometimes after lone mothers are forced to move to remote new towns, problems such as child caring and employment are intensified rather than solved.

Temporary solutions to housing problems

Because they lack resources, some lone mothers have to rely on temporary solutions such as living with friends and relatives or living in temporary shelters provided by welfare agencies. Very often, these 'temporary' arrangements can last for a long period before they really settle down. As I have pointed out earlier in this chapter, moving around between temporary dwellings becomes a way of life for many lone mother families - a series of 'temporary' accommodation becomes the permanent pattern.

This is especially common when a lone mother has just left her husband. In my survey, 5.7 per cent of the 88 lone mothers lived in temporary shelters and another 5.7 per cent lived with friends and relatives at the time of the study. However, most lone mothers interviewed in the case studies revealed that they had lived in shelter for women or with friends/relatives for a certain period of time after they left their husbands. In this section, I tried to question how far these temporary solutions were effective means of solving lone mothers' housing problems.

Living with friends and relatives

It is generally believed that in Chinese society we still have strong family ties, so that when a woman leaves her husband, she can still go back to stay with her parents. No doubt, going back to the parents is one of the most common solutions for lone mothers, especially immediately after leaving their husbands. In fact, relatives (mainly the mothers, and sometimes the sisters) are one of the major sources of help for many lone mothers. But these forms of help are rarely sufficient to solve lone mothers' housing problems permanently. Although some lone mothers have tried to stay with their parents, this seldom turned out to be a satisfactory long term solution.

One of the lone mothers tells us that after she moved back to stay with her parents, it created tremendous psychological pressure on her and her parents. A divorced daughter is considered as a disgrace for the family in traditional Chinese culture. It is believed that there must be something wrong with the daughter so that her husband deserted her. After Ms Chan moved back to live with her mother, she had to avoid meeting her neighbours in order to escape from gossip. She knew that her neighbours were gossiping about her, and that her mother felt very ashamed about her divorce. She could not stand it any longer after she had overheard her mother expressing a grievance to her neighbours.

> One day I heard my mother talking to the neighbour. The neighbour's daughter is going to get married soon. My mother said: 'you are very fortunate that your daughter is going to marry, you can release your burden very soon. But for me, I am really unfortunate, I have been working so hard to bring up my daughter, and shed the burden after she got married. But all of a sudden, the burden came back again'. I know that my mother feels ashamed and has lost face in front of her friends. I don't want the others looking down upon my mother, so I have decided to move out. (Ms Chan)

Here we can see that some women who have adopted traditional ideologies - Ms Chan's mother and her neighbours - can themselves become agents oppressing women themselves. That is an illustration of how gender oppression is so inconspicuous, and yet very potent.

Another practical problem in staying with parents is that in Hong Kong living space is so limited that it is difficult to accommodate additional members in the household. For example, after Ms Gon had left her husband, she lived with a friend for one week, and then lived with her mother for two months. Even though her friend and parents were very supportive, she still had to move out to find her own place.

> When I left my husband I didn't take my son with me, I stayed with a good friend who is also a lone mother with a young daughter. The place is very crowded indeed. After one week, I had to take my son out, it was really inconvenient staying there, so I moved to stay with my mother... My mother and father are living with my elder brother who has several children. Although we are very close relatives, I still feel very apologetic. It seems that my child and I have created too much trouble for them, so I decided to move out. (Ms Gon)

Moreover, it seems that those coming from middle or lower middle income families, such as Ms Gon, have better chances of staying with parents. Partly because their parents tend to be more open minded toward divorced women, and partly because they have more resources to take care of the divorced daughter. For working class or lower income groups it is practically impossible because their parents are living in extremely over congested conditions. Moreover, working class parents tend to be more traditional. That is they may feel ashamed to have a divorced daughter.

There are other conflicts in living with parents, such as the style of teaching children and disciplining children. Ms Pang's mother and sister are already very supportive, they accepted her to move back to live with them. In fact, the relationship between them is not too bad, but she still does not feel very good about living with her mother.

> From time to time, there are conflicts between me and them [her mother and sister], for example, on matters concerning my child. You know, sometimes it is good to see each other occasionally, but it is difficult to live together. Sometimes, when they become angry, they will say things like: 'you are a daughter "married out",[3] we are already very sympathetic in letting you stay, you shouldn't complain any more'. Sometimes, when I am angry, I may say things like: 'this is not my place anyway, I am only a sojourner'. This makes me seem like an outsider, not belonging to the family. (Ms Pang)

Ms Oi faced similar problems in teaching her child aged 4, when she lived with her mother. So, she moved out as soon as she can afford to rent her own place.

> You see, my mother is always my mother, she is always teaching me, including how to teach my child. Sometimes when I punish my son, he will run to his grandma, he knows that grandma will always protect him. So, he can avoid punishment and always repeat the same mistakes. This is my major reason for moving out. (Ms Oi)

Friends, parents and other relatives can be very helpful in a crisis situation. But such help is mostly on a short term basis only. Moreover, given the serious shortage of housing and living space in Hong Kong, it is unrealistic to rely on friends or relatives to provide long term solutions to housing problems.

Temporary shelter

For battered women, there is another temporary solution to their urgent needs for shelter. At present, there are two shelters for battered women. One is provided by the government and the other is run by a group of feminist social workers in a voluntary agency. These shelters have forty places each, and the maximum period of stay is three months, after which they have to find other solutions.

Due to lack of government support, and to the invisibility of lone mothers' housing problems, services in these shelters are very limited and fragmented. In general, services are literally only limited to the provision of shelter. Other services such as helping the lone mothers to find permanent accommodation, job placements, occupational training, or schools for children are not standard provision. That is, existing subsidies are not expected to cover these services. Moreover, the battered women have to move out after three months whether or not they have found a place to stay.

The provision of these shelters helps some battered women to escape from their violent husbands, but there is still no shelter service for divorcing women who are not threatened by physical violence. Some lone mothers in my case studies were not physically battered by their husbands, but were under such great psychological stress that they had to leave their home as soon as possible. They were really in need of shelter or some kind of residential service. However, this need is not recognized at present.

Lone mothers' experience in these shelters is not the major focus of this study, because obviously these are not permanent solutions to their housing problems. Of course, it does not mean that these services are unimportant. On the contrary, these services are very helpful in providing shelter for battered wives in a crisis situations. It is the inadequate support from the government for these shelter services and the lack of other related housing services that makes them ineffective in solving lone mothers' problems.

Conclusion

In this chapter we have seen that both private housing and public housing do not help lone mothers to solve their housing problems. Frequently, low income lone mothers can only obtain access to the worst quality housing whether public or private. They are not helped to solve their housing problems effectively. On the contrary, they often experience other problems such as threat of sexual harassment, isolation from friends and relatives, increasing child care burdens, and decreasing opportunities in employment.

Frequently, lone mothers can only obtain access to transitional and inadequate housing such as living with friends or relatives, or living in awful dwellings in slum areas. Many lone mothers are trapped in these 'temporary' housing solutions permanently. They are encouraged to believe that this is only a transitional arrangement. However, the reality is that as long as they remain lone parent families, they will be discriminated against and marginalized in the housing system and it is very unlikely that their housing problems will be solved. Under this circumstances, many women are forced to depend on men - either marrying another man or returning to their husbands - because of lack of practical alternatives.

Therefore it is not surprising to see that some women still have to go back to their husbands even when they have been seriously battered. Ms Jone's case is a vivid example. She left her husband once before, after she was beaten up by him.

But she had to return to her husband because she could not find a suitable place to stay with all her four children.

> The first time I left him, if I could have found a suitable place for my children to stay, surely I wouldn't have gone back. I missed my children very much, I was thinking about them the whole day, I couldn't sleep, couldn't eat, I lost weight seriously. A friend of mine advised me to move back, she said that I could not keep on like this. So, I moved back. But he beat me up again, I didn't stay very long before I needed to move out again. (Ms Jone)

Dobash and Dobash (1970, 1992) are right to point out that violence against wives is not simply pathological behaviour of individual men under psychological stress, it is backed up by our gender biased social system which reinforces men's domination over women. Here, we can see that the housing system is one of the most significant systems which perpetuates men's domination.

It has been demonstrated that lone mothers' disadvantageous position is socially constructed rather than the result of their own deficiencies. On the one hand, women are required to take up the child care burden and are charged with the responsibility for solving housing problems after the divorce. On the other hand, our patriarchal social system makes women, especially lone mothers, less competitive in the labour market and less capable of earning a living by themselves. To make the situation worse, not only housing services for lone mothers are extremely lacking, but also, the housing system discriminates against lone mothers or neglects their needs. Traditional patriarchal values penalize women who are not dependent on their husbands as in the social norm. Under these circumstances, it is extremely difficult for lone mothers to develop a new life after separation from their husbands.

Notes

1. Compassionate housing is a type of social housing services in Hong Kong (see Appendix C for an introduction of social housing services), in which public rental housing units are allocated to applicants on compassionate ground, with the discretion of the Housing Department and the Social Welfare Department. Please refer to the discussion in Chapter 3, especially table 3.2.

2. Income limit for public housing in 1993 is $7,600 for 2-person family (see Appendix C1). After vigorous protests from some lone mothers groups and women groups, starting from early 1994 the Housing Department has adopted the public housing application income limit, instead of the Public Assistance income limit, for compassionate housing.

3. This is a traditional Chinese concept, a married daughter is not considered as a member of her parents' family. She is an outsider, belonging to the family line of her husband.

Part Three

WOMEN IN NEW TOWNS

7 Confining women at home

It is indisputable that lone mothers are facing very limited housing opportunities. However, some people may argue that such difficulties are unique to lone mothers because they are a group of women in very special circumstances, and that ordinary women would enjoy similar housing opportunities as their husbands. In this part of the book (chapter 7 and 8) I am going to show that women in general living in new towns, who are not in extraordinary circumstances, can be adversely affected by their housing situation. Chapter 7 focuses on women's experience at home and in the community, while chapter 8 focuses on their experience in the labour market.

Suburbanization is a prime example of gender blindness in housing and urban planning. In Western countries, suburbanization is generally perceived as leading to an improvement in the living environment. While such an improvement may be true for middle class men, it may be a completely different story for women taking care of children, lone parents, the elderly and low income families. This is especially true for working class women in Hong Kong living in remote new towns such as Tuen Mun and Yuen Long.

In this chapter, we start by looking at the general problems arising from the failure of urban planning in Tuen Mun and Yuen Long new towns. Then we turn to look at how women experience these problems. These include: traffic, break down of social support networks and cutting down of social contacts, an increased burden of housework, lack of child care services, and lack of community services or facilities in the new towns in general. All these serve to reinforce women's confinement at home and their dependence on the family and their husbands.

The new town syndrome

Of course, women are not the only victims in the failure of new town planning. All people, whether male or female, young or old, working class or middle class, are affected some way or other. In fact, there are so many problems in new towns that this is always a hot topic of social research in Hong Kong, but unfortunately the gender dimension is frequently missing in these studies.

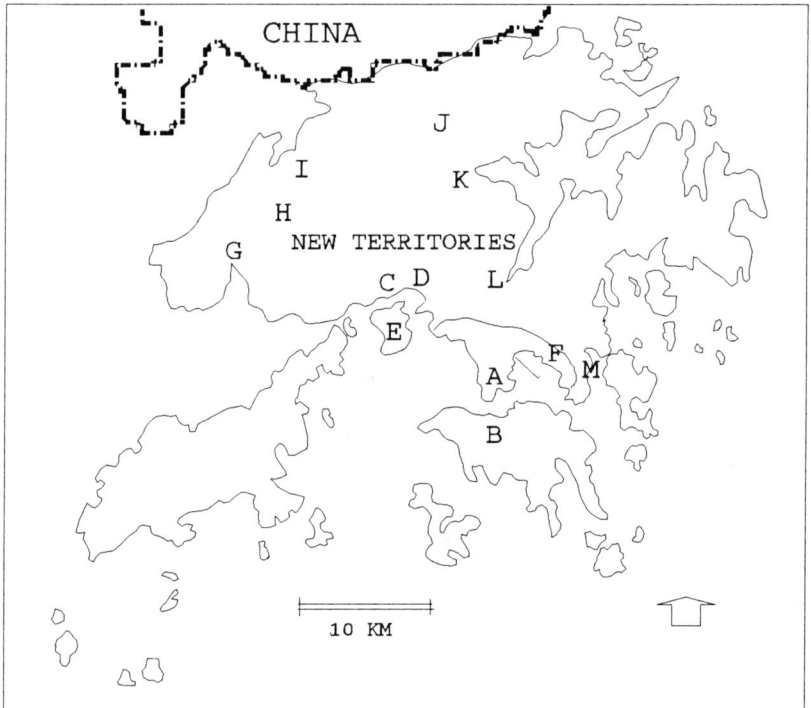

	Urban Area		Other New Towns
	A	Kowloon	G	Tuen Mun

Urban Area
A   Kowloon
B   Hong Kong Island
Early New Towns
C   Tsuen Wan
D   Kwai Chung
E   Tsing Yi
F   Kwun Tong

Other New Towns
G   Tuen Mun
H   Yuen Long
I   Tin Shui Wai
J   Sheung Shui/Fanling
K   Tai Po
L   Shatin
M   Junk Bay

Figure 7.1   **New towns in Hong Kong**

Before we proceed to analyze the case interviews, it may help to offer a brief description of the problems in developing new towns in Hong Kong, especially the problems in Tuen Mun and Yuen Long New Town (see fig. 7.1 for the location of new towns, and Appendix D for the geographic location of Hong Kong) which are the foci of our analysis. The development of new towns in Hong Kong can be traced back to the late 1950s and early 1960s (Bristow, 1989; Sit, 1981). At that time, the government was well aware that the urban area would soon reach full development, and that it would be necessary to decentralize the population to more remote areas to make way for economic development. That is one of the reasons why the government intervened in housing services massively from since the 1960s.

The scale of migration to new towns has been enormous. From 1971 to 1991, the proportion of the population in New Territories has risen from 16.9 per cent to 41.9 per cent (figure 7.2). Bearing in mind the rapid growth of population in Hong Kong, this means that the number of persons living in the New Territories has risen from 665,700 in 1971 to 2,374,818 in 1991, that is, it has nearly quadrupled within 20 years.

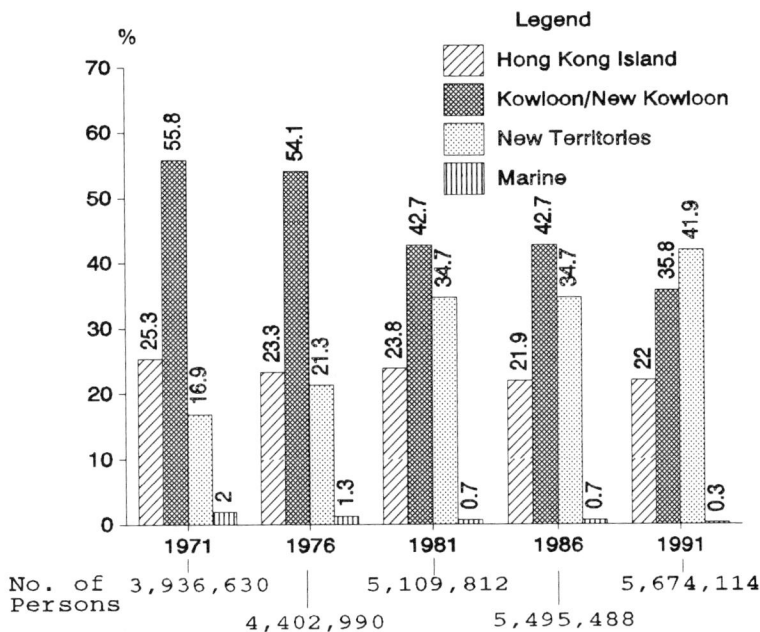

Figure 7.2 Population by broad area, 1971-91 census

Source: HK Census and Statistics Department (1993b), table 2.2, p.11.

This enormous population migration has been achieved largely through the development of public housing programmes in these new towns. Hong Kong's new town development has been very unlike the middle class suburbanization

141

movement in Western countries in which the better off middle class moved to suburban areas to enjoy a better living environment. In Hong Kong, it is mostly the low income working class, young families, and lone parent families which have been displaced to remote new towns because they could not afford expensive housing in the urban area. With limited housing options, they had to move to public housing in remote new towns. In table 7.1, we can see that in new towns the population living in social housing is much higher than that in the urban area, 67 per cent compared with 39.8 per cent. The social housing population in Tuen Mun (76.1 per cent) is even higher than the average of all new towns. The Yuen Long new town is relatively less developed, with 40.5 per cent of the population in social housing. Here, a significant proportion of the population is still living in rural villages.

Table 7.1
Social housing population in new towns (Tuen Mun, Yuen Long) 1991

	Total population	Population in social housing[a]	
		Number	%
Tuen Mun new town	356,819	271,583	76.1
Yuen Long new town	115,062	46,610	40.5
All new towns[b]	2,053,690	1,374,983	67.0
All urban area[c]	3,189,518	1,268,040	39.8
All Hong Kong	5,511,179	2,650,105	48.1

Notes:
a   Including all Housing Authority and Housing Society rental and ownership flats.
b   Including: Tsuen Wan, Kwai Chung/Tsing Yi, Tuen Mun, Yuen Long, Sheung Shui/Fanling, Tai Po, Sha Tin; but excluding other New Territories area outside the new towns (see figure 7.1).
c   Including Hong Kong Island, Kowloon and New Kowloon.

Sources: Complied from Hong Kong Census and Statistics Department (1992a), Table F8, p.236-7.

While arranging a massive migration of low income households, the government has been reluctant to develop community services and facilities in these new towns. In the beginning, these new towns were expected to be 'self contained' and 'socially balanced' (Bristow, 1989, pp.26-9). Self contained in the sense that the residents would find jobs, recreation facilities, education for children, social welfare services, etc. in the new towns without having to travel back to the urban area. Socially balanced in the sense that would be a normal mix of different social classes instead of the creation of a low income working class community. However these new town ideals are never achieved (see Bristow, 1989; Sit, 1981 for more detail discussion on failure of new town programme in Hong Kong). No wonder many families find tremendous difficulty in adjusting to the new environment in the new towns.

Table 7.2
Satisfaction with qualities of community services and facilities in Tuen Mun

Services & facilities	Degree of satisfaction (in %)				
	Very satisfied	Satisfied	Dis-satisfied	Very dis-satisfied	Total (no. of persons)
Employment opportunity	0.1	37.4	58.2	4.2	100% (697)
Transport	0.7	42.9	52.2	4.1	100% (892)
Markets	0.8	60.7	36.9	1.6	100% (894)
Cultural & recreational	0.2	50.1	47.5	2.1	100% (802)
School places	0.6	39.1	55.5	4.8	100% (813)
Medical	0.3	29.4	61.7	8.6	100% (871)
Consultative	0.6	61.2	36.3	1.6	100% (622)
Social welfare	0.6	46.3	50.4	2.7	100% (511)

Source: Chow (1990), table 3, p.55.

Given the fact that Tuen Mun is one of the most remote new towns coupled with government's failure in new town planning, it is not surprising to see that there are

143

numerous social problems in Tuen Mun and that the residents are largely dissatisfied with existing community services (e.g. see Han, 1982; Chow, 1988; Tuen Mun District Board, 1990). Chow's (1990) research on the quality of life in Tuen Mun indicated that more that half of the respondents were either dissatisfied or very dissatisfied with most of the essential services such as employment, transport, school places, medical facilities, and social welfare (table 7.2).

The lack of community facilities and services is detrimental to many families. Many families are under great strain because husbands have to travel long distances to work, while women are isolated in new towns, severed from their previous supportive networks and taking up all the caring burdens alone. In these domains, women are among the groups suffering the most from the mistake made in the development of new towns.

With this background, it is not surprising that Tuen Mun has developed very serious community problems and family problems. It is one of the districts in Hong Kong with the most serious rates of family breakdown, wife battering, child abuse, crime, and triad society activities.

There are already some research studies on Tuen Mun's housing problems, community problems, family problems, law and order, etc. However, most of these studies are gender blind. They failed to see that woman were one of the groups suffering most in the new towns. Some of the studies even tend to put the blame on families themselves (frequently implying the wife), for example for failing to take good care of the children. This only creates greater pressure on the women rather than helping them to solve problems.

Since the burden of new town existence is mostly born by women who are supposed to be responsible for caring duties with the family, it is not surprising to see that women living in new towns encounter tremendous difficulties.

The immobilizing transportation system

The first area we are going to discuss is the traffic problem, which is obviously one of the most serious problems for the residents. A survey by Chow (1988) shows that about 56 per cent of residents in Tuen Mun are dissatisfied or very dissatisfied with the transportation service (see table 7.2).

Most of the studies of Tuen Mun traffic problems seem to focus on home to work commuting, which implies that men who need to go to work in the city centre are badly affected while women who stay at home are better off. However, when I asked the women to name the most serious problems with their living environment, most women identified the traffic problem as one of the most important. Similarly, a survey on the needs of married women in Tuen Mun (Tuen Mun District Board, 1991, p.28) also showed that 57 per cent of the respondents identified transportation as the most important problem. That is, not only are men affected by poor traffic conditions, women are affected too.

144

Regarding transport to the city centre, the main complaint is about traffic jams on the Tuen Mun Highway. Tuen Mun is about 20 miles, and Yuen Long about 25 miles, from the city centre. Transportation between these new towns and the city centre mainly relies on the Tuen Mun Highway which is far from adequate in meeting the needs in these new towns.

It is already difficult for women on their own to endure jamming into an over crowded bus and getting stuck in traffic congestion on the Tuen Mun Highway, but it is much worse when they have to take their young children along. In fact, when women have to travel to the city centre, such as when shopping or visiting their parents, they usually have to bring the children along. So traffic jams become a terrible but commonplace, experience of women in Tuen Mun. Ms Sing had such an awful experience - trapped in the traffic jam on the highway, under the tropical sun in temperatures about 35°C, with three young children aged 9,10 and 11.

> Once, I took my children to visit my mother, we were trapped on the highway for over two hours. I was feeling very sick, you know, my health is no good; and all my children felt sick too. We really wanted to get out of the bus, but it was impossible, it was in the middle of the highway with no way to escape.... (Ms Sing)

Another major complaint is about the lack of choice of bus routes. Most of the bus services are geared toward travelling to and from the work place. Frequently, they fail to meet the needs of women who need to go for other social activities. For example, Ms Ngan found great difficulties in visiting her mother in the city centre.

> I seldom go to the city centre now... It is very troublesome that you have to changes several buses before you get to your destination. For example, if I go to visit my mother in Ngau Tau Kwok [in East Kowloon, urban centre], it takes more than one and half an hours, if the traffic is O.K. Otherwise, who knows?... (Ms Ngan)

Time wasting on transport has become a major deterrent, discouraging women's social activities. Not only in the wasting of time, but sometimes they may be embarrassed because of the lack of time control. Being one or two hours late is not an exceptional experience for Ms Ngan only, most of the interviewees have shared similar experiences with me.

> Once I needed to go to meet a friend in Kowloon, I was one hour late because of the traffic jam. My friend became very worried, thinking that I might have had an accident. It is very embarrassing .... You need to allow plenty of time for the traffic just in case there is a traffic jam, it is time wasting. (Ms Ngan)

Transportation expense is another major complaint. Especially in recent years, the bus company has introduced a more expensive air-conditioned bus service on some routes, which is quite costly for families with only moderate income. Sometimes, however residents are compelled to take this expensive service because of the lack of any alternative.

> Travel is a bit expensive... it is worse now because the bus company uses the air-conditioned bus which are much more expensive. I don't want to take that kind of bus, but sometimes there is no other buses, so we still have to take it. (Ms Oat)

Obviously, this air-conditioned bus is unnecessary in winter. But the bus company has to keep the air conditioner running because it can charge higher fares on these routes, and therefore be more profitable. The strategy of the bus company is completely absurd, it wastes energy and wastes consumer's money just for higher profits. It is another clear example of the inefficient utilization of resources in a capitalist system.

Do women in better off families have more resources to solve traffic problems? I have interviewed a few women in middle income families. Their situation is not much better. Even for those better off families who can afford to buy a car,[1] it is not common for women to be able to drive or use the car regularly. For example, although Ms Quart has a family car, she is not encouraged to drive. She has moved to Yuen Long more than 10 years ago, and started to learn to drive. However, after continual discouragement by her husband and other family members, she did not keep up her lessons regularly and failed the driving test several times. Finally, she has broke through all the obstacles and has recently got her licence.

> I don't agree that women are unsuitable for driving. It is only because they seldom need to, in most cases the husband will do the driving...it is good that I can drive, so I do not need to depend on my husband too much. (Ms Quart)

Because of the traditional concept that women are unsuitable for driving, most of them have to depend on their husband even if they have a family car. Moreover, most of the time the husband would drive the car to work, which is regarded as primary, leaving the wife very little chance to use the car even if she can drive.

Traffic within the new towns

In general, traffic design is geared toward meeting residents's needs in travelling to the work place, so that transportation within the new towns has been neglected. In 1988, a Light Rail system was set up within the Tuen Mun and Yuen Long district in the attempt to solve transportation problems within the community.

However, this does not seem to have had much effect on the problem. A major reason is that this public service is run by a private corporation on a commercial basis. In order to back up the Light Rail Corporation and guarantee its profit level, the government has banned buses and mini-buses from providing services in the local community. That is buses can only serve routes to and from the city centre, while the Light Rail has monopolized all local transportation services within the new town. Under this situation, it is not surprising to see that fares are high, while the service is unresponsive to community needs.

This has greatly influenced women's mobility within the new town. It has increased the burden on women performing essential social activities for daily living. For example, some women have complained about the difficulties of sending children to school in nearby housing estates, going to church, going to the health clinic, shopping, or meeting friends in the new town. Sometimes it is difficult to find a direct transport service from one place to another within the new town, so that they have to change routes or have to walk quite a long distance after getting off the Light Rail.

> I don't think that the Light Rail does any good for us. Sometimes you need to go round and round the town before you can get to your destination. For example, I used to go to the church in Tin King Estate [a nearby public housing estate], I have to change route several times in order to get there. Previously, without the Light Rail, there were many buses going directly to the church. Now, you cannot take the bus, you have no choice. If you don't take the Light Rail, what else can you do? The taxi? (Ms Oat)

The expensive Light Rail fare is another issue attracting a lot of complaints. The Light Rail fare is expensive for most residents, especially for short distance travel. Furthermore for most women, travel within Tuen Mun is mainly short distance, such as going to shopping in the town centre, taking children to school, or going to church in nearby estates. It seems that the fare structure of the Light Rail penalizes women for their short distance travel patterns. But, short distance travel is quite usual and necessary for women's normal daily activities.

> It is very expensive to take the Light Rail, the minimum charge is HK$2.70,...it is too expensive. Even if we take the bus to Tsuen Wan [the urban peripheral] it is only HK$3.6. But if you take the Light Rail for 1 stop you have to pay HK$2.7, it is unfair... (Ms Oat)

Because of the high expense, Ms Oat has to keep her travel to a minimum. In fact, she tries to stay home as far as possible in order to save money. Therefore, she is quite isolated from society.

As a result of this poor transportation system, many women are further deterred from leaving their homes and visiting friends. Even in better off families with private cars, very often, women have to depend on their husband to drive them around. In other words, these transportation problems serve to reinforce women's isolation from society and their dependency on their husbands.

Dismantling the social network

With this serious traffic problem, no wonder most women in new towns have to reduce their social activities and social contacts significantly. There are two significant impacts on women that require attention: 1) the dismantling of the social support network; and 2) reduction in contacts with friends or participation in social activities.

Social support network

The first major impact is the dismantling of their kinship support network. Before moving to Tuen Mun, most of the women had established their own kinship network, for example many have had mothers and sisters to help them in child caring. Once they moved to Tuen Mun, this support network cannot function as before. It is difficult for them to get help from their relatives any more.

> After I moved here, it greatly affected contact with my mother and sisters. They are all living in Sham Shui Po [in the urban centre]... I cannot ask them to help look after the children any more. (Ms Oat)

Table 7.3
Support from relatives in child caring

	With relatives support	Without support	Not applicable
Before moving to Tuen Mun/Yuen Long	11	3	
After moving to Tuen Mun/ Yuen Long	0	14	7

Table 7.3 shows the availability of help from relatives before and after moving to Tuen Mun. Among the 21 women interviewed, 3 received regular help from their relatives neither at present nor before; 7 cases are not relevant to this analysis because had been living in the community since childhood, or had no child before moving to Tuen Mun. On the other hand, a significant proportion, 11 cases, had received regular help from their mothers or sisters when they were living in the

city centre, but after moving to the new town, none were able to continue to use their support network any more.

Most women have had to take up all the burden of child care and homemaking, which had been partly shared with other relatives before they moved to Tuen Mun.

Reduced social contacts

The second major impact on women is the reduction in social contacts and social activities with relatives and friends. Not only is getting help from relatives in the city centre difficult, sometimes it is difficult simply to maintain regular contacts with them. It is not uncommon for women to reduce the frequency of visits to their relatives because of the time and expense of travelling to the city centre.

> I have reduced contacts with friends and relatives greatly, I think I leave home only about half as often as when I was living in the urban area, I try to stay at home as far as possible. (Ms Gam)

This reduction in contact with relatives can create stress on women who have to take up the responsibility of maintaining relationships with kin. Sometimes this social expectation can be very demanding in Chinese society in which kinship networks are very important. Some women, like Ms Oat, obviously get frustrated because of failure to maintain these links. Ms Oat is the youngest of her siblings, so she is expected to visit her siblings and parents to show respect to her elders. Although she expressed grievances about the long distance travel necessitated by these visits, she still needed to do so from time to time as socially expected.

> My relatives frequently accuse me of not going out to visit them or not joining family functions. They don't want to come here to visit us because it is too far away. Sometimes, I feel very unhappy about it, it seems that it is my responsibility to go out to see them. Why should I make this effort? I also need to travel a long way when I go out... (Ms Oat)

Less contact with friends and relatives not only implies less help for child care and more difficulty in maintaining links with relatives, it also means a significant reduction in social activities and further isolation from society.

> When I was living in the city centre, I had more chances to participate in various social activities, for example going to the city hall or to some cultural activities with friends. This broadens your perspective and lets you have more knowledge of what's going on in the society... but I cannot have all these now. (Ms Oat)

These social activities are extremely important for women, especially for full time housewives because it helps to keep them in touch with various social changes.

149

Without these social activities, they will be more isolated from society. Although some women are more sociable and are able to establish new social networks and join new social activities, most housewives I interviewed have experienced considerable difficulties. The problems they faced in adjusting to the new environment were largely neglected, and they were left on their own. Moreover, the heavy burden of housework and child care further hindered their participation in social activities and their building up of new social networks.

Never ending housework

No doubt housework is one of the major factors contributing to women's confinement at home and isolation from society. However, this factor is easily neglected because women are assumed to be natural homemakers. It is commonly believed that housework is not work, or is not heavy work. It is typically assumed that modern household appliances have made life much easier for housewives, and also that husbands in modern families help their wives with housework, which implies that women are released from this burden. In this section, I try to dispel these misconceptions about housework, and reveal how women experience housework.

Time use analysis

First of all, let us look at the enormous time women spend on housework. In this study I have attempted to plot the time use patterns of the respondents (see Bird and Fremont, 1991 for a similar application). They were asked to recall in as much detail as possible the time use pattern of the normal working day nearest to the interview. Then their activities were grouped into 5 major categories as follows:

1) paid work -   including full time and part time employment, time travelling to and from work, and take-home industry, etc.
2) housework -   including meal preparation, meal cleaning up, indoor cleaning, laundry, etc.
3) child care -   including baby care, cleaning and washing, teaching and supervising children's homework, giving orders and disciplining, indoor and outdoor playing, accompanying, taking to school, taking to medical service, etc.
4) leisure -   including sitting, relaxing, leisure telephone conversations, watching television, reading newspapers, outdoor sport, personal social activities, meeting friends, etc.
5) sleep.

The time they spent in these activities was carefully classified and rounded up to the nearest hour. The interviewees were divided into three categories: full time housewives, women with full time employment and men. The hours spent in different activities are summarized in table 7.4.

Table 7.4
Time use pattern (in hours) in a normal working day

	No. of cases	Paid work	House work	Child care	Leisure	Sleep
Full time housewife*	12	0.3	8.5	3.7	3	8.5
Women with full time jobs	9	9.1	4.3	1.4	1.4	7.7
Men with full time jobs	5	9.6	1	0	5.2	8.2

Note:
* In this category, one case is a housewife with part time job. Because she is only working 3 hours per day in paid employment, her time use pattern is closer to that of a full time housewife.

Before we proceed to the analysis, it must be stated that the classification of women's activities at home always has to face problems (see e.g. Bird and Fremont, 1991). One problem is that they are often doing several things at the same time. For example, they can be cleaning up the house while supervising the children's homework, or relaxing and reading the newspaper while accompanying and playing with the baby. In such cases, the interviewee is asked to give a rough estimate of the relative proportions of time used in the simultaneous activities. Another problem requiring attention is that homemaking activities can be very flexible; the 'normal working day' we are referring to in the interview does not imply a fixed schedule which the women will follow every day. Despite all these considerations, the time use pattern plotted is an important reference point for discussion of their activities at home.

From table 7.4 it is very clear that instead of 'having no work to do' the working hours for women are actually very long. For women with full time employment, although their paid working hours are similar to men (9.1 hours compare with 9.6 hours), they still have to spend 5.7 hours in housework and child caring in addition to their employment. On average, the men interviewed only spend 1 hour on housework, and are not involved in child care at all. Women with full time employment only have 1.4 hours available for rest or leisure in a day, while men have 5.2 hours for leisure - three times more. The situation is not much better for women doing full time housework, they have to spend 12.2 hours on housework and child care, which is a extremely long working day.

Housework is not work?

The misconception that housework is not work can be refuted easily by looking at the time and effort women spend on housework. In the 'time use analysis' of the respondents (see table 7.4), I have pointed out that full time housewives work about 12 hours per day while women with full time employment work 15 hours per days, which is far more than men who work about 10 hours per day including paid jobs and housework.

However, some would still insist that housework is not heavy work. This is erroneous, most housework is heavy manual labour. No one can say that it is not 'heavy work' to carry 20 or 30 pounds of food back from the market; or to clean up the house after the children and the husband have turned in into a mess. In modern jobs, even men's employment does not usually require very much manual labour. As I am going to show in the following chapter, it is not the nature of work that matters, but rather how housework is defined and remunerate (see chapter 8 for further discussion).

Of course, it is right to say that housework is flexible and women can space it out to suit their needs. Most of the women interviewed agree that housework is flexible. However, this does not imply that their work load is any lighter, it just means that their working hours are longer. On the other hand, with this lengthening of working hours, more work tends to be done. Many women pointed out that there is no limit to the quality and quantity of housework that can be done. It is unlike work in an office or factory, where your work can be 'done' after 8 hours. Whereas with housework, your work is never 'done', there is always something coming up or engaging you. It is literally endless.

Under patriarchy, one of the major judgements of a women's value lies in her contribution in the form of housework. That is why one of the most significant logic underlying housework is 'doing the best you can'. To women, housework is the medium through which they develop their identity and demonstrate the value of their existence. Therefore, housework is a 'commitment' rather than a simple task to be done, and most women feel that they should do the best they can. In this way the 'flexibility' of housework makes them do more not less.

Sometimes, some women even generate more housework than is necessary because it is so boring for them to stay at home. For example, some women go to the market or clean the floor twice everyday. So, in occasional cases, instead of finishing their work efficiently, some women look for more work to occupy their time.

Clearly, those who think that housework is not heavy do not understand the operation and the logic underlying housework. This devaluation of housework primarily reflects dominant patriarchal ideology (see chapter 8 for more detailed discussion of the ideology of work) rather than reality.

Another common belief is that more husbands are helping their wife to do housework, so women are much better off now. In reality, all the women interviewed, including those with full time employment, pointed out that they were taking up most, if not all, of the housework.

> My husband doesn't go into the kitchen, in my family men don't go to the kitchen. They have no need to do housework. Only my daughter will help me do housework sometimes. (Ms Iu)

This is supported by evidence in a research study in Tuen Mun on the social needs of married women (Tuen Mun District Board, 1991, p.19). Amongst 318 women interviewed, 85 per cent said that they were the principal carers in the family, while only 2.2 per cent said that their husbands took up the major responsibilities. The rest had to rely on paid domestic helpers or relatives (which are women, of course) for housework and child care.

If the husband helped occasionally, the women would be more than happy. For example, Ms Poon was very happy to tell me that her husband was so good that he helped to do some housework occasionally.

> Sometimes my husband helps me with housework, such as cleaning up after the meal and taking the garbage out.... I think it is very good already, I don't need to wash dishes after the meal. I don't have too much to do. (Ms Poon)

However, in saying this, Ms Poon seemed not to be aware that she also had a full time job like her husband. Most women completely internalize the view that housework is totally their own duty. If they only get a little help from the husband, they are still more than satisfied.

Most women firmly believed that men's paid work in employment was more difficult than housework, therefore they should take good rest after they come home. This is one of the major rationales for women excusing their husbands for not helping with housework.

> I don't insist that he should help because I don't think it is too difficult for me... Since I don't have a full time job, and my husband is working very hard, I don't mind doing more housework. (Ms Lai)

> My husband has no time to help me do the housework. He comes back from work at 9:00 pm.; after dinner, he needs to take a break, reading newspapers, watching T.V., and then goes to sleep. (Ms Fan)

They don't realize that even if their husband shared some housework, it would not take up a lot of their leisure time. Furthermore, if their husbands were more willing to take up some housework, they might have more opportunities to go out to work. Obviously, women unconsciously accept the ideology underlying the gender division of labour.

Even if some men share some housework, they do not assume equal responsibility with their wife. They only do housework if they have 'spare time', or it is only a favour to help their wife instead of a responsibility or duty.

For those husbands who help in housework occasionally or regularly, most are involved in minor things such as washing dishes after meals, disposing of rubbish, etc. Or, they tend to be involved in tasks regarded as technical. Quite often, this 'technical' aspect of the work is mystified to exaggerate its contribution to the housework. Ms Gam is quite happy that her husband helps her with some technical things, although he seldom helps in other types of household chores.

> My husband seldom helps me in housework, but he is responsible for things like throwing the rubbish out, repairing electrical appliances, sharpening knives, or some technical things. (Ms Gam)

However, men seldom help in more labour intensive or dirty work such as cleaning the kitchen and the toilet; or in jobs requiring more domestic skill such as cooking. Even if some husbands do help, they tend to leave a mess in the kitchen for the wife to clean up. Consequently, it deters the women from getting their husbands' help.

Many women do not feel good about asking their husbands for help because they have accepted the traditional role of homemaker. They will feel quite apologetic if they have other commitments that affect their household chores. For example, Ms Lai was an active member of the Residents' Association at her housing estate some years ago. She had to give up this commitment because she felt that it affected her role as wife and mother.

> I cannot afford the time to be involved in the committee. There is lots of housework waiting for me. I think it is no good if I leave all the things for my husband and children while I go out myself. (Ms Lai)

It may be true that nowadays men are involved more in housework than their counterparts in traditional feudal society. However, it is an exaggeration to say that men are sharing a significant proportion of the housework, let alone sharing equally with women. Obviously, most men's involvement in housework is still very marginal, or even non-existent. It is far from enough to relieve women from their burdens.

Modernization and socialization of housework?

The third important argument we are going to deal with is the modernization of housework. Some people argue that the advancement of technology in industrial and capitalist societies helps to minimize housework. With modern household electrical appliances, housework is becoming ever easier. Moreover, the argument goes, because capitalists have to enlarge markets, they have sought to penetrate consumption activities at home by means of the food production industry and some household services such as laundry. Consequently, housework has become more socialized, and women's burdens on housework have been reduced.

This seems to be too optimistic a view. No doubt, electrical appliances may help to reduce part of the manual labour, however, the extent of the relief is very much exaggerated (see Cowan, 1989; Roberts, 1991 pp.90-3). In reality, although most of the women interviewed point out that some household appliances can help, but only to a limited extent. Ms Hong and Ms Gam even pointed out that some 'new inventions' are labour adding rather than reducing the burden of housework, and that there is no short cut for some housework.

> ... some are helpful, but some are not. For example, I don't use the vacuum cleaner, it is time wasting and does not clean very well. I have to waste time cleaning the vacuum cleaner too. (Ms Hong)

> Some housework chores such as going to the market and cooking are time consuming, there is no short cut. You have to take time to do it. (Ms Gam)

At the same time, the standard of hygiene is much higher than before, so that women have to expend more effort in keeping the house clean. Consequently, the time spent on housework is not very much reduced. Or, at least the effect does not amount to the release of women from their housework chores.

Are the household services and food product industry helping to socialize housework and reduce women's work load? They do not seem to be too helpful in this respect. For example, although there is much ready made or instant food, these products do not appeal to housewives. Ms Gam is quite reluctant to buy them.

> I know there are some ready-to-cook packets, but they do not taste as good as freshly cooked food. You can eat them once in a while, but not frequently. It is no good for the family. (Ms Gam)

Putting aside the question of the quality of these products for a moment, many women think that as a full time housewife, it is their duty to have food freshly prepared. Food and eating is an important part of Chinese culture. A housewife will be considered too lazy if she relies on 'instant food'. They insisted that only freshly prepared food is best for their children and husband. Again, this relates to ideology underlying housework. That is, women have to demonstrate their competence in housework in order to be recognized as a good mother and a good wife. Their main concern is not how to save time and trouble, but rather to do the best they can.

Similarly, other household services provided in the private market, such as laundry and fast food restaurants, do not seem to be particularly helpful either. These services are so expensive that most women can only use them occasionally, if at all.

> It may be helpful if a cheap laundry service was available. If it was cheap enough, I would use this service. I do not use a privately run laundry service because it is too expensive. (Ms Fan)

Ms Fan has pointed out that if some cheap communal household services were available, it would help to reduce her burden of housework. However, it seems that the idea of 'communal household service' is only partly acceptable. Some items of housework are considered as more private and should be tailored to individual tastes, for example cooking.

> ... but, I don't think the idea of communal kitchen is suitable for families. Public kitchens lack individuality. In the family, if your cooking is good, your husband will show his appreciation, and you will feel very happy about that. (Ms Fan)

Obviously, convenience or minimizing work load is not the prime concern here. For women, the situation is more complicated than that. On the one hand, they hope that some housework can be reduced. On the other hand, housework has been mystified into carrying a symbolic meaning for women related to the demonstration of their ability. It is not that the very nature of housework means that it cannot be socialized. It is rather that most people, whether husband or wife, do not want to give up the underlying symbolic meaning.

As a concluding remark, the major purpose of capitalists is to expand their household consumption markets, not to socialize housework. There is no obvious trend of housework being socialized, or of women's burdens being reduced. Releasing women from housework burdens is only a selling point in advertisements, not a reflection of reality. Some new household appliances, new ways or new standard of housework are labour adding rather than labour saving. Furthermore, exaggerating the simplicity of housework through advertisements in the mass media further reinforces the myth that housework is not heavy work.

If housework were socialized, it would help to relieve women's work load. But obviously, socialization would be achieved through the development of industrial capitalism. As Crow (1989, pp.19-23) has pointed out, the growth of affluence and modernization push the family towards privatism. Women are more isolated from the community in this highly privatized family life. Of course, in the present social context of Hong Kong it is unlikely that many would advocate the complete socialization of housework, such as in the 'kitchenless houses campaign' (Hayden, 1981). Nevertheless, the socialization of part of the women's household chores should be encouraged. Socialization has to be based firmly on a fundamental reconceptualization of women's social roles and the traditional gender division of labour. Most probably, socialization of housework also implies that collective household services would be provided on a non-commodity, that is non-profit making, basis. It is only through the rejection of patriarchal and capitalist logic that women can have the chance of release from housework burdens.

The burden of child care

Child caring is another significant burden confining women at home (see chapter 3 for discussion on the lack of child care service in Hong Kong). A high proportion of the families moving to Tuen Mun are young families, that is nuclear families consisting of young couples with young children. For these families, the burden of child care is particularly heavy. Amongst the 21 women interviewed, only 4 had no children under the age of 12 (table 7.5). Some women even had two or three young children. Children aged below 12 are usually attending primary school or lower, and this is the time that most women think is unsuitable for them to go out to work.

Table 7.5
Respondents with children aged 12 or below

Number of children	Number of cases
3	2
2	7
1	8
0	4

Collective child care services

Here, an important question is that why don't the women put their children in a crèche, nursery or kindergarten and go out to work. There are two groups of typical answers. One group of women want to do that, but find that child care services are not available in the community, are inadequately provided, or are inaccessible or too expensive. The other group don't want to leave the children to collective child care service, thinking that individual care by the mother is the best.

The first group of women who want to have child care services, are frustrated by the situation in the new town. I have pointed out in chapter 3 that child care services in Hong Kong are extremely inadequate, and the situation in Tuen Mun is even worse than the norm. This is because in Tuen Mun the proportion of young families with small children is much higher than that of the general population. Consequently, places in government or subsidized child care services are so scarce that women in normal families have very little hope of getting them. These places are only just sufficient to meet the needs of families in extreme adverse situations such as when both parents are seriously ill or in jail. Ms Fan, who has three children aged 5, 7 and 9, was unable to get subsidized child care services even though she needed it very badly.

> Places are very limited. I applied for the nursery in Yan Oi Tong Community Centre [a subsidized nursery] when my child was small. But they turned me down.... For those who are successful, usually it takes half a year to get a place. (Ms Fan)

Most women can only turn to private services or pay full fees for services provided by voluntary agencies, which are much more expensive. Ms Fan told us that half day service (that is 3 hours) for a child costs HK$400 per month, while whole day service (8 hours) costs about HK$900 per month. It is too expensive for her to put all three children in this service.

> I can't put all my children in the nursery and go to work, it is too expensive. It will cost totally HK$1,800 for three children. You know, wages in Tuen Mun are extremely low, I can earn only about HK$3,000 per month. So, there will not be not much money left after paying for the nursery. (Ms Fan)

Given the low wages in the labour market and the expensive charges for child care services, most women are discouraged from going out to work. They prefer to stay home to take care of the children, which fits both the 'economic principle' and the traditional requirement of women's role as child carers.

The group of women who reject the idea of putting children in a nursery tend to distrust the quality of collective care services. Ms Poon, who had given up her employment to take care of her two children, thought that collective services were unreliable.

> I think it is better for me to take care of the children than to leave it to the nursery. For example, when the children are sick you can take special care of them. But I don't think that the nursery will do the same, they may forget to give medicine to the children. (Ms Poon)

In Hong Kong, which is a highly individualized and privatized capitalist society, coupled with traditional patriarchal Chinese culture, it is not surprising to find that some women are quite sceptical toward collective care. However further probing revealed that most of them have never seen the real operation of crèches or nurseries. Their conceptions are just common sense belief. Many women pointed out that they have never thought of putting their children in a nursery because it is virtually impossible in their community, this choice is completely out of their mind. Ms Poon explained why she had never thought of putting her two children in a nursery when they were small:

> There is only one nursery in this area. I can't take my children to Yuen Long town centre [about half hour by public transport] to the nursery and then go out to work, it is too troublesome, isn't it? That nursery in Kam Tin [the district where Ms Poon lives] is always full, and there are very strict regulations about family income levels to qualify for a place there [that is a government subsidized nursery]. (Ms Poon)

Instead of saying that many women don't like nursery or collective child care services, I would rather say that our society predisposes women to accept all the responsibility for taking care of the children. Additionally, child care services are provided at very minimal levels which further deters women from aspiring to use these services.

Another problem is that child care is a complicated task for women which cannot be solved by piecemeal services in nurseries. Usually, a family has two to three children of different ages that require different caring services. For example, those under the age of 6 need nursery services. But those attending primary school need after-school care services which are extremely inadequate in the new towns. It is only if a woman is successful in getting the various services to fit the different needs of her children at the same time that she is able to go out to work. This is nearly impossible in the case of Tuen Mun. So, those who want to go to work can only do so if they can get help from other relatives or they have to wait until their children are old enough to be independent.

Why women care

If child care and housework are such heavy burdens on women, why do women care? Are women satisfied with their roles as mothers and housewives? Do they like doing housework and taking care of their children?

It is commonly believed that women prefer to do full time housework rather than getting employment. This is very misleading. Of course, most women love their children and husband, but this does not equate to enjoying heavy caring related workload. In fact, in this study nearly all women described housework as boring, monotonous, dull, repetitive, etc. No women interviewed ever described housework positively such as enjoyable, lovely, funny, satisfying, creative, etc. In fact, doing full time housework is so boring that most of the women prefer to go out to work instead of staying at home (see chapter 8 for more detail on women's conception of work). Ms Lai's (a full time housewife, mother of three children) response to housework is very typical rather than exceptional.

159

It is very boring to stay at home and do housework. You are repeating the same things every day, cooking, going to the market, washing clothes, looking after the children, etc. (Ms Lai)

Most women even said that they are really making sacrifices for the family. Child care and housework are not enjoyed, this is sacrifice rather than enjoyment.

If women do not enjoy housework, why do they accept their roles as carers and homemakers? When confronted by these questions there are two common responses: one group of women has never questioned this gender division of labour, while the second group is reluctant to accept this division but is compelled to do so because of social sanctions and social expectations.

Ms Iu, mother of 6 children, living in a rural village in Yuen Long, is a typical case within the first group. She was very puzzled by this question because she has never thought about it. Women in this group think that there is no other alternative, women are born to be carers and homemakers.

... unfair? I don't know. Life is always like that, all women are born to work like that. Isn't this so? (Ms Iu)

The second group of women are quite reluctant to accept the traditional social division of 'public men - private women'. However, they have no choice other than to accept reality because they will be penalized if they do not perform their roles well as mothers and wives.

Some women are aware that this unfair division of labour is harmful, rather than functional, to their family relations. For example, Ms Hong has summarized neatly that a more equal division of labour will lead to a happier family life:

I disagree with the traditional division between men and women. If both husband and wife have jobs and also do the housework together, they will have more common experience to share with each other. Life would be happier like that... You feel your home is warmer and happier when your husband helps in the housework. (Ms Hong)

Ms Hong continued to share her experience after her husband started to go to market together with her:

Previously, he sometimes complained that I was spending too much. But now he comes to the market with me occasionally, so he knows that food is expensive, he has no more complaint now. (Ms Hong)

However, it is interesting to note that while most women reject traditional ideology on the conceptual level, in practice they do not break away from this traditional pattern of social division. Some women feel that there is no chance to break through or there is no alternative.

160

Other women turn to traditional ideology to rationalize their acceptance of the conventional gender division of labour. For example, they will say that it is more suitable for them to take care of the children by themselves, or that they would not be able to earn much if they went out to work. So, it is better for them to stay home. Obviously, this common sense belief is self contradictory. Ms Lai's opinion is one of the typical examples.

> I don't agree with the traditional division between men and women. If husband and wife both go out to work, they should share the housework together. But in my case, I don't have employment; so it is acceptable that I do all the housework. (Ms Lai)

This example illustrates how common sense beliefs can twist logic around. Women believe that it is fair for them to stay at home doing all the housework because they have no full time employment, not because of gender inequality. When Ms Lai, and most women as well, uses this rationale to justify that she should do all the housework, she failed to realize that her lack of employment opportunity is the consequence of traditional gender division of labour (this will be further elaborated in chapter 8 on 'Women and Employment'). In accepting this rationale, she also accepts the traditional gender division of labour.

As a concluding remark, we can see that the domination of patriarchal ideology operates on multiple levels. Most women, and of course men, accept the traditional patriarchal ideology. Very often, the ideology dominates to such an extent that the formulation of other alternatives is inhibited. For example, many women think that there is no alternative other than taking care of the children themselves, or becoming a full time housewife after marriage. Even though they are not happy with existing child care and housework duties, they still think that this is the only, if not the best, possible arrangement. Those who start to question gender inequality are easily diverted to other sets of ideology regarding housework and employed work (also see chapter 8), such as regarding the existing division of labour as most 'efficient' and 'economical', which helps to rationalize women's subordination at home.

Inadequate community facilities and services

Besides transport problems and the child care problems, in this study the interviewees also identified numerous problems which have significant impact on their daily lives. These ranged from school places for children, medical services, and welfare services, to law and order problems, and other difficulties arising from the poor design and management of the housing estates. Women suffer from these problems to various degrees depending on family conditions, employment status and living location.

Again, we can see that the patriarchal and the capitalist ideologies, which we have discussed in chapter 2, are operating behind the planning and development of these community services. The consequence is that women's needs are being neglected and women's position of subordination and dependency is reinforced. Once again, we must remind the readers of the danger of reducing the argument to 'environmental determinism' (see chapter 2) which postulates women as passive objects totally controlled by their environment. The process is much more complicated than that. Taking the risk of over simplification, we can say that it is because of economic reasons that the state only provides limited facilities and services in new towns. However, this produces a more significant impact on women than men because of the gender division of labour in patriarchal society.

Of course, most community problems will affect men as well as women. But, usually, women have to bear most of the burden because of their role as carers in the family. Moreover, since women have to spend most of their time at home and in the community, they suffer more directly from these problems. That is what Ms Fan is grumbling about:

> It is always the mother who needs to take up these worries. Living in Tuen Mun, you have to worry about the lack of school places, the lack of teachers in schools, the lack of doctors in hospitals; worry about delinquent behaviour of your children, etc. Men do not need to face these problems. (Ms Fan)

Education services

Education for their children is one of the greatest problems which concern women. Taking care of the children and ensuring that they have the best education is supposed to be the mothers' responsibility.

However, this responsibility is difficult to fulfil in new towns because the lack of school places for children. The problem arises mainly because the provision of school places is not flexible enough to respond to local community needs. Instead, it merely follows strictly a single Hong Kong-wide planning standard. As I have pointed out, a high proportion of the families moving to Tuen Mun are families with young children. At the early stage of developing the new town women have to face the problem of lack of crèches and nurseries. A few years later, when the babies have grown up, there are insufficient primary schools, and later on, insufficient secondary schools. This problem has not been solved ever since Tuen Mun started to develop in the late 1970s. The same problem is repeated continuously whenever a new housing estate is built in Tuen Mun. Up to the present, many children still cannot find a school place in the local community. Ms Fan, who has two children in primary school and one in a nursery, was suffering badly from this problem.

> Here there is a serious lack of primary school places. If your children are lucky enough to get a place in this area, it is just like winning in a lucky

draw... Otherwise, your children have to go to schools in other areas. We are very worried about small children taking school buses on their own... and the private school buses are expensive too... Some women are so worried that they take the children to school themselves, it is difficult and time consuming. (Ms Fan)

The lack of school places increases the burden on women, resulting in more taking children to school. This time consuming task also minimizes women's chances of getting employment. Although sometimes privately run school bus services are available, this is provided on a profit making basis which incur further financial burdens for the family.

Social services for women

Social services for women is another area that the interviewees were most concerned about. In chapter 3 we have discussed the social welfare services closely related to women's role as family carers, such as child care service. Here, we focus on social services geared toward the individual needs of women, such as a women's community centre.

In general, women's individual needs are invisible within the social welfare system in Hong Kong. Literally, in Hong Kong there are no welfare services specifically designed to meet women's needs. Although undoubtedly most welfare services recipients are women, they are just fulfilling the roles as mothers and wives; and getting services on behalf of the family rather than for their individual needs. In recent years, some feminist groups in Hong Kong have advocated the development of social services for women, such as the establishment of women's centres. The government's response has been women's needs are being taken care of through other welfare services such as community centres and family service centres. The underlying logic seems to imply that woman are important only as a part of the family - as mothers and wives - not as individuals in their own right. Obviously, with this ideology women's needs are not being taken care of.

Limited by their duties in child caring and homemaking, women are not free to join other social activities organized for adults in general in community centres. Obviously, they need services which are specifically designed to suit their available time and interests. Ms Gam told us the difficulties she faced in trying to join some community activities:

Actually, I like to learn new things and join activities in the community centre. For example, I have thought about taking adult education classes or interest classes. But they only offer evening classes. As a housewife, I have to cook for my husband. My husband doesn't like me to join these activities in the evening, he says that I will be too busy. Actually, he is afraid that I would have no time to cook for him. (Ms Gam)

In addition to time restriction, she also faces pressure from her husband who objects to her joining these activities.

The need for social services is more obvious if we understand that full time housewives in Tuen Mun are more socially isolated when compared to their counterparts in the urban area. Many of them cannot find any place to go or activities to join besides staying home and doing housework. It is so boring that some women indulge in playing 'Mahjongh' (a traditional Chinese game of gambling) to kill their spare time. This indulgence frequently develops into serious gambling. It has become a common entry point used by the triad society to exploit and control women through illegal loan services and prostitution.

Some social service agencies have realized these problems and have tried to start some services for women in the community, albeit with very little financial support from the government, or none at all. Many of them try to channel more resources to organize women's group in children and youth centres. Although such limited resources cannot have a great impact in solving the problems, it seems that they do benefit some women who have participated. Ms Ngan, a full time housewife with two children, shared her experience of joining a women group organized by a social service centre in her housing estate:

After I joined this activity I learned to use time more efficiently. I feel that there are a lot of things I can do, I don't feel as bored as before. (Ms Ngan)

Contrary to common sense belief, joining these social activities does not necessarily adversely affect housewives' performance of housework. More frequently, it results in better time management and work efficiency. Of course, orientation of these services for women is problematic: that is, whether they aim at raising consciousness, or just serve to kill women's spare time. Although this is not a major concern of my study, it is an important question regarding women services.

Anyway, the lack of social services for women means that the problems they encounter in the new town are less likely to be solved. In addition, they are being deprived of the chance for self development beyond fulfilling their traditional roles as mothers and wives.

Law and order

In recent years, the rising crime rate, especially relating to rape and sexual attacks, in Tuen Mun has been alarming. Although crime affects both men and women, it is women and children who are more vulnerable. Women not only worry about loss of property, they also have to take special care to avoid sexual attack. Women have to assume a far greater psychological burden. For example, Ms Oat is extremely worried about her 11 year old daughter, who was amongst the most vulnerable to sexual attack.

Last week, a sex attacker disguised as a doctor raped a child in her home in this housing estate. My daughter was very frightened when she heard about this. I am very worried too... Of course, I cannot prevent her from going out, but I am really worried about her safety. (Ms Oat)

Patriarchal culture has placed the responsibility on women to protect themselves. That is why frequently women are blamed for 'asking for it' because of indecent or seductive clothing. Many feminists have pointed out that sexual attacks do not stem mainly from men's sexual urges, rather it is the urges for power and control over women (Smart, 1976; Scully, 1990; Abbott and Wallace, 1990 pp.171-2). Here, my main concern is not to develop a comprehensive explanation for violence against women, but to point out that the threat of violence in these poorly designed housing estates or community limits women's social life (Hanmer and Saunders, 1984; Radford, 1987).

Putting the blame on women becomes a mechanism of social control to confine women to their home, to limit women's social activities to a certain prescribed 'safe' arena, safe time, and safe place. They can only participate in 'out-of-bounds' activities under the protection of men. This creates further dependency on men. For example, Ms Kwok has to avoid going out in mid afternoon, and Ms Hong's daughter needs her father to accompany her home whenever she comes home after 9:00 p.m.

Recently, there has been a 'sex attacker' around this housing estate, I am very worried. The attacker usually takes action in mid afternoon when the estate is very quiet. Therefore I try to avoid going out in the mid afternoon, and avoid taking the lift alone. I also seldom go out at night. (Ms Kwok)

Now, when my daughter has to return home late, say after 9:00 in the evening, I will ask my husband to wait for her at the bus stop, outside the entrance of the village. (Ms Hong)

'Physical' design?

It is commonly believed the physical design of housing units and housing estates is purely technical and there is no inherent gender bias. However, the women I interviewed have shown us how they were badly affected by gender blind housing design. There were numerous complaints, but due to limitation of space I can only cite a few examples such as the design of kitchens, the location of clothes drying racks in high rise buildings, and the lack of communal space.

Kitchen design The first example is kitchen design. Although the kitchen is the major work place for women, most architects seem not to understand well enough how women work in the kitchen. That is why there are numerous complaints that everything seems to be in the wrong place. Moreover, it is common that the kitchen is designed to be as small as possible in Hong Kong. This not only reflects the lack of space in Hong Kong, but also reflects the logic that the kitchen is not important for the family, but is only the concern of the housewife. Housewives are so submissive and tolerant, or so powerless, that there is no strong demand for change. On the other hand, the interests and concerns of men always govern housing decisions so that the kitchen is given only a very low priority.

> The kitchen design is very bad indeed. Many facilities are located in the wrong place, it is difficult to use, for example, the washing basin which is installed in a peculiar way so that it makes your work much more difficult... My children seldom come to the kitchen to help me because there is not enough space. (Ms Ming)

The small kitchen design, which is underpinned by the gender biased assumption that only women work in the kitchen, further deters other family members from coming to help in the kitchen and reinforces this division. No wonder it is argued that the place of the kitchen in modern domestic architecture is 'to make visible and institutionalize the dominant role of women in the family' (Craik, 1989, p.62).

Moreover, a small kitchen inevitably means poor ventilation. That is why many women in the interviews complained about the situation. This is especially true for Chinese cooking which generates lots of heat and smoke. Coupled with the hot tropical weather in Hong Kong, this becomes unbearable. This is Ms Lai's experience of cooking in a poorly designed kitchen in a public housing estate.

> The kitchen is poorly designed, there is no window in the kitchen, it is extremely hot. After I have cooked the meal, I am so hot and tired that I really don't want to eat. I have to take a shower before I can eat anything. (Ms Lai)

Clothes drying rack Another common design problem is the dangerous clothes drying rack in high rise public housing blocks. When using these racks, women have to lean outside the window with a heavy load of wet clothing. It is not uncommon for women to twist their back or arms in hanging out clothes for drying. There are even some cases of serious accident in which women have fallen to their death or been badly injured when using these racks.

> The clothes drying rack is really very dangerous. It is very easy to drop the clothes and the bamboo stick [for hanging clothes] down the street and hurt someone on the street. I know that some women have even fallen out of the window and died. Now I do not use it any more. (Ms Lai)

However, the architects in the Housing Department have denied that there is anything wrong with the design. They claimed that the problem is caused by the women themselves because they are too small and weak to use these racks.

Clearly, this is another gender blind design which has taken no consideration of the physical attributes of the women using these facilities.

Communal space The lack of communal space is another problem. Although there is quite a lot of open space in new towns as compared to the urban centre, such space is not utilized effectively to facilitate community support or communal life. Therefore it is difficult for the residents to develop community support systems, which is very important for women wanting to share responsibility for child caring. Some architects and scholars in Western countries have pointed out the significance of public and communal space in developing community support and neighbourhood relations (Boys, 1984, pp.44-52; Woolly, 1994, pp.253-4). For example, a common sitting room or activity room shared with neighbours can help to develop support networks amongst women.

In Hong Kong it should not be too difficult to provide such communal space because the population is highly concentrated. One storey in a high rise public housing block can accommodate 20 to 30 families. It is not difficult to reserve one unit in every storey for communal activities. This is not provided not became of lack of space, especially in new towns where space is not as precious as that in the urban area. Of course, the provision of communal room incur extra financial and administrative costs. But these costs would be very minute as compare to the construction and administrative cost of a housing estate. If planners and architects are more aware of the importance of mutual support networks among neighbours in general, and among women in particular, there would be greater improvement in this aspect.

These few examples demonstrate that 'physical' housing design is not that 'neutral' as commonly believed. Gender blind design practices, such as a poorly designed kitchen, not only creates more difficulties for women, but also reinforces the gender division of labour by discouraging men from going into the kitchen. Other design practices, such as the lack of communal space, hinder women from developing mutual support networks and increases women's burden in child caring. Some gender blind designs, such as the clothes drying racks in high rise buildings, even threaten the safety of women. Although it is problematic to say that planners and architects are deliberately designing these environments to oppress women, the lack of gender consciousness in urban planning and housing design could create tremendous difficulties for women.

Conclusion

We have seen how the living environment and related social practices are acting against women in new towns. Consequently, they are further isolated from the public sphere and confined at home after migrating to new towns. This isolation is not due to women's inability to adjust to the new environment, but rather because policy planners are blind to women's needs and to the problems created for women by circumstances in new towns.

For example, women are 'immobilized' because of the poor transportation system, which is geared toward meeting needs in travelling to work while women's needs in taking care of the family and in other social activities are being neglected. Insufficient attention is paid to the break down of old social support networks and the reduction of social contacts and social activities, which resulted in heavier burden in child caring and homemaking in addition to further isolation from the public sphere. This burden is grossly underestimated, so that related supportive services such as collective child care, children's education and medical service are extremely under-provided. It is no need to mention that the possibility of developing more gender conscious services, such as collective homemaking service and developmental service for women, are largely excluded under the existing patriarchal ideology. This 'anti-women' housing system is also echoed in the housing design and housing management, which resulted in numerous problems such as the severe crime rate, especially sexual attacks, the poor kitchen design and the lack of communal space.

On top of all this, the employment system, which we are going to discuss in the following chapter, has an important role to play in reinforcing women's subordination in the family and dependency on men.

Note

1. In Hong Kong, private car is not as common as in UK or USA. In 1992, there are 237,000 private cars for a population of 1,640,000 households (Hong Kong Census and Statistics Department, 1993a, pp.28 & 6). That is, on average only about 14 per cent of the households own a car. Bear in mind that because of the high cost in running a car, car ownership is concentrated on the high income groups, of which some may own two or more cars. Therefore, the actual percentage of households owning a car is much less than 14 per cent.

8 Marginalizing women at work

Women's problems in new towns are partly due to their being marginalized by and subordinated in the employment system and partly due to their isolation in the home. After seeing how women are confined to their home in chapter 8, we now turn to look at how women are being subordinated in, marginalized by or even being excluded from the employment system.

This chapter starts with a brief discussion of how the ideology of work serves to reinforce women's subordination in the working sphere. My main concern here is how women are affected by these ideologies. Readers should refer to chapter 2 for an analytical discussion of these ideologies. In the second part of this chapter we will turn to look at women's experience at work both outside and within Tuen Mun to show how women's marginal position in work is exacerbated by moving to new towns. Here, the term 'marginalizing women at work' refers to the processes through which women's importance is underplayed in the employment system. This comprises two aspects, firstly women's work, whether paid employment or unpaid housework is regarded as unimportant. Secondly, women are pushed to the margins of the labour market. That is, they often occupy marginal, part time, temporary, dirty jobs. In effect, they are subordinated within the working sphere, whether in paid work or in the unpaid housework they carry out within the family.

Ideology of work

As I have pointed out in chapter 2, marginalization of women at work hinges on some mythical misconceptions of women's work developed in patriarchal and capitalist societies. Women's work, especially housework, is regarded as unimportant and unproductive. The genuine reason does not lie in the essence of the housework itself, but in how work is being defined and remunerated. Housework is as productive as any other paid work. The separation of domestic and industrial labour (or consumption and production activities) is one of the major characteristics of industrial capitalism. Home and work are separated, whereby paid work is considered as a production process and home is regarded as a place for consumption. With the help of this ideology, capitalists are able to minimize their production cost by not paying part of the labour reproduction process, i.e. housework (e.g. see Cowan, 1989; Dex, 1985, pp.104-10; Oakley, 1974).

In this section, we are going to focus on women's experience in three areas. First, how the definition of work serves to marginalize women and create dependency on men. Second, how women are being confined to the 'domestic sphere' and how this shapes their career development. And, finally we turn to the question 'do women like to work?'.

Defining work

The first issue we will address is how the definition of work marginalizes women's position and creates dependency on men. In general, women's housework is defined as unproductive and therefore is unpaid. Of course, this separation of production and consumption activity is problematic. This conceptualization serves predominantly as an ideology legitimizing the unpaid nature of women's domestic labour.

With this degradation of the value of housework, many full time housewives feel that they are useless or unproductive. For example, Ms Ding insisted on having a paid job even though her husband did not like her to. The most important reason was not the money, it was because she felt useless and unproductive as a full time housewife.

> When you go out to work it is very tiring, but you feel that you are useful. If I am doing full time housework, I have to ask my husband for money, I feel useless. (Ms Ding)

Ms Ngan shared similar views when she compared the differences between paid employment and unpaid housework.

> You feel more freedom, more satisfied and more productive, when you go out to work... Although you [being a full time housewife] can also make friends with the neighbours in the community and kill your spare time, you don't think that you are productive... (Ms Ngan)

I have pointed out that many women dislike housework because it is monotonous and uncreative (see the discussion on women's experience in housework in the chapter 7). However, this is not the only reason because most paid jobs in modern capitalist societies, especially those available to middle age working class women, are also monotonous and uncreative. For example, Ms Ding has a temporary part time job as a cleaner and her job is as monotonous as the housework.

One of the most important differences in her job as compared to housework is that this is a 'paid' job. In modern capitalist society, one's competence is largely judged by one's ability to earn. No wonder women doing full time unpaid housework are regarded as useless, and are not respected.

> It would be better if you've got a job, your husband would respect you more. He would think that you are able to earn your own living, not merely depending on him. As my mother said frequently: 'you are only a women, what can you do? You have to accept it even if you are not happy, you can do nothing'. Now it is different, my husband has to respect me more, I am not totally dependent on him. (Ms Ding)

Some people would try to contend that women's housework is not unpaid, instead women are paid through their husband's wage. Or, some may even argue that housewives are in a far better position because they have money to spend without going to work.
Here is a typical response from a man I have interviewed who claimed that men are protecting women by keeping them at home.

> I don't want her to work, I hope that she could enjoy her life at home... That is, in marrying her I want to make her happy, I want her to have an easy life, it is difficult enough for me to go to work, she shouldn't be in this difficult situation. She should enjoy her life, taking care of the children, cleaning the house, shopping, going to restaurants, this is a happier life, isn't it? (Mr Zeto)

Putting aside the problem that Mr Zeto has grossly underestimated the difficulties of housework (see chapter 8 for detailed discussion of women's experience in housework and child caring), there are still two major problems with this argument. The first problem is that women do not share household resources equally with men, but rather they are getting far less than they deserve. They are doing the same work as child carers and domestic helpers in paid employment, who get several thousand dollars per month. However, they getting far less from their husbands for doing housework. In fact, most of the money they get from their husband is used to cover family expenses, not their own consumption.

> Sometimes I feel that it is very unfair that housewives do not have their own wage. Of course, when we use the family income to buy a dress for ourselves, it is just like claiming our own wage. But, when I am using the money for myself, I feel that this money is not mine. It is different from the money you earn yourself, this belongs to your husband, it is not yours. (Ms Ngan)

Another typical example is Ms Chu's situation. Ms Chu was an accounting clerk before she gave up her work to take care of the children. Even though her household income has increased substantially because of her husband's career advancement, she felt that she was much poorer than before. This seems contradictory, but it is real. The reason is that housewives do not have equal access to their husband's income. In other words, frequently women are poor in relation to their spouse.

> I feel even poorer than before [when she was working]. Of course, our family income is higher now, but, literally I have no money for myself. All the money I receive is for the family. When I want to buy something for myself, for example a dress, I need to think very carefully because I feel that I am using the family wealth. I feel that I am poorer now, very poor indeed. (Ms Chu)

In Western society, 'feminization of poverty' has become an important issue in poverty and feminist studies (e.g. see Glendinning and Millar, 1992; Scott, 1984; Townsend, 1993, p.106-11). However, in Hong Kong this issue is largely being neglected. Up to the present, there is still a lack of systematic study of the sharing of household resources between husband and wife.

This leads to the second problem in the argument that housewives are being paid through their husband's wage - that is, the underplaying of the power inequality between men and women within the family. It is through this process of getting their 'wage' from their husbands that women are compelled to depend on men. It is a clear capitalist principle that the person who controls the money controls the power. Therefore, by making the wife dependent on her husband's income, we construct women's subordination and dependency. No wonder Ms Chu, a full time housewife who quit her job three years ago to take care of the family, felt that her husband is her boss.

> He is more wealthy than I, he has his own business. He gives me money and I depends on him. He is just like my boss, he pays me every month... depressing, isn't it? (Ms Chu)

Women are compelled to depend on men, even though they contribute on equal amount, if not more, toward the family resources. Ms Earl neatly expresses their significant contribution to the family.

> I don't think women are unproductive, there are lots of family chores, who does all this work? It's women. They go to the market, they cook, they clean up the house... There is a lot of work for women, isn't there?... If I don't have employment, it is because of the family, isn't it? If you employ a Filipino maid, you have to pay her HK$3,000 or so per month, you also have to provide food and lodging. You save all these with a housewife at home. (Ms Earl)

Unfortunately, Ms Earl's voice is not heard. Women's significant contribution in producing family resources are being neglected completely. On the contrary, housework is considered as unproductive and housewives are not sharing equal social status with their husbands.

Defining women's social roles

Not only is women's work subject to degradation, women's social role is also confined mainly to the domestic sphere. Patriarchal ideology insists that physically, psychologically, and naturally, men are more suitable for the public world and women are more suitable for the private sphere. In chapter 2, I have already pointed out the flaw of this 'public men - private women' conceptualization, now let us look at how this misconception limits women's employment opportunities.

> My husband doesn't like me to go out to work, he thinks that I should take care of the children and the family first. He is a very traditional - male chauvinist. He says that he prefers to be poor than letting me go to work. If we were poor, we could spend less. But if I go to work, no one would take care of the family. (Ms Lai)

Here, we can see that Ms Lai's husband firmly sticks to the 'private-public' division of gender role. Although Ms Lai is clearly unhappy about this social division, she is powerless to fight for a better deal. Ms Lai was a factory worker before she moved to Tuen Mun New Town in 1980. After she moved she gave up her full time employment to take care of the family.

Another more dramatic case is Ms Bob, who had started her own business in the late 1970s. Although it was not a big business, it seemed promising because she was developing business in Mainland China during the early era of its economic reforms. However, after she gave birth to her elder son, she decided to wind up her business to look after the family. Although she still worked full time throughout these years, she changed to much lower paid clerical work, so as to take care of the family.

> The main reason for closing down [her business] was the birth of my elder son. It was extremely difficult to take care of the business and the family at the same time. At that time, I had to travel to China frequently because of the business. I always worried about my son, that was a really difficult time for me... I don't know, maybe because of my marriage, after I married, my attitude changed. I was not working as hard as I did before... Maybe it is not an issue of making sacrifice for the family, I just don't want to be so stressed. You know it is very difficult to be successful in business, you need to invest a lot of effort, I just don't want to do that any more. (Ms Bob)

Of course, we are not sure whether Ms Bob has the right personality to be a successful business women. But, imagine if Ms Bob were a man, the whole story would be different. Then the most possible outcome would be that her spouse would quit the job to take care of the family so that she could concentrate on her business. Of course, most probably a man would not give up his career to take care of the family and support his wife's business even though she may have far better potential to succeed. On the contrary, in the interviews I have heard numerous stories of how the wife gave up her employment to support the husband.

Ms Chu is one of the common examples of a woman who has given up work to support her husband. I interviewed both Ms Chu and her husband. Let us look at their career paths to illustrate the differences in employment opportunities for males and females. About ten years ago, before they got married, Ms Chu and her husband were colleagues in a small company. They started at similar rank in clerical work, and they had similar education and qualifications. But after they married, Ms Chu's husband changed to work in a larger company, because he felt that the previous company was too small and the boss was not aggressive enough for further expansion. On the other hand, Ms Chu stayed on because her job was stable and secure. In case there was anything wrong with her husband's new job, they would still have some stable income. Moreover, she pointed out that she treasured the good relationship between colleagues in this company, although she knew that career prospects were not outstanding. Later on, her husband pursued further training at the Polytechnic and got promotion while she still stuck to her old job.

About three years ago Ms Chu's husband started his own business, so he became very busy. At about the same time, Ms Chu gave birth to her second child. The extra stress on the family was significant, the husband had started his own business while the wife was still working full time and taking care of two children. Ms Chu's husband had kept on asking her to quit her job ever since they had the first child, and he increased this pressure tremendously after they had the second child. Although Ms Chu was very keen to have employment, she finally had to give it up. She quit her job about three years ago to take care of the family so that her husband could concentrate on his own business.

> My husband objected to me going out to work after we had a child... After I stopped working he doesn't need to care any more, he doesn't need to help in household chores such as cleaning the toilet, cleaning the flat, etc. He only thinks about his work. Before I stopped working, sometimes when our children were sick he was able to take them to see the doctor if I was really very busy in my work. But now he doesn't need to care any more, he knows that I am always there. (Ms Chu)

Here, we can see that even though both Ms Chu and her husband started with similar jobs and similar qualifications, the man ended up as a boss while the woman became a full time housewife depending totally on her husband.

Some people here tried to argue that because women usually earn less in their jobs than their husbands, it is a pragmatic rather than a gender biased decision for the wife to quit the job to take care of the family. Of course it is partly a pragmatic decision, but this explanation fails to answer the question why women so often have lower wages than their husbands and why almost always it is the woman who has to make the adjustment.

In fact, if we look at Ms Chu and Ms Bob's career paths, it is clear how patriarchal ideology works to limit women's career prospects. Even though Ms Chu was starting on similar ground and Ms Bob had better career prospects as compared to their husbands, they ended up giving up their opportunities. Obviously, these are not 'pragmatic' or 'utilitarian' decisions, but manifestations of the patriarchal ideology.

It is interesting to note that in cases where women are required to work because of financial necessity, the ideology of 'private-public division' still continues to operate. Under these circumstances, women are only considered as 'reserve army of labour' for the family.[1] That is, their labour is utilized only if their family needs extra income to make ends meet.

When I interviewed Mr Zeto, the husband of Ms Earl whom we also interviewed, he clearly expressed the view that he did not like his wife to have employment. It was only because of financial difficulties that his wife started to work again about three years ago.

> I don't like her to go to work, she should enjoy her life at home. But... economics, because of economic reason, there is no alternative, is there? (Mr Zeto)

Mr Zeto was a seaman until he retired from his job several years ago. In the past, finance was not a problem, so Mr Zeto did not allow his wife to work. His wife, Ms Earl, had given up her job to look after the family ever since they moved to Tuen Mun. In recent years, Mr Zeto has retired from this relatively better paid job and the family budget has tightened up substantially. So, the reserve army of labour - his wife - has to work again.

This conceptualization of women as the 'reserve army of labour' helps to trivialize or marginalize women's contribution to family resources. Women's financial contribution to the family is regarded as marginal, notwithstanding the fact that their contribution has been increasing significantly due to their increasing participation in the labour force.

Another point to note is that women's need and interest has no role to play in Mr Zeto's decision. It is not because of her wife's need to participate in society that he encourages her to take up employment. The needs of the family are more important, women are only a tool to serve the needs of the family. In fact, in the interview, his wife Ms Earl pointed out that she has always liked to go to work, whether now or in the past. Ironically, it is only because her family is in financial difficulties that she has the chance to go out to work again.

This leads us to the last question we are going to address in this section: 'do women like to have paid jobs?'. Or, what is women's attitude to work? I have to re-emphasize that all women have to work, it is just a matter of whether this is paid employment or unpaid housework. Ironically, in most situations women even work more than men (see chapter 8 table 7.4).

Concerning paid jobs, it is not surprising to see that most women are quite ambivalent since they are under the influence of very conflicting ideologies. On the one hand, capitalist logic defines one's value according to one's earning ability in the labour market. That is why most women feel that they are useless or unproductive if they are doing unpaid housework full time. On the other hand, patriarchal ideology tells women that it is their natural and sacred duty to do unpaid domestic work. Before we go to another point, it must be clarified that the conflict between capitalist and patriarchal ideology does not necessarily imply that capitalism helps to minimize gender inequality. Even if more women are participate in the labour market because the capitalists need their cheap labour, this does not necessarily lead to gender equality. On the contrary, they have to carry the double burden of employed work and work at home, and they still occupy marginal and subordinate positions in the labour market. It is more exact to say that capitalism transforms the manifestation of gender inequality, rather than reduces it.

Patriarchal ideology works so powerfully because not only do men accept it, but women also buy this ideology consciously or unconsciously. When Ms Chu was asked why it is that her husband has become a boss while she has become a housewife, given the fact that they were starting with similar qualification and working in the same office about ten years ago, she admitted that she has adapted to her husband's expectation.

> I am less ambitious, he is more ambitious... My husband doesn't like me to be outstanding, too ambitious, he doesn't like it. That is you shouldn't be too clever, mmm... women... women shouldn't be too smart, maybe he is selfish, a male chauvinist. (Ms Chu)

In criticizing her husband as a male chauvinist, Ms Chu does not mean to reject this gender division completely. She is quite ambivalent in that on one hand she likes to work, and on the other hand she feels that she should fulfil her duties as a wife and a mother.

Ms Bob, who had to wind up her business about ten years ago to take care of the family, is more explicit in expressing her commitment to the family. When she was asked whether she was sacrificing her career development for the family, she clearly pointed out that she preferred to have a happy family than attain outstanding achievements in her career.

No, no, it is not sacrificing. When you choose something you must give up the others. For example, some of my old friends, whom I first met in the days when I was doing my own business, are very successful now. But many of them got divorced. When I met them, they always said that they were jealous of me, I have a happy family, a good husband, two nice kids... That is, I think, if you make a choice you have to take all the good and bad with it. (Ms Bob)

The major problem here is that women are torn between these pseudo choices. There is no real choice for women. If they choose to develop their own career, they would be blamed if the family got into trouble because they are supposed to be the one who cares for the family. In other words, the whole social structure, the family, the labour market, the social welfare system and other state policies are working to tie women down to their family commitments. At the same time, support for women to participate in the labour market or in social activities, such as child care services, is extremely scarce. Women are left on their own to bear the double burden of employment and family if they insist on keeping their employment. Consequently many women are obliged to give up their career opportunities.

However, it would be wrong to say that women are happy to accept this 'public-private' division of social roles. On the contrary, when they were asked whether they would like to have employment if they were free to choose, almost all women, including the full time housewives and those who had paid jobs, preferred to go out to work rather than stay at home.

A major reason for preferring to have paid jobs is that full time housework restricts their social exposure and perspective. That is why many full time housewives feel that they are 'ignorant', 'useless' and know nothing about the world. They hope to go out to work not so much for the money they earn, but for widening their social exposure and for personal development.

I like to go to work, you know more friends in the work place, and you know more about what is going on in the world, you will be happier. (Ms Lai)

Because most women are bound by family duties, they have to strike a compromise between family and work. One of the major strategies is to stick to a less demanding job, such as a part time or temporary job with flexible working hours, a manual or clerical work which requires little training. A major consideration is that these jobs allow them to take care of the family simultaneously. Ms Ding was doing a temporary job as a cleaner in a child care centre near her home. She was quite satisfied with this job as it did not interfere too much with her housework.

My husband can accept me doing this job, I am working quite near my home, no need to take a bus. This is a temporary job, I am not working everyday, so I can take care of the children most of the time. If I work full time regularly, I don't think he likes it. The best jobs are those that suit my housework schedule. (Ms Ding)

As women are restricted to jobs that minimally affect their housework schedule, their choices are extremely limited. Consequently, many housewives are confined to marginal, part time, temporary jobs without prospects or job security.

Speaking overall, we can see that the ideology of work exerts a powerful influence on women's employment opportunities. Women are marginalized at work but not because they are less productive or less skilful. It is mainly because their work is socially defined as less important. Moreover, women's major social role is defined as taking care of the family. Consequently, women are marginalized within the employment system, and are compelled to depend on their husbands' income. Through this process, the subordination and dependency of women is socially constructed, and further reinforced.

Women's experiences in work

We have seen how the patriarchal ideology marginalizes women in work by defining women's housework as unproductive and confining women's role to the 'private sphere'. This marginalization from paid employment is further exacerbated by the scarcity of employment opportunities in remote new towns like Tuen Mun. Let us look at women's experience in work in Tuen Mun to see how they are marginalized in or excluded from work.

In this section, we are going to focus on three major difficulties women in Tuen Mun faced in getting jobs: 1) difficulties in travelling to work outside the new town; 2) lack of job opportunities in the new town; and 3) discrimination against women in the job market.

Before we go into detail of women's experience in work, I want to remind readers that in the last chapter I have pointed out that many problems in the Tuen Mun New Town are the direct consequence of a failure of state housing policy and new town planning. Low income households and young working class families are being pushed out to remote new towns on a massive scale, without proper consideration of employment opportunities, child care services, education for children, medical services and other community services. Under these circumstances, women are amongst the groups hardest hit.

Difficulties in working outside the new town

Employment opportunities would be improved substantially if women would travel to work in the city centre. However, transportation services to and from Tuen Mun New Town are extremely poor (see our discussion in chapter 7). In peak hours, it usually takes more than one and a half hours to travel from the city centre back to Tuen Mun. Given their duties in homemaking, it is extremely difficult for women to undertake long distance travel to work. Even among those women who used to have jobs before moving to Tuen Mun, most had to give up their jobs sooner or later.

Table 8.1 shows the changes in employment status after moving to Tuen Mun for the women interviewed. Among the 21 women interviewed, all had worked for some years before they got married. Only one woman could continue to work full time after moving to Tuen Mun, but she had given up a more promising career to change to a relatively low paid clerical job so that she could spare more time to take care of the family. Five women had to stop working completely after they moved to Tuen Mun, and 8 women changed to work part time, changed to unstable temporary jobs, or became out-workers at home. Three of the women interviewed were not working before moving to Tuen Mun. Four women were not relevant to this discussion because they had been living in Tuen Mun or Yuen Long from birth or since they were small. Most of the women interviewed suffered from loss of employment opportunity after moving to the new town.

Table 8.1
Changes in employment status after moving to Tuen Mun

Changes in employment status	Number of cases
Continuing to work full time after moving	1
Ceded employment completely after moving	5
Changed to part time, or temporary job, or to take home industry in tuen mun	8
No employment before moving to new town	3
Not applicable	4

This picture is also reflected in evidence from research on the social needs of married women in Tuen Mun (Tuen Mun District Board, 1990, p.16). Among 307 women in employment before marriage, 78 per cent stopped working temporarily or permanently, and 90 per cent of these respondents said that this was because of pregnancy and child rearing.

Ms Gam is one of the women who had to give up their jobs after moving to the new town. Ms Gam was working in a garment factory before moving to Tuen Mun about one and half years ago. She has a child aged 4. Although she was very keen to keep on working and had tried very hard to do so, she had to give up at the end.

I like to work, so I kept on working in the factory after I moved here. But it was really very tiring to travel to and fro everyday... I felt great pressure on me, I was completely exhausted after working everyday, but I still had to do all the housework, it was very difficult indeed. Therefore my husband advised me to stop working. (Ms Gam)

Ms Ding had given up her full time job in a garment factory after moving to Tuen Mun. Because of the need to take care of her two children aged 9 and 12, she could only find a temporary job as a cleaner. Although she realized that job opportunities in the city centre were much better, she is too worried about leaving the children behind to work in the city centre.

Job opportunities in the city centre are better, you look at the newspaper, most of the jobs advertised are in the urban area. There are many suitable jobs for us, but we cannot afford the time to travel, we have to take care of the family. If we leave our children behind, no one will care about them, I am worried that they would become juvenile delinquents. (Ms Ding)

That is why among the 10 women who had full time or part time employment, only 2 of them, Ms Ann and Ms Ult, were able to work in the city centre. They were able to do so because their jobs did not interfere with their housework duties very seriously. In addition, their husbands were quite supportive of their work. Ms Ann was working as an office assistant in a mail delivery company. Her major duty was delivering mail to other offices, therefore she could come home as soon as she had finished her daily quota. Ms Ult was working in a garment factory in the urban area. Since she started working at 8:00 am. and finished at 4:00 pm., she could come back early to cook for the children and her husband. Circumstances for these two were the exception rather than the norm.

Of course, the lack of employment opportunities in new towns and the poor transportation does not only affect women, it affects men as well. However, men and women react to this situation very differently. I have interviewed five men living in Tuen Mun new town. They have never thought of giving up their jobs in the city centre to change to lower paid jobs in the new town.

...the prospect and... the working conditions in the factories here are not attractive enough, in fact, they are very bad. I think I would get one third less pay if I worked here [in the new town]. (Mr Zeto)

Of course, Mr Zeto's decision to not getting a job in the new town seems very normal from the male perspective. But, if we compare career decisions between males and females, it would be clear that Mr Zeto had never considered the need to spare more time for the family, especially when they had to adjust to the new environment in this remote new town. On the contrary, his wife, Ms Earl, had given up her job without a second thought to take care of the family after they moved to the new town.

Of course, it is possible for men to keep on working in the city centre because they don't have to take responsibility for homemaking as their wives do. On the contrary, if they are the one mainly responsible for taking care of the family, such as the case of lone fathers, their employment opportunity and career prospect will be affected most probably. Obvious examples can be found in my interviews of lone fathers (see chapter 5). In these situations, lone fathers' employment opportunity are being affected because of their family commitment.

The impact of poor transportation and lack of employment opportunities in new towns on men and women are different. For men, this may means longer and more exhausting journeys to work and more transportation expenses. They will, however, never be cut off from the public sphere completely. But for women, the effect is worse. Many women are being from work completely and thus confined to their home. Or at best, some women have to change to much lower paid and less promising jobs in the new town.

Limited opportunities in the new town

The employment opportunities within Tuen Mun new town are much worse as compared to the city centre. As I have pointed out in chapter 7, because of the 'non-interventionist' attitude of the laissez-faire capitalist state, the development of Tuen Mun new town has failed to achieve the original objective of 'self containment'. Without active government intervention, factories and offices are not moving into the new towns as expected. Consequently, job seeking is extremely competitive in Tuen Mun, both for men and women. The situation has worsened in recent years because of the restructuring of the economy of Hong Kong (see chapter 3). The main base of the economy of Hong Kong has shifted from labour intensive industries to financial and commercial services. Manual work in factories for working class women is becoming scarce. On top of this problem, jobs in financial and commercial service are concentrated in the urban centre, which is out of reach for most working class women in the new town.

Let us look at the employment status of the 21 women interviewed. In the sampling process, I selected 10 women with full time or part time employment at the time of interview, while the other 11 women were full time housewives. Amongst the 10 women with employment, only 1 could get a job in the urban centre, while the other 9 were working in the Tuen Mun and Yuen Long area. Moreover, all women were in low paid jobs such as cleaners, domestic helpers, clerical workers, office assistants, shop assistants, etc., except one who was a nursing officer in a hospital in Tuen Mun. Summarizing the employment situation of the 10 women: 4 were part time or full time cleaners, 2 were office assistants and clerical assistants, 1 drove mini school bus for a kindergarten on part time basis, 1 was a shop assistant in a cake shop, 1 was a factory worker, and 1 was a nursing officer.

Obviously, the choices of employment were extremely limited. In fact many of the women interviewed, whether currently with or without employment, were skilled workers in factories earning much higher wages before they moved to Tuen Mun or before they had children. In the 1970s and 1980s, when jobs in factories were abundant, many middle age women could still find jobs in the factories after their children had grown up. But now they had much less choice and the situation in new towns was even worse.

For example, Ms Ding was working in a garment factory before she moved to Tuen Mun. After she moved to Tuen Mun and had the second child, she gave up her work and became an outworker. However, these take-home industries have declined in recent years. As Ms Ding's children had just grown up, she wanted to work again in the factory. However, she was frustrated to discover that there were few factories remaining.

> But now we really don't have much choice, many factories have moved back to Mainland China. There are not many factories and not many take home industries available. Previously there were really a lot, but now it has all gone.... Here, jobs are really very exploitative, Macdonald's gives only HK$10 per hour to part time workers, they don't have any welfare, no holiday, no other benefits. They know your weakness, you can't work outside Tuen Mun, there are no other jobs available, you may feel that low pay is still better than having no job at all, so they exploit you. (Ms Ding)

Ms Ding could only get a job as a temporary part time cleaner in a child care centre, earning HK$12 per hour. The employer requested her to stop working for one week after every three weeks of work, so as to escape from labour regulations protecting worker's rights. The employer did not want to employ her on a regular basis under which she was entitled to annual leave, medical services, a provident fund and other employment benefits. In fact, she had been working for the agency under these 'temporary' terms for more than 7 months, frequently working 9 to 10 hours per day.

Ms Earl was in a similar situation, after had stopped working for some years to take care of her three children, she could only find a job as a cleaner earning HK$3,250 per month.

> Very difficult indeed, many factories have moved back to Mainland China, many of my friends cannot find jobs in the factories. Some of them become cleaners, or work in the fast food restaurants, Macdonald's, or Coral Fast Food... Here the wages are extremely low, you can only get about HK$3,000 per month by working in these fast food restaurants, unless in the city centre normally you can get HK$4,000 to HK$5,000 in such jobs. Here, there are a lot of housewives looking for such jobs. They have to accept HK$10 per hour. (Ms Earl)

So, many women have to accept these low paid and unstable jobs under very exploitative terms because of the lack of alternative opportunities in Tuen Mun. That is, moving to the new town contributes to the further marginalization and subordination of women in the work sphere.

Discriminating against women

The lack of employment opportunities for middle age housewives does not only reflect the competitiveness of the capitalist labour market, it also reveals discrimination regarding age and sex within the employment system. Lack of opportunities results not because women are not competent enough, but rather because of discrimination in the employment system.

As I have pointed out in chapter 3, economic restructuring in recent years has displaced manual work in factories with jobs in the financial and service sectors. However, it should be noted that not all women have been displaced. In fact, in the service sector, a significant proportion of the jobs are occupied by women because of their readiness to accept lower wages, their submissiveness, and their caring and concerned personalities which are considered ideal for service workers. However, these positions in the service sector are mostly for young women or women with better education, rather than for middle aged housewives.

Middle aged housewives are unable to benefit from this economic restructuring. On the contrary, they are amongst the groups suffering the most. In Hong Kong, there is no labour regulation to guard against discrimination on grounds of age or sex. When employing female workers such as shop assistants and service workers in restaurants, many employers specify young women. This is especially true in the Tuen Mun new town where jobs are scarce while the supply of cheap labour is abundant.

Ms Ann has suffered from such discrimination, and her case is one of many. After she moved to Tuen Mun 9 years ago, she gave up her full time job to take care of the children. She started to try to find a job few years ago. As soon as she began her job hunting, she was extremely frustrated to discover that there was strong discrimination against middle age women.

> It is very difficult for us, those in their 40s and without much education [she is aged 42 with secondary education]. I had attended numerous interviews for jobs in Tuen Mun, but all of them said that I was too old, they need younger ones... For example, I applied for a job as store keeper in a factory and another job as cashier in a supermarket, both of them said that they required women aged under 40. There is no chance for us aged above 40. (Ms Ann)

Ms Ann is a lucky one, because finally she was able to get a full time job as an office assistant. Many other women are not so lucky. For example, Ms Chu was still trying to find a job, without success, after three years without work due to taking care of the children. She was only 35, with secondary education and several years of experience as an accounting clerk. This is not a bad qualification by Hong Kong standards. However, it was not easy for her to get a suitable job in Tuen Mun.

What can I do? A women in her mid 30s. They don't even employ you as a cleaner, it is true, it is up to age 35 only. I have seen an advertisement outside the Welcome Supermarket recruiting female cleaners - aged 35 or less, not 35 or above. I really don't know what I can do. Going to work at Macdonald's? Only HK$10 per hour, that's the work for us!? (Ms Chu)

There is no apparent reason for such age restrictions on these jobs for women. Why cannot a women of aged over 35, be a cashier, store keeper, shop assistant, or cleaner? Clearly this is a form of discrimination on grounds of age and sex.

An important point to note is that this form of discrimination applies only to women. It is very uncommon that employment for men is restricted to young men only. Men are assessed by their qualifications and work experience. On the other hand, it is common place for women to have to be young, beautiful, nice and good looking in order to be qualified for a job. This is another clear reflection of the underlying patriarchal ideology that women are judged by their physical appearance and their ability to please men, not by their ability to work.

Sometimes it is difficult for these women to accept the reality that they can only take up marginal work in this discrimination-based labour market. Ms Gam, aged 36, was earning about HK$5,000 per month as a skilled worker in a garment factory three years prior to moving to Tuen Mun. She had given up her job to look after her children. But now, she found that she was unable to get a job unless she accepted low pay. This was very frustrating indeed.

There are not many choices. The only job I can get is working as a cleaner in a fast food restaurant. But I really don't want to do that, most of the workers in these jobs are old women, but I am not that old. (Ms Gam)

Consequently, middle aged, married, working class women, especially those living in new towns, are marginalized by and excluded from the labour market. At best, they can turn only to low paid or 'dirty' jobs such as cleaning, washing dishes in restaurants, etc. There is so much competition, even for these low paid jobs, in Tuen Mun new town, that workers are paid less than their counterparts in the urban area.

Conclusion

Our examination of women's experience in the labour market has clearly demonstrated that they are marginalized, discriminated against and subordinated. Their discrimination is systematised and endemic in society. Their contribution, whether in the form of unpaid domestic labour or paid employment is grossly undervalued. In the worst case, full time housewives doing housework for over 12 hours per day are regarded as 'not working'. At the same time, the employment system, underpinned by patriarchal ideology and capitalist logic, serves to push women into marginal positions with low pay and unstable jobs.

This marginalization of women at work is exacerbated when they move to a remote new town like Tuen Mun. Their chances of getting employment are even worse. In Tuen Mun, many women can only find unstable and low paid work such as cleaning. Those who are lucky enough to find jobs are more susceptible to exploitation because of the lack of alternative choices. For example, one woman whom I interviewed was still working under 'temporary terms' - that is without occupational benefits - even though she had been working full time as a cleaner for more than 7 months with the same employer. Another example of marginalization is the discrimination against middle age women - many jobs such as shop assistants are restricted to women aged 30 or less.

This disadvantageous position in the labour market together with the lack of community services and facilities in the new town that we have discussed in the last chapter have firmly tied women down and confined them to their home; subordinated within the family and dependent on their husbands.

Note

1. Women as the reserve army of labour for the capitalist is an important debate in Marxist and feminist studies (see Bruegel, 1986), which is out of the scope of our discussion. Here, the term 'reserve army of labour for the family' is only used to refer to the presumed marginal position of women's employment within the family.

Part Four

CONCLUSION AND DISCUSSION

9 Social construction of gender inequality

Although this research deals primarily with women in two specific situations - lone mothers and women in new towns, it has a much wider significance. The arguments can be extended to analyze the housing problems of women in other situations, albeit with some adjustment. I have attempted to develop a more comprehensive theoretical explanation of the causes of women's housing problems, or alternatively, have contributed to the explanation of women's subordination in society at large. This discussion also has important implications for policy analysis in general and for the improvement of existing social policy in Hong Kong.

Explaining gender inequality in the housing system

The most important argument put forward in this book is that women's housing problems are not a consequence of individual inadequacy as commonly believed in Hong Kong, but are socially constructed in our social system at the ideological level, the structural level and in everyday social interaction. In Hong Kong, women's housing problems are either completely ignored or at best regarded as individual inadequacy or mishap. For example, lone mothers' problems are usually regarded as resulting from women's inability to maintain the family both before and after the divorce. Women's problems in the new towns are usually perceived as individual maladjustment to the new living environment. It seems to imply that there is no need for government intervention, and that these 'temporary' problems will be resolved eventually. Contrary to common sense belief, evidence from this research shows that women's housing problems are socially constructed and women are trapped in this disadvantaged position. Women are left alone to take up the full burden of a wider social problem.

Why does gender inequality in the housing system exist and persist? It is not simply arising out of negligence, but is the result of systematic bias within our social system. That is why we have to start with fundamental questions such as how we perceive or conceptualize this social inequality.

Patriarchal ideologies dominate our housing system. We have identified two such ideologies: the domestic ideal and the familial ideology. In portraying home as haven, domestic ideal obscures the fact that home is a work place for women, thereby ignoring women's burden of homemaking and further isolating women at home. Moreover, homes, like factories, can have very poor working conditions and can be more dreadful than factories. Familial ideology promotes the traditional family as the basic unit in society. On the one hand, this ignores the power inequality between the two sexes in the family. On the other hand, this marginalizes families not conforming to this 'conventional' model such as lone parent families. In other words, the housing system actively coerces or induces women to conform to patriarchal expectations.

By arguing that the housing system is coercive or oppressive, we need to clarify that housing is not a simple tool used by men to oppress women. Care should be taken to avoid the pitfall of 'environmental determinism' which argues that the design of housing and the community as such oppresses women. The real problem lies in the social relations embedded in housing design and in the facilities and functions associated with the physical construction of the home, not the physical environment itself. Similarly, simply giving a detailed account of women's limited access to housing resources, as in the 'add on' approach, is insufficient to challenge the patriarchal orientation underpinning the housing system. On the other hand, it reinforces the misconception that women are 'vulnerable' or less capable of solving their own problems (Clapham and Smith, 1990; Marcuse, 1989a).

Therefore, in my research, at the same time as revealing women's disadvantaged position in the housing system, I also emphasize the importance of deconstructing the myth and showing the reality of the social functions of housing. The manifestation of power inequality between the two sexes is subtle, but very potent. It permeates our social systems. Male domination is so potent not only because men accept patriarchal practices, but very often women themselves are part of the mechanism constructing inequality. For example, many lone mothers I have interviewed had tried to maintain a 'two-parent model' even though they and their children were battered seriously. Many women moving to new towns have no hesitation to give up their employment to support their family and their husbands. Therefore, it is important to study gender inequality at different levels including the ideological level, the structural level, and in everyday social interactions.

In my study, I have focused on two domains of women's activities - home and work - to examine how women's subordination in the housing system results from the interplay between these two axes. Within the patriarchal ideology of public-private division, women are confined to the domestic duties of homemaking and child caring. At the same time, they are marginalized or subordinated in the labour market. These forces work together to reinforce women's disadvantaged position in the housing system.

The capitalist state also plays its part in reinforcing patriarchy. Although we cannot say that the capitalist state and patriarchy is unitary, in practice, state policies largely reinforce gender inequality. For example, housing policy in Hong Kong marginalizes 'unconventional' families. That means that women not depending on a traditional family (or not depending on men) could find great difficulties in solving their housing problems. Social welfare policy fails to see the need to support the family in taking care of the children, thereby shifting the burden to women. At the same time, labour policy in Hong Kong fails to protect women against sex discrimination in the labour market.

Housing problems of lone mothers and women in new towns

The disadvantaged housing position of women is constructed by these 'anti-women' social policies and social practices. I have selected two groups of women - women as lone mothers and women living in new towns - as illustrations. The acute housing problems of lone mothers serve to illustrate how urgent housing needs of women can be ignored in our gender blind society. In addition, the study of women in new towns shows that women's housing problems are not confined to 'vulnerable' groups such as lone mothers. On the contrary, women's housing problems widely exist even under more common circumstances such as women living in new towns, albeit less conspicuously.

Lone mothers are charged with the duty of looking after the children after divorce, and very often, they are the one responsible for solving housing problems after the family breaks down. Their problem solving ability is restrained under the present gender biased social policies and social practices. For example, access to child care services for lone mothers is extremely limited because women are assumed to be the 'natural carers'. Lone mothers' disadvantaged position in the labour market significantly reduces their financial resources for problem solving. For those depending on Public Assistance, the situation is even worse. They are trapped in poverty without adequate child care, housing and job placement support, and lacking other services. Exploitation and discrimination of lone mothers are echoed in the wider social context. Women without husbands are considered unprotected, loose women, wicked or 'undeserving' because they have failed in their duties of taking care of the family. They are discriminated against by neighbours, their children's teachers, social welfare officers, and housing officers. That is why they have to face such great difficulties in solving their housing problems.

We have found that more divorced women have to move out of their matrimonial home than common sense has led us to expect. Many lone mothers are virtually homeless, continuously moving around from one appalling dwelling to another.

It is extremely difficult for lone mothers to secure accommodation in the private market not only because of their limited financial ability, but also because they are regarded as problematic and frequently rejected by private housing market landlords/landladies or vendors. In the study, many women told us that they had to cover up their identity as lone mothers before they could find accommodation. Even if they could find accommodation, most probably this was an appalling dwelling in a slum area. This does not help at all to solve their housing problems and instead creates further problems, such as the hazard of sexual harassment and difficulties in looking after the children.

The public housing system is ineffective for solving lone mothers' housing problems. Lone mother families are not regarded as a priority group in the public housing allocation system in Hong Kong. The criteria for compassionate public housing are so stringent that only a few cases of the most desperate kind succeed. For example, a lone mother has moved 7 times in one year from one urban slum to another before the Housing Department was convinced that she had genuine needs. Lone mothers are often desperately in need of accommodation, but are discriminated against or exploited by housing officials. They are offered the worst quality and type of housing in the worst housing locations.

Temporary solutions such as living with friends and relatives (mostly living with parents), or living in shelters provided by welfare agencies are common ways for lone mothers to solve their problems, at least temporarily. In the housing and social welfare system in Hong Kong, shelter services for lone mothers and their children are extremely underdeveloped. On the other hand, because of lack of space in the parent's family (especially in working class families in Hong Kong), and sometimes because of social stigma, it is extremely difficult for the lone mothers to live with their parents. For example, a lone mother has told us that she had to move out of her mother's place to avoid gossip amongst the neighbours and to minimize the social pressure on her mother. So, these are never satisfactory long term solutions.

Women living in new towns are another illustrative example of the wide existence of gender inequality in the housing system. Due to the gender blind new town development policy, women in new towns are being further marginalized or subordinated in the labour market on the one hand, and further confined to the home and isolated from the public world on the other hand.

Women's isolation in the home is exacerbated by the government's failure in the new town programme and related policy planning. In general, there are several common problems women in Tuen Mun need to face. First, the underdevelopment of the transportation system limits women's mobility. This creates extra burdens for women in taking care of the family or in daily activities such as taking children to school and to hospital, paying bills, going to the bank, meeting friends or participating in other social activities. Second, in moving to new towns, women are isolated from the support network they had experienced in the city centre. Especially in the early years of migration when new support networks are not yet established, the pressure on women is tremendous and they have to shelter difficulties alone without support.

The heavy burden on women is closely related to women's domestic duty for homemaking and child care, which are the third and fourth problems we have studied. New towns are developed with the patriarchal assumption that women stay at home to take care of the children and the family. Hence, child care services are extremely scarce, not to mention services supporting women's homemaking duties.

Fifth, the design of housing units and the quality of management also affects women. Aspects of the poor design or poor management threatens the safety of women. For example, many women interviewed expressed concern about safety in their community, they have to avoid going out at night or in the early afternoon, when the crime rate is highest. This seriously restricts the time and scope of women's social activities. Other poor aspects of the design of housing units may also endanger women and children's safety at home, for example the design of the kitchen, clothes drying racks outside the window of high rise buildings, unsafe electrical or gas appliances, all contributing to increase the burdens on women in homemaking.

Employment opportunities in new towns are restricted for both men and women because of the failure of urban planning. Women's employment is regarded as unimportant or secondary to their roles as homemakers. Therefore, it is extremely common that women have to adjust their paid work to take care of the family such as changing to a less demanding job, changing to work part time, or quitting the job completely. That is why in general women are further isolated from the public world after moving to the new towns.

Constructing women's subordination

The disadvantaged position of women in the housing system does not only increase their burden of homemaking, it also creates women's dependency on men and women's subordination in society at large.

Since women are charged with duties in child care, looking for new accommodation and solving financial problems after divorce, in order to avoid these burdens many lone mothers are compelled to stay with their husband in the 'conventional' family even under very adverse situation. A lone mother told us that she had been battered by her husband for over 10 years before she could really break away from him because of the housing problems and the financial difficulties she would face after separation. In this way, many women are literally forced to live with violent husbands, or to endure unnecessarily lengthy psychological pressures within a broken marriage.

Those lone mothers who dared to leave their husbands are discriminated against and marginalized by the housing system, the employment system, the welfare system, and by society at large. For example, lone mothers are discriminated against by landlords/landladies in private housing, lone mother families are given low priority for public rental housing and Home Ownership schemes. Lone mothers find extra difficulties in job hunting because of discrimination, or they are exploited intensively in jobs because a lack of alternative choice in the labour market. Those who depends on Public Assistance are trapped in poverty, stigmatized and even humiliated.

Under these circumstances, it is extremely difficult for lone mothers to re-establish normal social life after divorce. In order to solve these problems, women are forced to return to their violent husband, or depend on another men - that is, re-marry (Maclean, 1991, p.63-81). In other words, their subordination in the family and dependency on men are reinforced.

For women living in new towns, the housing system also contributes to their subordination within the family and their dependency on men, albeit in a more subtle form. I have shown that failures in new town planning such as the underdeveloped transportation system, lack of employment opportunities, and inadequate child care services have created tremendous difficulties for women in taking care of their family.

Almost all the women I have interviewed have been compelled to make adjustments to their employment such as changing to less demanding jobs, working part time, or even quitting their job completely in order to take care of their family. With all these changes, they have been compelled to depend more on their husbands and have less opportunities for self development. For example, a woman I have interviewed told us that her husband seems to be more like her boss since she gave up her employment to look after the family. Very often, for women, living in new towns implies further isolation from the public sphere and confinement to the home.

State and policy analysis

There are several important lessons we can learn from this study for the analysis of policies relating to women's subordination within the housing system and within society at large.

State policy and antagonization of gender relations

Traditional policy analysis tends to focus on the quantity and quality of service provision without challenging the orientation of the policy, this is especially true in Hong Kong. It seems to assume that the state is a benevolent state trying to satisfy the social needs of its citizens as far as possible with its limited resources.

A major limitation of this 'benevolent state' assumption is that the role of the state and the social context in which the policy operates is completely ignored (Marcuse, 1986). The state is a system of political domination, whereby dominant ideologies and social practices are reflected in its policies. In this research, I have shown that housing policy is not 'neutral', the housing system contributes to reinforce women's subordination within society at large. That is, housing policy does not necessarily benefit all members in the family equally. In fact, there is increasing evidence that housing and urban policies serve to widen existing social inequalities on various dimensions such as class, race, ethnicity, age and sex (Marcuse, 1989b, 1993; Harloe and Fainstein, 1992, p.253; Harloe, 1995, pp.545-7). The oppressive nature of housing policy (Marcuse, 1989a, pp.71-2) and its contribution to the widening of social inequality is very much underplayed or underestimated in traditional policy analysis.

Under the laissez-faire capitalist state in Hong Kong, there is also another dominant myth about the role of the state. It tries to argue that social services intrude upon personal life and are ineffective in solving social problems, so it is better to turn to privatized services. This 'meddling state' argument should not be alien to Western countries with a New Right government (Marcuse, 1986), like Britain. However, evidence in this research shows that the failure of social services to solve social problems, like those of lone mothers' housing or those of women in new towns, does not implies that public services can never work. Instead, a major cause of the failure of public service is the problematic orientation of the policy itself.

More exactly, because existing policy and services are underpinned by patriarchal ideology, they are not only ineffective for solving social problems but literally they create more problems. For example, fragmented social services fails to help lone mothers to re-establish a new life after divorce. The lack of child care support and the lack of employment services does not encourage lone mothers to obtain paid employment and be financially independent. In addition, the inadequate housing service for lone mothers means that it is extremely difficult for them to settle down, get a job, or find schools for their children. This increases women's dependency on social security. Consequently, the government may end up with spending more money in the social security system for lone mothers than providing them with adequate housing services, employment services, and subsidized child care services so that the lone mothers can be financially independent.

Similarly, the problems in new towns are mainly due to the failure of state policies. Because the policy planners failed to see the extra difficulties for women in taking care of the family in new towns, they are not provided with adequate support services such as child care services, after school service for children, or collective homemaking services. As a result of this failure, the government has ended up paying more for having to deal with serious social problems in new towns such as broken families, family violence, abandoned elderly, juvenile delinquency, vandalism or law and order problems.

Instead of maintaining stable families and a stable society as generally believed, these gender blind housing policies and state policies literally antagonize gender relations and sharpen the conflicts in the family. Very often, not only women suffer, but men suffer as well. For example, husband and wife are forced to compete for the matrimonial home because the state refuses to take care of the housing needs of the lone parent family and the absent partner in a divorce. That is why some men are reluctant to leave the matrimonial home for the wife and the children because they will become homeless. In the new towns, women are isolated at home while men take up less of the burden of homemaking. The consequence is that the gap between the husband and the wife widens, and family conflicts intensify. No wonder that many women in new towns have complained that their husbands pays less attention to the family; and that the understanding between husband and wife deteriorates after moving to the new town.

In summary, inadequate service provision and gender biased policy are among the major causes of social problems, instead of solutions to these problems as commonly believed. The state is not a benevolent one, it is part of the system which creates the social problems. Of course, what we required to do is to improve social policy and services, not doing without them completely, and not ruling out all forms of state intervention completely.

Policy discourse: beyond state policy

Another significant implication of this study is that social policy analysis should go beyond the scrutiny of the 'state policy' as such. Social inequality is structured in daily social interactions as well as in social structures and social policies. This is especially true when analyzing inequality between the two sexes, where the manifestation of power is subtle and obscure. That is, more attention has to be paid to the social discourse underlying particular policies and the definition of social problems. Here, we want to remind the readers of Saunders' (1989, 1990) study on the 'meaning of home' which we have discussed in chapter 2. It is problematic for Saunders to conclude that the home is not oppressive to women because women love their home as much as men do. Obviously, Saunders has neglected the subtlety of power manifestation. In more general terms, it is not only important to analyze the causes, effects or the extent of a social problem, it is also important to study why some problems are treated as important ones while others are regarded as 'non-issues'.

The process of formulating my research question is an illustrative example. At the beginning of my research, most of my colleagues (who are also academics in social science disciplines) in Hong Kong were very puzzled by my research question. To them, this was not an issue at all. They thought that either there is no gender inequality in the housing system, or that was too insignificant for a PhD study. Here, we should be aware that the academics and the professionals are part of the system contributing to the reinforcement of gender inequality. Frequently, women's problems were defined as not a problem at all. That is why even though there were a number of academic research studies on lone mothers and family problems in new towns, gender inequality or the subordination of women was never put on the agenda of these studies.

This process of constructing gender inequality is more obvious within women's daily experience. For example, holding the dominant belief that two-parent families are better than lone parent families, many lone mothers interviewed had tried to put up with physical or psychological abuse from their husbands in order to maintain the two-parent family model. It is only after they had broken this myth and divorced their husband that they realized that they could maintain a lone parent family, which in many cases proved to be happier than their two-parent families. As Chandler has pointed out, very often children in lone parent families are involved more in family decision making and thus have better relations with their parents (Chandler, 1991, pp.131-50). Of course, some lone mothers are still quite ambivalent about divorce because they have to face social pressure, discrimination and stigmatization which work against lone parent families.

Similarly, women's problems in new towns are not considered as an 'issue' by the husbands, or quite often by the women themselves. In my interviews it is common to hear from both men and women that the major worries in moving to the new town is the issue of men's journey to work and schooling of the children. It seems that women's isolation and confinement at home and their loss of employment opportunities are never treated with concern, since it is taken for granted that women's primary role is carer of the family.

That is, by defining problems within a patriarchal framework, women's problems are regarded as 'non-issues' or trivialized, and thus women's subordination is maintained. This reminds us of Lukes's (1984) classical study on power which emphasized the importance of paying attention to 'non-issues' and how social demands are being moulded, or Foucault's emphasis on the 'capillary' nature of power which is build up from below rather than impose from top down (Dreyfus and Rabinow, 1982; Smart, 1985, pp.76-80; McNay, 1992, pp.38-40; Foucault, 1986). Only by exposing the absurdity and unfairness of existing gender relations is there better hope for the improvement of our social policy.

Policy implications

From this study, it is clear that the choices of existing policies and services in Hong Kong is neither best nor inevitable. Throughout the study, the women I interviewed gave various invaluable suggestions for improving housing and related social services. Although my main concern in this book is not to develop detailed alternative policy proposals, it may be useful to summarize these suggestions as indications of how existing policy can be improved. Needless to say, these highly simplified abstractions are only general principles for the development of related policies rather than detailed programmes for implementation.

First, as a result of the ideology that family violence is the 'private affair' of individual families, sheltered housing services for battered women are extremely underdeveloped. At present, there is only one government run shelter for battered women and one run by a voluntary agency. Because of scarcity of resources, this service is mainly limited to women suffering from physical violence. Sheltered services should be expanded substantially and extended to women seeking divorce, but not under the threat of physical violence. In this research, many lone mothers who were not threatened by violence before divorce reflected that it would be extremely helpful if this service had been available to them. That is, a broader definition of gender violence, such as the one proposed by the United Nations, should be adopted:

'Violence against women' includes any act of gender based violence that results in, or is likely to result in physical, sexual or psychological harm or suffering to women, including threats of such acts, coercion or arbitrary deprivation of liberty, whether occurring in public or private life (World Health Organization, 1993, p.78).

Moreover, besides developing temporary shelter services, the government should also explore other alternatives such as 'halfway houses' or small group homes for lone parent families, which help them to adjust to new family patterns and to develop mutual support. This implies that the government needs to abolish the out dated 'private-public division', and recognize that these 'private' family affairs are in fact social problems.

Because of the extremely limited resources put into these services, other than the provision of temporary shelter, it has been impossible to develop more comprehensive services, such as employment placements or job training, or help in seeking permanent accommodation, finding school places for children, and in making applications for Public Assistance. In fact, battered women are only allowed to stay for a maximum period of three months whether they can find other suitable permanent accommodations or not. Of course, temporary shelter should not be a permanent place for lone mother families, but the government should provide permanent accommodation before they are required to move out. As I have pointed out earlier, if more comprehensive services are developed for lone mother families, they can settle down and re-establish normal social life sooner and depend less on the government.

Second, lone mother families should be considered as a priority group in the public housing system. At present, with the exception of the elderly, the allocation of public housing in Hong Kong does not give priority to groups with special social needs such as lone parents, the physically or mentally handicapped, and the chronically sick. On the contrary, 'unconventional' families such as lone parent families are discriminated against. In the interviews, some lone mothers pointed out that they were not qualified to apply for public housing because there were only two members in their families - a mother and a child. In contrast, most public housing is geared towards meeting the needs of 'conventional' nuclear families with three or more members - two parents and at least one child. Similarly, some lone mothers applying for the government Home Ownership flats complained that they were given lower priority than 'conventional' nuclear families. Under existing housing policy, lone parent families do not even have a fair chance to compete with 'conventional' families, let alone getting higher priority. We need to re-orientate our housing policy to remove this unreasonable discrimination and channel more housing resources to support lone parent families and other women with housing needs such as single women, elderly women, and women taking care of physically or mentally handicapped family members.

Third, existing new town development does not take into consideration women's needs. Urban planners and policy makers ignore the fact that the spatial isolation of new towns creates tremendous pressures for women. New towns should be designed with more gender consciousness. For example, more attention should be paid to women's needs for transportation services, women's employment opportunities, child care services, after school services, and supportive services for homemaking. Housing and community design in new town should facilitate the carrying out of domestic duties and the development of neighbourhood support. Special consideration should be taken of the alternation of housing design and community facilities to suit families of different composition, such as elderly women, lone mothers or women taking care of disabled family members.

Fourth, legislative protection for women's housing rights needs to be improved. Although women's access to housing wealth is not a main focus in this research, obviously housing wealth transfer and inheritance have significant impact on social inequality (Hamnett, 1991; Smith, 1990; Forrest and Murie, 1988a). Many women I have interviewed channelled their grievances toward this area. For example, a lone mother I have interviewed complained that she was obliged to give up her right to her Home Ownership flat before she was qualified for any housing services. Similarly, some women I have interviewed in the Tuen Mun new town told us that before they got married they used to live with their parents in private housing and shared the mortgage repayment with their siblings. However, after they got married, they had to leave the flat without any share in the property. Housing becomes the property of the family sons. Worse still, some women living in a rural village in Yuen Long complained that under existing village customs they were not entitled to inherit housing property in their family, inherence being restricted to men only. Of course, legislation alone does not change the patriarchal assumption that men are the owners of family property and that women have no contribution to family wealth. However, legislation against discrimination is an essential basic step to guarantee equal access to housing property between men and women.

In order to solve women's housing problem effectively, housing policy and other related policy should be integrated and consistent. Therefore the fifth policy we are going to discuss is the improvement of Public Assistance and the social security system. Given a minimal level of service provision and an insensitivity to women's needs, there is not much that can be achieved by existing services, except the maintenance of lone mother families at subsistence level. Lone mothers are trapped in poverty, degraded and humiliated within the system instead of being helped to re-establish normal social life after divorce. Lone mothers should be provided with more comprehensive services such as stable accommodation, help in employment placements, and adequate child care services. If these were provided, more women could become financially independent, and make less demands on social subsidies, and further social problems would be prevented.

Sixth, the inadequacy of child care services is a major obstacle against women obtaining work. This is true not only for lone mothers and women living in new towns, but also applies to other women. The government should provide more subsidized child care services and encourage the development of non-profit making services run by voluntary agencies or employers. In recent years, many employers have complained about the shortage of labour in Hong Kong. If the government were more willing to invest in child care services, more women would be released from their domestic duty and participate in the labour market. Certainly, this would greatly benefit the economy of Hong Kong.

Seventh, housework is another significant obstacle to women getting out of the home. In this study, we have seen that technological developments and the modernization of housework alone has not helped women to get rid of their burdens as has been commonly believed. We need a complete re-conceptualization of housework and family relations in modern society. The government should provide public education encouraging men and other family members to share the housework, instead of putting all the burden on to women. At the same time, collective homemaking services or socialization of housework should be encouraged as far as possible. On the one hand, this enhances mutual understanding and cooperation between family members, and prevents family breakdown. On the other hand, this helps to release women from the burden of homemaking.

Eighth, women are marginalized from, subordinated to, or excluded from the employment system, which is a major contributor to women's subordination in society in general. So, the government should improve labour legislation to protect women's rights in employment, to remove all forms of sex discrimination in employment. An example is to enlarge the right to return to employment after paid or unpaid paternity as well as maternity leave. Moreover, employment benefits and labour protection should be extended to cover part time and temporary jobs, in which many women are being employed.

Lastly, in this study we have seen that many professionals such as housing officers, social security officers, social workers, teachers, policy planners, urban planners and government officials are part of the mechanism constructing women's subordination; not to mention the academics who help to trivialize studies on women's issues. Therefore, we should pay more attention to the training of professionals and academics. More emphasis should be placed on gender consciousness and social equality in the training.

In arguing for the improvement of social policies and services for women, it should be emphasized that we do not imply that women need more care and attention because they are less capable, or they are a 'vulnerable' group that need extra resources. On the contrary, in this study I have found that quite often, women take more of the burden, working longer hours than men. It is only because most social policies and the social structure work against women that they have to face so many problems. Therefore, we are arguing for a removal of these constraints on women, and for giving them a fair deal.

Another point we should note is that by arguing for the improvement of state policy and services we are not simply shifting women's dependency from men to the state. In Western welfare states, a widespread criticism has been made that state welfare can be oppressive, intrusive, and patriarchal and can create dependency in women (Sassoon, 1992). Therefore care must be taken that we do not simply copy a Western style welfare state for Hong Kong, and force women to depend on the state. However, at the same time, the limitations of Western style welfare state should not be used as an excuse for the Hong Kong government to shed its responsibility for solving social problems.

On the one hand, the lack of social services such as the inadequate child care service and the minimal level of Public Assistance for lone mothers can create tremendous difficulties for women. On the other hand, the development of social services underpinned by patriarchal ideology such as in existing housing services and in the development of new towns can reinforce women's subordination. Therefore, before women's housing problems can be solved, we must re-orientate our policy and develop our services through gender consciousness. In fact, if more 'non-sexist' services are developed, social problems such as family violence, family break down, juvenile delinquency and other related family problems may be reduced significantly.

Appendix A
Interview guidelines

Appendix A1   Guideline for interviewing lone parents

Name of interviewee:
Date of interview:
Time of interview:
Place of interview:

---

1   Difficulties in finding accommodations
   1.1   Do you need to move out after separated from your husband?
   1.2   If yes, describe the difficulties in finding accommodation.
   1.3   Do you think that the difficulties in finding accommodation affect your decision to leave your husband? How?
   1.4   Describe your housing situation before you separated from your husband.

2   Experience in compassionate housing
   2.1   Have you ever applied for Compassionate Housing?
   2.2   If yes, describe the process and the difficulties in detail.
   2.3   If no, why don't you apply?
   2.4   Comment on the policy in compassionate housing for lone mother?

3   Difficulties for lone mother in caring of the family and children
   3.1   Are you being discriminated by your neighbours, friends, relatives, or the society at large?
   3.2   Is it more difficult for lone mothers to take care of their children?
   3.3   Do you think that it is better or worse for your children, if you are still staying with your husband?

3.4 Please list out the details of your time use pattern in a normal working day.

3.5 Do you like housework or not? What do you like or dislike about it?

3.6 Do you face financial difficulties? How does this affect your family and your children?

4 Work experience

4.1 Do you have an employment now?

4.1.1 If yes, what is your occupation, position, income, place of work...?

Who help you to take care of the children if you go to work?

4.1.2 if no employment, why don't you work?

4.2 Do you prefer to work, or to depend on Public Assistance?

4.3 Do you like to go out to work, or like to do full time housework?

4.4 Have you ever go out to work before you separated from your husband?

4.5 Do you think that you are sacrificing your job/career for your family?

4.6 Do you think that you are being discriminated in the job market?

5 Background of respondents

Age, marital status, number of children living together at present, any other relatives living together, education, new immigrants or local born, age/year of marriage and divorce, family income, whether depend on social security, maintenance from ex-husband, employment, number of accommodation lived after separated from husband, type of present accommodation.

--- END ---

Name of interviewee:
Date of interview:
Place of interview:
Time of interview:

---

1   Housing history
    1.1 What are the significant changes in housing in your life time?
    1.2 What are the determining factors in making these housing decision? Especially, describe your decision making process before moving to the Tuen Mun new town.
    1.3 Compare the female respondents' experiences with their male siblings or with their husbands.

2   Social network
    2.1 Does moving to Tuen Mun limit your social activities?

3   New town problems and community facilities
    3.1 What are the services most in lack of here?   And, how does this affect you?
    3.2 Do you feel safe at home or going around in your community?

4   Housework
    4.1 Describe your time use pattern in a normal day.
    4.2 Does the pattern of housework and the pattern of social support being affected after moving to new towns?
    4.3 Does your husband/children help in housework and child caring?
    4.4 Does modern household appliances and modern food industry help to reduce your housework?

5   Child caring
    5.1 Does moving to this new town change your pattern/strategy in child caring?
    5.2 What is your comment and your experience in using local child care services?

6   Concept of home, child caring and housework (why women care)
    6.1 Do you agree that 'child caring and housework is not heavy work'?
    6.2 Do you enjoy child caring and housework?
    6.3 Do you accept traditional gender division of labour?   And what is the situation in your family?

6.4 Do you like your home or dislike it? In what way?

7 Women and employment
7.1 Describe your work history. Give details of your present job, if any.
7.2 Have you ever tried to find a job in Tuen Mun or outside Tuen Mun? Why or why not? And, what are the difficulties involved?
7.3 Do you think that moving to Tuen Mum has affected your work opportunity?
7.4 Do you think that you have less opportunities in employment than men?
7.5 Do you have any experience of being discriminated in employment or in finding a job? How?

8 Conception of work
8.1 Do you prefer to have an employment or to be a full time housewife?
8.2 Does your husband prefer you to go out to work or to be a housewife?
8.3 Do you feel that housework is 'unproductive', or housewife is useless?
8.4 Do you think that housework should be paid? why or why not?
8.5 Do you think that your domestic labour is 'fairly paid' or you have a fair share of the family wealth?
8.6 Do you think that women are less skilful, less efficient, or less committed in work? Why or why not?
8.7 Have you ever thought of developing your own career?
8.8 Do you think that you are sacrificing your employment for your family? Is it worth?

9 Housing resources (inheritance and ownership)
9.1 Have your parents assisted you, financially or in other ways, in establishing your home?
9.2 Do you think that men get more help from their parents than women in solving housing problem?

10 Background information
Age, education, marital status, age when married, number of children and age, other family members, employment and salary (present/past), family income, years of residence in Hong Kong and in Tuen Mun, self identification of class position.

11 Do you think that your husband would also like to be interviewed?

--- END ---

Appendix B
Background of respondents

Appendix B1   Background of respondents - lone mothers

Total 17 female and 3 male

ID	Housing type	age/ education/ yrs. of separation	children (with age)	work/ income (HK$/month)
L01 AU	compassionate housing	38/ F.1/ 3 yrs.	2 (age 8,10)	P.T. office assistance/ HK$2,500
L02 BAO	private, rent a room	29/ P.3/ 1 yrs.	1 (age 1)	no/ Public Assistance
L03 CHAN	private, rent a room	29/ F.3/ 2 yrs.	1 (age 3)	care taker/ HK$5,810
L04 DENG	private, rent a room	33/ P.5/ 1 yrs.	1 (age 6)	no/ Public Assistance
L05 ELL	private, rent a room	40/ F.3/ 2 yrs.	1 (age 3)	no/ Public Assistance + maintenance

ID	Housing type	age/ education/ yrs. of separation	children (with age)	work/ income (HK$/month)
L06 FUNG	private, rent a room	26/ P.6/ 2 yrs.	2 (age 10, 4)	no/ Public Assitance
L07 GON	private, rent whole flat	32/ F.5/ 5 yrs.	1 (age 7)	Senior clerk/ HK$8,000
L08 HONG	public housing	45/ F.3/ 2 yrs.	1 (age 17)	factory worker/ HK$3,000
L09 IP	compassionate housing	32/ P.6/ 3 yrs.	2 (age 10, 8)	no/ Public Assistance
L10 JONE	private, rent a room	47/ nil/ 3 yrs.	1 (age 9)	P.T. cleaner/ HK$3,000
L11 KAM	private, village house, whole flat	40/ P.6/ 2 yrs.	1 (age 4)	no/ Public Assistant
L12 LEE	private, rent a room	38/ P.6/ 2 yrs.	2 (age 4, 7)	no/ Public Assistant
L13 MAN	compassionate housing	40/ F.3/ 5 yrs.	1 girl	P.T. health worker/ HK$4,500
L14 NG	public housing	37/ P.6/ 4 yrs.	2 (age 16, 13)	Hawker/ HK$3,000 + Maintenance
L15 OI	private, rent whole flat	34/ F.6/ 5 yrs.	1 (age 4)	Secretary/ HK$15,000

ID	Housing type	age/ education/ yrs. of separation	children (with age)	work/ income (HK$/month)
L16 PANG	public housing	32/ F.3/ 3 yrs.	1 (age 9)	Office Assistant/ HK$8,050
L17 QUAN	public housing	32/ tertiary/ 3 yrs.	1 (age 7)	Merchandiser/ HK$8,000 + maintenance
L18 ROD (male)	public housing	58/ F.2/ 3 yrs.	3 (age 10,11,7)	no/ Public Assistance
L19 SIU (male)	public housing	48/ F.3/ 4 yrs.	1 (age 9)	manual worker/ HK$4,000
L20 TANG (male)	Public housing	42/ F.5/ 5 yrs.	1 (age 8,13)	Workmen/ HK$6,000

Appendix B2   Background of respondents - women in new towns

Total 21 female and 5 male

ID	Type of housing /Years in new town	Age/ Educa -tion	Children (with age)	employment/ Own income/ family income	remark
T01 Ann	public rental/ 9 years	42/ F.5	2 (age 8,13)	office assistance/ HK$5,300/ HK$15,000	husband T22
T02 Bob	private, Home Purchase Scheme/ 11 years	37/ F.5	2 (age 5,11)	clerk/ HK$5,900/ HK$22,000	husband T23
T03 Chu	Home Ownership Scheme/ 10 years	35/ F.5	2 (age 3,5)	no/ family income HK$20,000	husband T24
T04 Ding	public rental/ 10 years	36/ F.1	2 (age 9,12)	temporary P.T. cleaner/ HK$2,000/ HK$10,000	husband T25
T05 Earl	public rental/ 10 years	47/ P.4	3 (age 11,14, 17)	Cleaner/ HK$3,250/ HK$9,000	husband T26
T06 Fan	private, ownership/ 11 years	38/ F.3	3 (age 5,7,9)	no/ family income HK$16,000	
T07 Gam	Home Ownership Scheme/ since 90	36/ P.6	1 (age 4)	no/ family income HK$10,000	

ID	Type of housing /Years in new town	Age/ Educa -tion	Children (with age)	employment/ Own income/ family income	remark
T08 Hong	village hut, renting/ since 1973	42/ nil	4 (age 10,13, 17,18)	cleaner/ HK$3,000/ HK$9,000	
T09 Iu	village house, owner/ since birth	62/ P.1	6 (youngest age 23)	retired/ family income HK$3,000	
T10 Jan	village house, owner/ since 1971	27/ P.6	3 (age 2,4,5)	p.t. mini-bus driver/ HK$3,000/ HK$10,000	
T11 Kwok	public rental/ since 1978	38/ P.6	3 (age 7,14,20)	no/ family income HK$9,000	
T12 Lai	Home Ownership Scheme/ since 1980	38/ P.5	3 (age 10,15, 18)	no/ family income HK$20,000	
T13 Ming	public rental/ since 1982	45/ P.6	4 (age 10,14, 16,19)	no/ family income HK$12,000	
T14 Ngan	public rental/ since 1984	36/ P.6	2 (age 13,19)	no/ family income HK$9,000	
T15 Oat	public rental/ since 1984	35/ P.3	2 (age 6,11)	no/ on Public Assistance	
T16 Poon	Village house, owner/ since birth	40/ F.3	2 (age 13,16)	care taker/ HK$5,000/ HK$16,000	

ID	Type of housing /Years in new town	Age/ Educa -tion	Children (with age)	employment/ Own income/ family income	remark
T17 Quart	village house, owner/ since 1981	39/ P.6	2 (age 11,15)	shop assistant/ HK$3,800/ HK$24,000	
T18 Row	public rental/ 10 years	32/ F.3	2 (age 15,19)	cleaner/ HK$7,500/ HK$15,000	
T19 Sing	compassionate housing/ since 1991	45/ P.1	2 (age 9,10,11)	no/ on Public Assistance	
T20 Tao	Home Ownership Scheme/ since birth	43/ F.5	2 (age 8,9)	nurse/ HK$23,000/ HK$40,000	
T21 Ult	Public rental/ 8 years	32/ P.6	2 (age 4,10)	factory worker/ HK$2,500/ HK$10,000	
T22 Van (male)	public rental/ 10 years	47/ P.6	2 (age 9,12)	own business/ HK$12,000/ HK$16,000	wife T01
T23 Wong (male)	private, Home Purchase Scheme/ since birth	45/ F.5	2 (age 5,11)	Chemical Analyst/ HK$15,000/ HK$23,000	wife T02
T24 Xan (male)	Home Ownership Scheme/ 10 years	37/ ter- tiary	2 (age 3,5)	own business/ HK$20,000/ HK$20,000	wife T03

ID	Type of housing /Years in new town	Age/ Educa -tion	Children (with age)	employment/ Own income/ family income	remark
T25 Yan (male)	Public rental/ 10 years	36/ pri- mary	2 (age 10,12)	renovation worker/ HK$10,000/ don't know	wife T04
T26 Zeto (male)	public rental/ 10 years	50/ P.3	3 (age 12,13, 18)	manufacturing worker/ HK$5,000/ HK$8,000	wife T05

Appendix B3 **Background of informants interviewed - housing managers and social workers**

Code/ Name	Job	Sex	Area/ Type of housing
S01 Mui	Social worker (Shelter for battered women - NGO)	F	urban/ Temporary Housing Area
M01 Ming	Housing Officer (Government)	M	new town/ Temporary Housing Area
M02 Fun	Housing Officer (Government)	F	urban/ public rental housing
M03 Lai	Housing Manager (Government)	M	new town public rental housing and Home Ownership Scheme
M04 Ying	Assistant Housing Manager (Government)	F	Housing Department Headquarters

214

Appendix C
List of social housing services in Hong Kong

Appendix C1   Public rental housing

Families can join the general waiting list for public rental housing if they satisfy the following criteria:

1. The applicant's age is at least 18.
2. The household consists of at least 2 related persons living together. Single persons can also register on a separate list.
3. Household monthly income does not exceed the income limits which are reviewed annually. Income limits effective from 1 April 1993 are as follows:

Family Size (Persons)	Maximum Income Limit (HK$)
1	4,600
2	7,600
3	9,500
4	11,400
5	12,300
6	14,100
7	15,300
8	17,300
9	18,600
10	20,000

4. Applicant or family members must not be the owner of any domestic property; or must not have entered into any agreement to purchase such property.
5. On allocation, applicant and the majority of family members must have at least 7 years of residence in Hong Kong; for two-person families both members must have lived in Hong Kong for at least 7 years.

Appendix C2   Home Ownership Scheme and Home Purchase Loan Schemes

There are four different ownership schemes:

1. Home Ownership Scheme for applicants in public sector (green form application)
   a) Two categories of applicants are eligible to apply:
      i)   Housing Authority/Housing Society estates tenants and authorized occupants of the Housing Authority's Temporary Housing Area/Cottage Area
      ii)   Prospective public housing tenants whose eligibility has been established. They consist of: waiting list applicants; clearees and disaster victims; and Junior Civil Servants applying under the Civil Service Quota.
   b) Successful applicants will have to surrender their existing flats or public housing eligibility.
   c) No income limit for the household.
   d) No property ownership restriction for household members.

2. Home Ownership Scheme for applicants in private sector (white form application)
   a) Two categories of applicants are eligible to apply:
      i)   Nuclear families living in private sector housing.
      ii)   Separate family units who wish to live apart from their present households in Housing Authority and Housing Society estates, temporary housing areas and cottage areas managed by the Housing Authority.
   b) Household income not exceeding HK$20,000 per month (effective from 1 April 1993).
   c) No family member may own any domestic property.

3. Home Purchase Loan Scheme
   a) Interest free loan are granted to successful applicants to buy their own flats.
   b) Eligibility of applicant is similar to those in Home Ownership Scheme (for both public and private sector).
   c) The amount of interest free loan was increased to HK$200,000 in April 1993, repayable over 20 years. Or, the successful applicant can choose to receive a monthly subsidy of HK$2,600 for 36 months (effective from April 1993).

4. Home Purchase Loan Scheme for 'Sandwich Class'
   a) This is a new scheme started in 1993, which extends the Home Purchase Loan to household with higher income; this scheme is under the auspices of the Housing Society.
   b) All families without domestic property in the past 12 months, with household income between HK$20,000 and HK$40,000 and with wealth worth less than 1 million dollars are eligible to apply.
   c) Each successful applicant is granted HK$550,000 loan (effective from 1993), repayable over 20 years with 2 per cent interest rate.

All applicants for home ownership loan scheme and home purchase loan scheme must also satisfy three criteria:

1. The age of the applicant is at least 18.
2. There are at least 2 related persons in the family, and priority is given to nuclear family with 3 or more members.
3. The applicant and at least one family member must be permanent residents and have lived in Hong Kong for at least 7 years.

Appendix C3   Other housing services

1. Compassionate Housing
   a) Public housing may be granted to some applicants on compassionate ground, instead of joining the queue in the general waiting list.
   b) In most of the situation, decision is jointly made by the Housing Department and the Social Welfare Department.
   c) However, the eligibility criteria is extremely stringent and the number of compassionate housing units granted each year is extremely limited. For example, in 92/93 compassionate housing only constitute 4.3 per cent of the total flats available for allocation (see Chapter 3 table 5).

2. Temporary Housing Area
   a) These are temporary structure built and managed by the Housing Department. Only very basic facilities are provided. Residents have to share toilets and shower rooms on communal basis.
   b) Provide interim accommodation for the homeless and people not yet eligible for permanent public housing in clearances, fires and natural disasters (e.g. new immigrant living in Hong Kong less than 7 years).

Appendix C4   Provision of various types of housing (as at 31 March 1993)

1. Public Rental Housing	
No. of flats	639,660
Authorized Population	2,357,931
2. Home Ownership Scheme	
No. of flats	159,049
Estimated Population	510,600
3. Temporary Housing Area	
Authorized Population	63,245

Source: All information in Appendix C is extract from HK Housing Authority (1993), Appendix 6, and pp.60,139.

Appendix D
Geographic location of Hong Kong

Bibliography

Abbott, Pamela and Wallace, Claire (1990), 'The Production of Feminist Knowledge', in *An Introduction to Sociology: Feminist Perspectives*, Routledge: London.

Allen, John and Hamnett, Chris (ed.) (1991), *Housing and Labour Market: Building the Connections*, Unwin Hyman: UK.

Alcock, Pete (1993), *Understanding Poverty*, Macmillan: UK.

Anderson-Khleif, Susan (1981), 'Housing Needs of Single-parent Mothers', in Keller, Suzanne I. (ed.), *Building for Women*, Lexington Books: USA.

Antipode, (1984), vol.6, no.3, special issue on 'Women and Environment'.

Association for the Advancement of Feminism (A.A.F.) (1990), *Women and Social Welfare Policy in Hong Kong*, Association for the Advancement of Feminism: Hong Kong, (Published in Chinese).

Association for the Advancement of Feminism (A.A.F.) (1993), *Hong Kong Women's File*, Association for the Advancement of Feminism: Hong Kong, (Published in Chinese).

Austerberry, Helen and Watson, Sophie (1983), *Women on the Margin*, Housing Research Group, City University: UK.

Bardo, J.W. and Hartman, J.J. (1982), *Urban Sociology*, Peacock: USA.

Barrett, Michele and McIntosh, Mary (1982), *The Anti-social Family*, Verso: UK.

Birch, Eugenie Ladner (ed.) (1985), *The Unsheltered Women: Women and Housing in the 80s*, the State University of New Jersey: USA.

Bird, Chloe E. and Fremont, Allen M. (1991), 'Gender, Time use, and Health', *Journal of Health and Social Behaviour*, vol.32, June, pp.114-29.

Bowlby, Sophie (1988), 'From Corner Shop to Hypermarket: Women and Food Retailing', in Little, J.; Peake, L. and Richardson, P. (ed.), *Women in Cities*, Macmillan: UK.

Boys, Jos (1984), 'Women and Public Space', in MATRIX (ed.), *Making Space: Women and the Man Made Environment*, Pluto Press: UK.

Bradshaw, Johnathan and Millar, Jane (1993), *Lone Parent Families in the UK*, HMSO, Department of Social Security Research Report No.6: UK.

Brion, M. and Tinker, A. (1980), *Women in Housing*, Housing Centre Trust: UK.

Bristow, Roger (1989), *Hong Kong's New Towns: a Selective Review*, Oxford University Press: Hong Kong.

Brown, W. (1992), 'Finding the Men in the State', *Feminist Studies*, vol.18, no.1 pp.7-34.

Bruegel, Irene (1986), 'The Reserve Army of Labour 1974-1979', in Feminist Review (ed.), *Waged Work: A Reader*, Virago Press Ltd.: UK.

Built Environment, (1984), vol.10, no.1, special issue on 'Women and Built Environment'.

Castells, Manuel (1977), *The Urban Questions*, Edward Arnold: UK.

Castells, Manuel (1992), 'Four Asian Tigers With a Dragon Head: A Comparative Analysis of the State, Economy, and Society in the Asian Pacific Rim', in Appelbaum, Richard P. and Henderson, Jeffery (ed.), *States and Development in the Asian Pacific Rim*, Sage Publication: USA.

Castells, Manuel; Goh, L. and Kwok, R. (1990), *The Shek Kip Mei Syndrome: Economic Development and Public Housing in Hong Kong*, Pion Limited: UK.

Central Statistical Office (1994), *Social Trends: 1994 edition*, HMSO: UK.

Chan, Kam Wah (1985), *Privatization of Public Housing in Hong Kong*, University of Essex, unpublished MA Dissertation: UK.

Chan, Kam Wah (1993), *A Study on Housing Problems of Lone Parent Families in Hong Kong*, Department of Applied Social Studies, Hong Kong Polytechnic: Hong Kong, (Published in Chinese).

Chan, Kam Wah and Ng, Chun Hung (1994), 'Gender, Class and Employment Segregation in Hong Kong', in Lau, S.K.; Lee, M.K.; Wan, P.S. and Wong, S.L. (ed.), *Inequalities and Development: Social Stratification in Chinese Society*, Hong Kong Institute of Asia Pacific Studies, the Chinese University of Hong Kong: Hong Kong.

Chandler, Joan (1991), *Women Without Husbands: An Exploration of the Margins of Marriage*, Macmillan: UK.

Cheung, Bing Leung (1988), 'Political Implications and Pragmatic Considerations of the Government in Setting Up "Independent Authorities"', *Ming Pao Monthly*, February 1988, (Published in Chinese).

Chow, Nelson W.S. (1986), 'The Past and Future Development of Social Welfare in Hong Kong', in Cheng, J.Y.S. (ed.), *Hong Kong in Transition*, Oxford University Press: Hong Kong.

Chow, Nelson W.S. (1988), *The Quality of Life of Tuen Mun New Town Inhabitants*, Department of Social Work and Social Administration, University of Hong Kong: Hong Kong.

Chow, Nelson W.S. (1990), 'Community Building in Tuen Mun New Town', *Hong Kong Journal of Social Work*, vol.24, pp.52-9.

Clapham, David and Smith, Susan J. (1990), 'Housing Policy and "Special Needs"', *Policy and Politics*, vol.18, no.3 193-205.

222

Cochrane, Alan (1993), 'Looking for a European Welfare State', in Cochrane, Alan and Clarke, John (ed.), *Comparing Welfare States: Britain in International Context*, Sage Publication and the Open University: UK.

Coleman, Alice (1990), *Utopia on Trial*, revised edition, Hilary Shipman: UK.

Coleman, L. and Watson, S. (1987), *Women Over Sixty: A Study of the Housing, Economic and Social Circumstances of Older Women*, Australian Institute of Urban Studies: Australia.

Cowan, Ruth Schwartz (1983), *More Work for Mother: the Ironies of Household Technology from the Open Hearth to the Microwave*, Free Association Books: UK.

Craik, Jennifer (1989), 'The Making of Mother: The Role of the Kitchen in the Home', in Allen, Graham and Crow, Graham (ed.), *Home and Family: Creating the Domestic Sphere*, Macmillan: UK.

Crow, Graham (1989), 'The Post-War Development of the Modern Domestic Ideal', in Allan, Graham and Crow, Graham (ed.), *Home and the Family: Creating the Domestic Sphere*, Macmillan: UK.

Crow, Graham and Hardey, Michael (1991), 'The Housing Strategies of Lone Parents', in Hardey, M. and Crow, G. (ed.), *Lone Parenthood: Coping With Constraints and Making Opportunities*, Harvester Wheatsheaf: UK.

Dahlerup, Drude (1992), 'Confusing Concept - Confusing Reality: A Theoretical Discussion of the Patriarchal State', in Sassoon, A.S. (ed.), *Women and the State*, reprinted, Routledge: UK.

Dalley, Gillian (1988), *Ideologies of Caring: Rethinking Community and Collectivism*, Macmillan Education Ltd.: London.

Davidoff, L.; L'Esperance, J. and Newby, H. (1976), 'Landscape With Figures: Home and Community in English Society', in Mitchell, Juliet and Oakley, Ann (ed.), *The Right and Wrong of Women*, Penguin: Britain.

Dex, Shirley (1985), *The Sexual Division of Work*, Harvester Press: Brighton.

Dickens, Peter (1989), 'Human Nature, Society and the Home', *Housing Studies*, vol.4, no.4, Oct., pp.227-37.

Dobash, R. Emerson and Dobash, Russell P. (1970), *Violence Against Wives*, the Free Press: USA.

Dobash, R. Emerson and Dobash, Russell P. (1992), *Women, Violence and Social Change*, Routledge: UK.

Dominelli, Lena and Mcleod, Eileen (1989), *Feminist Social Work*, Macmillan: UK.

Dreyfus, Hubert L. and Rabinow, Paul (1982), 'Afterword', *Michael Foucault: Beyond Structuralism and Hermeneutics*, The Harvester Press: UK.

Dunleavy, Patrick (1986), 'Explaining the Privatization Boom: Public Choice Versus Radical Approaches', *Public Administration*, vol.64, Spring, pp.13-34.

Eichler, Magrit (1988), *Non-sexist Research Methods*, Allen and Unwin: London.

Elshtain, J.B. (1981), *Public Man Private Woman*, Martin Robertson: UK.

Esping-Andersen, Gosta (1990), *The Three Worlds of Welfare Capitalism*, Princeton University Press: USA.

Fee, Elizabeth (1983), 'Women's Nature and Scientific Objectivity', in Marian Lowe and Ruth Hubbard (ed.), *Women's Nature: Rationalization of Inequality*, Pergamon: USA.

Fetterman, David M. (1989), *Ethnography: step by step*, Sage Publication: USA.

Finch, Janet (1983), *Married to the Job: Wives Incorporation in Men's Work*, Allen and Unwin: UK.

Finch, Janet and Groves, Dulcie (ed.) (1983), *A Labour of Love: Women, Work and Caring*, Routledge and Kegan Paul: UK.

Forrest, Ray and Murie, Alan (1986), 'Marginalization and Subsidized Individualism', *International Journal of Urban and Regional Research*, vol.10, no.1, pp.46-65.

Forrest, Ray and Murie, Alan (1988a), 'Differential Accumulation: Wealth, Inheritance and Housing Policy Reconsidered', *Policy and Politics*, 1988 Winter.

Forrest, Ray and Murie Alan (1988b), *Selling the Welfare State: Privatization of Council Housing*, Routledge: Britain.

Foucault, Michael (1986), 'Disciplinary Power and Subjection', in Lukes, Steven (ed.), *Power*, Blackwell: UK.

Franklin, Adrian (1990), 'Ethnography and Housing Studies', *Housing Studies*, vol.5, no.2, pp.92-111.

Gilroy, Rose and Woods, Roberta (ed.) (1994), *Housing Women*, Routledge: UK.

Gittins, Diana (1985), *The Family in Question*, Macmillan Education: UK.

Glendinning, Caroline and Millar, Jane (1992), *Women and Poverty in Britain: the 1990s*, Harvester Wheatsheaf: UK.

Goldthorpe, John H. (1983), 'Women and Class Analysis: in Defence of the Conventional View', *Sociology*, vol.17, no.4.

Goldthorpe, John H. (1984), 'Women and Class Analysis: A Reply to the Replies', *Sociology*, vol.18, no.4, pp.491-9.

Gottdiener, M. (1985), *The Social Production of Urban Space*, University of Texas Press: USA.

Graham, Hilary (1983), 'Caring: A Labour of Love', in Finch, J. and Groves, D. (ed.), *A Labour of Love*, Routledge and Kegan Paul: London.

Hammersley, Martyn (1992), *What's Wrong with Ethnography?*, Routledge: UK.

Hammersley, Martyn and Atkinson, Paul (1990), *Ethnography Principles in Practice*, reprinted, Routledge: UK.

Hamnett, Chris (1991), 'A nation of Inheritors? Housing Inheritance, Wealth and Inequality in Britain', *Journal of Social Policy*, vol.20, no.4, pp.509-36.

Han, Daniel (1982), 'Migration and Residential Satisfaction in a New Town: the Case of Tuen Mun', in Leung, C.K.; Cushman, J.W. and Wang, G. (ed.), *Hong Kong: Dilemma of Growth*, reprinted, University of Hong Kong: Hong Kong.

Hanmer, J. and Saunders, S. (1984), *Well-Founded Fear*, Hutchinson: UK.

Hardey, Michael (1989), 'Lone Parents and the Home', in Crow, Graham and Allan, Graham (ed.), *Home and Family*, Macmillan: UK.

Hardey, Michael and Glover, Judith (1991), 'Income, Employment, Daycare and Lone Parenthood', in Hardey, M. and Crow, G. (ed.), *Lone Parent: Coping with Constraints and Making Opportunities*, Harvester Wheatsheaf: UK.

Harding, Sandra (1987), 'Introduction: Is There a Feminist Method?', in Harding, S. (ed.), *Feminism and Methodology*, Open University Press: UK.

Harloe, Michael (1981), 'The Recommodification of Housing', in Harloe, M. and Lebas, E. (ed.), *City, Class and Capital*, Arnold: UK.

Harloe, Michael (1995), *The People's Home? Social Rented Housing in Europe and America*, Blackwell: UK.

Harloe, Michael and Fainstein, Susan (1992), 'Conclusion: the Divided Cities', in Fainstein, S.; Gordon, I. and Harloe, M. (ed.), *Divided Cities: New York and London in the Contemporary World*, Blackwell: UK.

Harman, Elizabeth J. (1983), 'Capitalism, Patriarchy and the City', in Baldock, C. and Cass, B. (ed.), *Women, Social Welfare and the State*, Allen and Unwin: Sydney.

Hartmann, Heidi I. (1979), 'Capitalism, Patriarchy and Job Segregation by Sex', in Eisenstein, Z. (ed.), *Capitalism, Patriarchy and the Case for Socialist Feminism*, Monthly Review Press: New York.

Hartmann, Heidi I. (1981), 'The Unhappy Marriage of Marxism and Feminism: Towards a More Progressive Union', in Sargent, L. (ed.), *Women and Revolution*, South End Press: Boston.

Harvey, David (1978), 'The Urban Process Under Capitalism: A Framework for Analysis', *International Journal of Urban and Regional Research*, vol.2, pp.101-31.

Harvey, David (1987), 'Flexible Accumulation Through Urbanization: Reflections on "Post-Modernism" in the American City', *Antipode*, vol.19, no.3.

Hayden, Doleres (1980), 'What Would a Non-sexist City Be Like? Speculations on Housing, Urban Design, and Human Work', *Signs*, vol.5, no.3, supplement, S170-87.

Hayden, Doleres (1981), 'Two Utopian Feminists and Their Campaigns for Kitchenless Houses', in Keller, S.I. (ed.), *Building for Women*, D.C. Health and Co.: USA.

Hayden, Doleres (1984), *Redesigning the American Dream*, W.W. Norton & Co.: USA.

Henderson, Jeffrey and Appelbaum, Richard P. (1992), 'Situating the State in the East Asian Development Process', in Appelbaum, R.P. and Henderson, J. (ed.), *State and Development in the Asian Pacific Rim*, Sage Publication: USA.

Henderson, Jeffrey and Castells, Manuel (ed.) (1987), *Global Restructuring and Territorial Development*, Sage Publication: UK.

Hillier, B. (1986), 'City of Alice's Dreams', *The Architects' Journal*, 9 July, pp.39-41.

Ho, Shuet-Ying (1986), 'Public Housing', in Cheng, Joseph Y.S. (ed.), *Hong Kong in Transition*, Oxford University Press: Hong Kong.

Hong Kong Census and Statistics Department (1986a), *Hong Kong 1986 By-Census Main Report Volume 2*, Government Printer: Hong Kong.

Hong Kong Census and Statistics Department (1986b), *Hong Kong Annual Digest of Statistics 1986 Edition*, Government Printer: Hong Kong.

Hong Kong Census and Statistics Department (1991), *1989/90 Household Expenditure Survey and the Rebasing of the Consumer Price Indexes*, Government Printer: Hong Kong.

Hong Kong Census and Statistics Department (1992a), *Hong Kong 1991 Population Census: Main Tables*, Government Printer: Hong Kong.

Hong Kong Census and Statistics Department (1992b), *1991 Census Summary Result*, Government Printer: Hong Kong.

Hong Kong Census and Statistics Department (1993a), *Hong Kong - 25 Years' Development: Presented in Statistical Data and Graphics (1967-92)*, Government Printer: Hong Kong.

Hong Kong Census and Statistics Department (1993b), *Hong Kong Annual Digest of Statistics 1993 Edition*, Government Printer: Hong Kong.

Hong Kong Census and Statistics Department (1993c), *Hong Kong 1991 Population Census: Main Report*, Government Printer: Hong Kong.

Hong Kong Census and Statistics Department (1994), *Annual Report on the Consumer Price Index 1993*, Government Printer: Hong Kong.

Hong Kong Christian Family Service Centre (HKCFSC) (1986), *A Survey on the Family Life of Lone Parent Families in Kwun Tong*, Hong Kong Christian Family Service Centre: Hong Kong, (Published in Chinese).

Hong Kong Commissioner for Resettlement (1955), *Annual Report: 1955*, Government Publication: Hong Kong.

Hong Kong Family Welfare Society (H.K.F.W.S.) and Law, Chi Kong (1991), *Need of Single Parent Families: A Comparative Study*, Hong Kong Family Welfare Society: Hong Kong.

Hong Kong Government (1977), *Help for Those Least Able to Help Themselves*, Government Printer: Hong Kong.

Hong Kong Government (1993), *Green Paper on Equal Opportunities for Men and Women*, Government Printer: Hong Kong.

Hong Kong Government (1994), *Hong Kong 1994: A Review of 1993*, Government report of the year, Government Printer: Hong Kong.

Hong Kong Housing Authority (1986), *Hong Kong Housing Authority Annual Report 1985/86*, Hong Kong Housing Authority: Hong Kong.

Hong Kong Housing Authority (1987), *Long Term Housing Strategy: a policy statement*, Hong Kong Housing Authority: Hong Kong.

Hong Kong Housing Authority (1991), *Hong Kong Housing Authority Annual Report 1990/91*, Hong Kong Housing Authority: Hong Kong.

Hong Kong Housing Authority (1993), *Hong Kong Housing Authority Annual Report 1992/93*, Hong Kong Housing Authority: Hong Kong.

Hong Kong Housing Authority (1994), *Hong Kong Housing Authority Annual Report 1993/94*, Hong Kong Housing Authority: Hong Kong.

Hong Kong Housing Authority (1995), *Long Term Housing Strategy: A Policy Statement (April 1987), A Report on the Mid-term Review (October 1993), Final Report on the Mid-term Review (June 1994)*, Hong Kong Housing Authority: Hong Kong.

Hong Kong People's Council on Public Housing Policy (1984), *The Challenge of the Housing Problems in 1980s (A White Paper)*, Hong Kong People's Council on Public Housing Policy: Hong Kong, (published in Chinese).

Hong Kong Rating and Valuation Department (1993), *Hong Kong Property Review 1993*, Government Printer: Hong Kong.

Hong Kong Rating and Valuation Department (1994), *Hong Kong Property Review 1994*, Government Printer: Hong Kong.

Hong Kong Social Welfare Department (1991a), *The Five Year Plan for Social Welfare Development in Hong Kong - Review 1991*, Government Printer: Hong Kong.

Hong Kong Social Welfare Department (1991b), *Social Welfare into the 1990s and Beyond: Hong Kong Social Welfare White Paper*, Government Printer: Hong Kong.

Hong Kong Social Welfare Department (1992), *Report on Single Parent Families - Based on the 1991 Population Census Data*, Hong Kong Social Welfare Department: Hong Kong.

Hong Kong Social Welfare Department (1993), *The Five Year Plan for Social Welfare Development in Hong Kong - Review 1993*, Government Printer: Hong Kong.

Hong Kong Society of Social Security (1990), *Response to 'Social Welfare Services into the 1990's and Beyond*, Hong Kong Soceity of Social Security: Hong Kong.

Imaray, L. and Middleton, A. (1983), 'Public and Private: making the boundaries', in Gamarnikow, E. et al. (ed.), *The Public and the Private*, Heinemann Education Books Ltd.: UK.

International Journal of Urban and Regional Research, (1978), vol.2, no.3., special issue on 'Women and the City'.

Katz, Michael B. (1993), *The 'Underclass' Debate: Views from History*, Princeton University Press: USA.

Kephart, George (1991), 'Economic Restructuring, Population Redistribution, and Migration in the United States', in Gottdiener, M. and Pickvance, Chris (ed.), *Urban Life in Transition*, Sage Publication: USA.

Keung, John (1985), 'Government Intervention and Housing Policy in Hong Kong: a Structural Analysis', *Third World Planning Review*, vol.7, no.1, February, pp.23-44.

Kemeny, Jim (1992), *Housing and Social Theory*, Routledge: UK.

Land, Hilary (1991), 'Time to Care', in Maclean, M. and Groves, D. (ed.), *Women's Issues in Social Policy*, Routledge: UK.

Langan, Mary and Day, Lesley (ed.) (1992), *Women Oppression and Social Work: Issues in Anti-discriminatory Practice*, Routledge: UK.

Lather, Patti (1988), 'Feminist Perspectives on Empowering Research Methodologies', *Women's Studies International Forum*, vol.11, no.6, pp.569-81.

Lau, Kwok Yu (1994), 'Public Housing', in McMillen, Donald and Man, Si Wai (ed.), *The Other Hong Kong Report: 1994*, Chinese University Press: Hong Kong.

Law, Cheng Sik Sze (1991), *Public Finance Decision Making in Hong Kong*, Wide Angle Press Ltd.: Hong Kong, (Published in Chinese).

Lee, Ming Kwan (1985), 'Housing Policy and the Changing Family', *The Changing Hong Kong Society*, Commercial Press: Hong Kong, (Published in Chinese).

Lee, Ming Kwan (1991), 'Family and Social Life', in Lau, S.K.; Lee, M.K.; Wan, P.S. and Wong, S.L. (ed.), *Indicators of Social Development: Hong Kong 1988*, Chinese University Press: Hong Kong.

Leonard, Diana and Hood-Williams, John (1988), *Families*, Macmillan: UK.

Leung, Lai Ching (1993), *Research Report on Pattern of Health and Illness Amongst Lone Mothers in Hong Kong*, Department of Applied Social Studies, City Polytechnic of Hong Kong: Hong Kong.

Lewis, Oscar (1969), 'The Culture of Poverty', in Moynihan, Daniel P. (ed.), *On Understanding Poverty*, Basic Books: USA.

Little, Jo; Peake, Linda and Richardson, Pat (ed.) (1988), *Women in Cities: Gender and the Urban Environment*, Macmillan Education: UK.

Logan, John R. and Molotch, Harvey L. (1987), *Urban Fortunes: the Political Economy of Place*, University of California Press: USA.

Lonsdale, Susan (1992), 'Patterns of Paid Work', Glendinning, C. and Millar, J. (ed.), *Women and Poverty in Britain the 1990s*, Harvester Wheatsheaf: UK.

Lukes, Steven (1984), *Power: A Radical View*, reprinted, Macmillan: UK.

Maclean, Mavis (1991), *Surviving Divorce: Women's Resources After Separation*, Macmillan: UK.

Madigan, Ruth; Munro, Moria and Smith, Susan J. (1990), 'Gender and the Meaning of the Home', *International Journal of Urban and Regional Research*, vol.14, no.4.

Malpass, Peter (1990), *Reshaping Housing Policy: Subsidies, Rents and Residualization*, Routledge: UK.

Marcuse, Peter (1986), 'Housing Policy and the Myth of the Benevolent State', Bratt, Rachel G.; Hartman, Chester W. and Meyerson, Ann (ed.), *Critical Perspectives on Housing*, Temple University Press: USA.

Marcuse, Peter (1989a), 'The Pitfalls of Specialism: Special Groups and the General Problem of Housing', in Rosenberry, S. and Hartman, C. (ed.), *Housing Issues of the 1990s*, Praeger: USA.

Marcuse, Peter (1989b), 'Dual City: A Muddy Metaphor for a Quartered City', *International Journal of Urban and Regional Research*, vol.13, no.4, pp.697-708.

Marcuse, Peter (1993), 'What's So New About Divided Cities?', *International Journal of Urban and Regional Research*, vol.17, no.3, pp.355-65.

Marsden, Dennis (1973), *Mothers Alone: Poverty and the Fatherless Family*, Pelican: UK.

Matrix (1984), *Women and the Man Made Environment*, reprinted 1985, Pluto Press Ltd.: UK.

McDowell, Linda (1983a), 'Towards an Understanding of the Gender Division of Urban Space', *Environment and Planning D: Society and Space*, vol.1, pp.59-72.

McDowell, Linda (1983b), 'City and Home', in Evans, M. and Ungerson, C. (ed.), *Sexual Divisions: Patterns and Process*, Tavistock: UK.

McDowell, Linda (1991), 'Restructuring Production and Reproduction: Some Theoretical and Empirical Issues Relating to Gender, or Women in Britain', Gottdiener, M. and Pickvance, Chris G. (ed.), *Urban Life in Transition*, Sage: USA.

McLaughlin, Eugene (1993), 'Hong Kong: A Residual Welfare Regime', in Cochrane, Allen and Clarke, John (ed.), *Comparing Welfare States: Britain in International Context*, Sage and the Open University: UK.

McNay, Lois (1992), *Foucault and Feminism*, Polity: UK.

McNeill, Patrick (1985), *Research Methods*, Tavistock Publication: London.

Miliband, Ralph (1969), *The State in Capitalist Society*, Weidenfeld and Nicolson: London.

Millar, Jane (1987), 'Lone Mothers', in Glendenning, C. and Millar, J. (ed.), *Women and Poverty in Britain*, Wheatsheaf: UK.

Millar, Jane and Bradshaw, Johnathan (1987), 'The Living Standard of Lone Parent Families', *The Quarterly Journal of Social Affairs*, vol.3, no.4, pp.233-52.

Miller, S.M. (1978), 'The Recapitalization of Capitalism', *International Journal of Urban and Regional Research*, vol.2, no.2.

Miners, N.J. (1989), *The Government and Politics of Hong Kong*, Oxford University Press: Hong Kong.

Mok, Hing Luen (1993), 'Housing Problems of the Singleton and Two-person Family', in Lee, Kin Ching and Chan, Kam Wah (ed.), *Analyzing Housing Policy in Hong Kong*, Publishers' Cooperative: Hong Kong, (Published in Chinese).

Morris, Jenny and Winn, Martin (1990), *Housing and Social Inequality*, Hilary Shipman: UK.

Moser, Caroline O.N. and Peake, Linda (1987), *Women, Human Settlement and Housing*, Tavistock Publication: UK.

Munro, Moria and Smith, Susan J. (1989), 'Gender and Housing: Broadening the Debate', *Housing Studies*, vol.4, no.1, pp.3-17.

Murgatroyd, L. (1982), 'Gender and Occupational Stratification', *Sociological Review*, vol.30, no.4, November, pp.574-602.

Murray, Charles (1984), *Losing Ground: American Social Policy 1950-1980*, Basic Books: USA.

Murray, Charles (1990), *The Emerging British Underclass*, Institute of Economic Affair: UK.

Ng, Agnes M.C. (1985), 'A Study on Juvenile Delinquency in Hong Kong', in Ying, M.W. and King, Ambrose Y.K. (ed.), *Hong Kong Development*, Chinese University Press: Hong Kong, (Published in Chinese).

Nicholson, Linda J. (1992), 'Feminist Theory: the Private and the Public', in McDowell, Linda and Pringle, Rosemary (ed.), *Defining Women: Social Institutions and Gender Divisions*, Polity and the Open University Press: UK.

Oakley, Ann (1972), *Sex, Gender and Society*, Temple Smith: UK.

Oakley, Ann (1974), *The Sociology of Housework*, Martin Robertson: UK.

Oakley, Ann (1989), 'Women's Studies in British Sociology: To End at Our Beginning?', *The British Journal of Sociology*, vol.40, no.3, pp.442-70.

Oakley, Ann (1990a), 'Interviewing Women: A Contradiction in Terms', in Helen Roberts (ed.), *Doing Feminists Research*, reprinted, Routledge and Kegan Paul: UK.

Oakley, Ann (1990b), 'Who is Afraid of Randomized Controlled Trial?', in Helen Roberts (ed.), *Women's Health Counts*, Routledge: London.

O'Connor, James (1973), *The Fiscal Crisis of the State*, St. Martin's: USA.

Offe, C. (1984), *Contradictions of the Welfare State*, MIT Press: USA.

Oppenheim, Carey (1990), *Poverty: the Facts*, Child Poverty Action Group: UK.

Organization for Economic Cooperation and Development (OECD) (1990), *Lone Parent Families: the Economic Challenge*, OECD Social Policy Studies, No.6, OECD: Paris.

Pateman, C. (1987), 'Feminist Critiques of the Public/Private Dichotomy', Phillips, Anne (ed.), *Feminism and Equality*, Basil Blackwell: UK.

Payne, Sarah (1991), *Women, Health and Poverty*, Harverster Wheatsheaf: UK.

Phillips, Anne and Taylor, Barbara (1986), 'Sex and Skill', in Feminist Review (ed.), *Waged Work: A Reader*, Virago: UK.

Pickup, Laurie (1988), 'Hard to Get Around: A Study of Women's Travel Mobility', in Little, J.; Peake, L. and Richardson, P. (ed.), *Women in Cities: Gender and the Urban Environment*, Macmillan Education: UK.

Poulantzas, Nicos (1973), *Political Power and Social Classes*, New Left Books: London.

Pryor, E.G. (1983), *Housing in Hong Kong*, Oxford University Press: Hong Kong.

Pugh, Cedric (1990), 'A New Approach to Housing Theory: Sex, Gender and the Domestic Economy', *Housing Studies*, vol.5, no.2, pp.112-9.

Radford, J. (1987), 'Policing Male Violence - Policing Women', in Halmer, J. and Maynard, M. (ed.), *Women, Violence and Social Control*, Macmillan: UK.

Reinharz, Shulamit (1983), 'Experiential Analysis: A Contribution to Feminist Research', in Bowles, G. and Duelli-Klein, R. (ed.), *Theories of Women's Studies*, Routledge and Kegan Paul: London.

Ribbens, Jane (1989), 'Interviewing - an "Unnatural Situation"?', *Women's Studies International Forum*, vol.12, no.6, pp.579-92.

Roberts, Helen (ed.) (1990), *Doing Feminist Research*, reprinted, Routledge and Kegan Paul: UK.

Roberts, Marion (1984), 'Private Kitchen, Public Cooking', in Matrix (ed.), *Making Space*, Pluto Press: UK.

Roberts, Marion (1991), *Living in a Man-Made World: Gender Assumptions in Modern Housing Design*, Routledge: UK.

Rowbatham, Sheila (1979), 'The Trouble with "Patriarchy"', *New Statesman*, December 1979.

Saegert, S. (1980), 'Masculine Cities and Feminine Suburbs: Polarized Ideas, Contradictory Realities', *Sign*, vol.5, pp.96-112.

Salaff, Janet W. (1990), 'Women, the Family, and the State: Hong Kong, Taiwan, Singapore - Newly Industrialized Countries in Asia', in Stichter, Charon and Parpart, Janet, L. (ed.), *Women, Employment and the Family in the International Division of Labour*, Macmillan: UK.

Sargent, Lydia (ed.) (1981), *Women and Revolution*, South End Press: Boston.

Sassoon, Anne Showstack (ed.) (1992), *Women and the State*, reprinted, Routledge: UK.

Saunders, Peter (1986), *Social Theory and the Urban Question*, 2nd edition, Hutchinson: UK.

Saunders, Peter (1989), 'The meaning of "home" in Contemporary English Culture', *Housing Studies*, vol.4, no.3, pp.177-82.

Saunders, Peter (1990), *A Nation of Home Owners*, Unwin Hyman: UK.

Saunders, Peter and Williams, Peter (1988), 'The Constitution of the Home: Towards a Research Agenda', *Housing Studies*, vol.3, no.2, pp.81-93.

Sayer, Andrew (1989), 'Postfordism in Question', *International Journal of Urban and Regional Research*, vol.13, no.4, pp.666-95.

Schiffer, J. (1991), 'State Policy and Economic Growth: A Note on the Hong Kong Model', *International Journal of Urban and Regional Research*, vol.15, no.2, pp.180-96.

Scott, A.J. and Storper, M. (ed.) (1986), *Production, Work and Territory: the Geographical Anatomy of Industrial Capitalism*, Allen and Unwin: USA.

Scott, Hilda (1984), *Working Your Way to the Bottom: The Feminization of Poverty*, Pandora Press: UK.

Scully, Diane (1990), *Understanding Sexual Violence: A Study of Convicted Rapists*, Unwin Hyman: UK.

Segal, Lynne (ed.) (1983), *What is to be Done About the Family?*, Penguin Books: UK.

Sexty, Carol (1990), *Women Losing Out: Access to Housing in Britain Today*, Shelter Publication: UK.

Signs, (1980), vol.5, no.3, special issue on 'Women and the American City'.

Sit, Fung Shun (1981), 'New Towns for the Future', in Sit, Fung Shun (ed.), *Urban Hong Kong*, Summerson Eastern Publisher Ltd.: Hong Kong.

Skocpol, T. (1985), 'Bringing the State Back In: Strategies of Analysis in Current Research', in Evans, P.B.; Rueschemeyer, D. and Skocpol, T., *Bringing the State Back In*, Cambridge University Press: USA.

Skocpol, T. and Amenta, E. (1986), 'States and Social Policies', *Annual Review of Sociology*, vol.12, pp.131-57.

Smart, C. (1976), *Women, Crime and Criminology*, Routledge and Kegan Paul: UK.

Smart, Barry (1985), *Michael Foucault*, Routledge: UK.

Smith, Susan J. (1990), 'Income, Housing Wealth and Gender Inequality', *Urban Studies*, vol.27, no.1, pp.67-88.

Somerville, P. (1989), 'Home Sweet Home: A Critical Comment on Saunders and Williams', *Housing Studies*, vol.4, no.2, pp.113-8.

Spicker, P. (1987), 'Poverty and Depressed Estates: A Critique of Utopia on Trial', *Housing Studies*, vol.2, no.4, pp.283-92.

Stacey, Judith (1988), 'Can There be a Feminist Ethnography?', *Women's Studies International Forum*, vol.11, no.1, pp.21-7.

Stanley, Liz (ed.) (1990), *Feminist Praxis: Research, Theory and Epistemology in Feminist Sociology*, Routledge: London.

Stanley, Liz and Wise, Sue (1983), *Breaking out*, Routledge and Kegan Paul: London.

Stanworth, M. (1984), 'Women and Class Analysis: A Reply to Goldthorpe', *Sociology*, vol.18, no.2, pp.159-70.

Sullivan, Oriel (1986), 'Housing Movement of the Divorced and Separated', *Housing Studies*, vol.1, no.1, pp.35-48.

Tang, Shu Hung (1992), *Public Finance in Hong Kong in the Post-transition Era*, Joint Publishing (HK) Co. Ltd.: Hong Kong, (Published in Chinese).

Thompson, Paul (1989), *The Nature of Work: An Introduction to Debates on the Labour Process*, 2nd edition, Macmillan: London.

Townsend, Peter (1979), *Poverty in the United Kingdom: A Survey of Household Resources and Standards of Living*, Penguin: UK.

Townsend, Peter (1993), *The International Analysis of Poverty*, Harvester Wheatsheaf: UK.

Treiman, D. and Hartmann, H. (1981), *Women, Works and Wages: Equal Pays for Jobs of Equal Value*, National Academy of Sciences: USA.

Tuen Mun District Board (1990), *Social Needs of Married Women in Tuen Mun: Survey Report 1990*, Tuen Mun District Board: Hong Kong, (Published in Chinese).

Walby, Sophie (1989), 'Theorising Patriarchy', *Sociology*, vol.23, no.2, pp.213-34.

Walby, Sophie (1990), *Theorising patriarchy*, Polity: UK.

Walker, Alan (1982), *Community Care*, Basil Blackwell and Martin Robertson: Britain.

Walker, Alan (1988), *Social Policy Versus Economic Policy: the Future of Social Planning*, Peter Hodge Memorial Lecture, University of Hong Kong: Hong Kong.

Wan, Chi Kei (1985), *Political Representation of Women in Hong Kong*, Unpublished BSc thesis, University of East Asia: Macau.

Warde, A. (1990), 'Production, Consumption, and Social Change: Reservation Regarding Peter Saunders' Sociology of Consumption', *International Journal of Urban and Regional Research*, vol.14, no.2, pp.228-48.

Watson, Sophie (1986a), 'Housing and the Family: The Marginalization of Non-family Households in Britain', *International Journal of Urban and Regional Research*, vol.10, no.1, pp.8-28.

Watson, Sophie (1986b), 'Women and Housing or Feminist Housing Analysis?', *Housing Studies*, January 1986, pp.1-10.

Watson, Sophie (1988), *Accommodating Inequality: Gender and Housing*, Allen and Unwin: Australia.

Watson, Sophie (1991), 'The Restructuring of Work and Home: Production and Reproduction Relations', in Allen, J. and Hemnett, C. (ed.), *Housing and Labour Markets*, Unwin Hyman Ltd.: UK.

Watson, Sophie (ed.) (1990), *Playing the State: Australian Feminist Intervention*, Verso: UK.

Watson, Sophie and Austerberry, Helen (1986), *Housing and Homelessness: A Feminist Perspective*, Routledge and Kegan Paul: UK.

Weisman, Leslie Kanes (1992), *Discrimination by Design: A Feminist Critique of the Man-made Environment*, University of Illinois Press: USA.

Westkott, Marcia (1979), 'Feminist Criticism of the Social Science', *Harvard Educational Review*, vol.49, no.4, pp.422-30.

Willmot, P. and Murie, A. (1988), *Polarisation and Social Housing*, Policy Study Institute: UK.

Wilson, Elizabeth (1977), *Women and the Welfare State*, Tavistock: UK.

Women and Geography Study Group of the Institute of British Geographers (1984), *Geography and Gender: An Introduction to Feminist Geography*, Hutchinson and Explorations in Feminism Collective: London.

Wong, Luke S.K. (1978), 'An Overview of Housing Provision and Housing Needs in Hong Kong', in Wong, Luke S.K. (ed.), *Housing in Hong Kong: A Multi-disciplinary Study*, Heinemann Education Book (Asia) Ltd.: Hong Kong.

Wong, Yue Chim and Liu, Pak Wai (1988), 'The Distribution of Benefits Among Public Housing Tenants in Hong Kong and Related Policy Issues', *Journal of Urban Economic*, vol.23, no.1, pp.1-20.

Woolley, Tom (1994), 'Innovative Housing in the UK and Europe', in Gilroy, Rose, and Woods, Roberta (ed.), *Housing Women*, Routledge: UK.

World Health Organization (WHO) (1993), 'Violence and Health', *World Health Statistics Quarterly*, vol.46, no.1, World Health Organization Publication: United Nation.

Yin, Robert K. (1993), *Case Study Research: Design and Methods*, 2nd edition, Sage: USA.

Young, Iris (1981), 'Beyond the Unhappy Marriage: A Critique of the Dual System Theory', in Sargent, Lydia (ed.), *Women and Revolution*, South End Press: USA.

Young, Katherine P.H. (1985), *A Report on Single Parent Families in Hong Kong*, Department of Social Work, University of Hong Kong: Hong Kong.